The Righteous Judgment of God

Aspects of Judgment in Paul's Letters

John R. Coulson

FOREWORD BY
Michael Bird

WIPF & STOCK · Eugene, Oregon

THE RIGHTEOUS JUDGMENT OF GOD
Aspects of Judgment in Paul's Letters

Copyright © 2016 John R. Coulson. All rights reserved. Except for brief quotations in critical publications or reviews, no part of this book may be reproduced in any manner without prior written permission from the publisher. Write: Permissions, Wipf and Stock Publishers, 199 W. 8th Ave., Suite 3, Eugene, OR 97401.

Wipf & Stock
An Imprint of Wipf and Stock Publishers
199 W. 8th Ave., Suite 3
Eugene, OR 97401

www.wipfandstock.com

PAPERBACK ISBN: 978-1-4982-9034-0
HARDCOVER ISBN: 978-1-4982-9036-4
EBOOK ISBN: 978-1-4982-9035-7

Manufactured in the U.S.A.

Unless otherwise indicated, indented quotations from the Bible throughout the book are from Today's New International Version®, TNIV®. Copyright© 2001, 2005 by Biblica, Inc.™ Used by permission of Zondervan. All rights reserved worldwide.

In memory of another Paul

—Paul Grant—

father in the faith and faithful servant of the gospel

Contents

Foreword by Michael Bird | ix
Preface | xi
Abbreviations | xv

1 **Judgment in the Old Testament and in the Teaching of Jesus** | 1
   Judgment in the Old Testament | 1
   Judgment in the Teaching of Jesus | 5
   Summary of Main Points | 7

2 **Overview of God's Judgment in Paul's Letters, Part 1** | 8
   Romans | 9
   First Corinthians | 23
   Second Corinthians | 30
   Galatians | 35

3 **Overview of God's Judgment in Paul's Letters, Part 2** | 42
   Ephesians | 42
   Philippians | 45
   Colossians | 48
   First Thessalonians | 52
   Second Thessalonians | 55
   First Timothy | 58
   Second Timothy | 62
   Titus | 66
   Philemon | 68
   Concluding Observations | 69

4 **The Fallen Human Condition as God's Judgment** | 74
   Summary concerning the Fallen Condition of Humanity | 75
   Reflections | 76

Contents

5   **God's Temporal Judgment** | 84
    Summary of Paul's Teaching on Temporal Judgment | 84
    Romans 1:18–32: Increasing Sinfulness as Judgment | 86
    What about Human and Natural Disasters as God's Judgment? | 92
    Unbelief as Temporal Judgment | 95
    Judgment of Evil Spiritual Powers in Gospel Ministry | 96
    Judgment through Civil Authorities | 97
    Disciplinary Judgment of God's People | 100

6   **God's Judgment at the Cross** | 108
    Summary concerning the Cross and God's Judgment | 108
    Romans 3:25 and "Propitiation" | 109
    Penal Substitution? | 115
    Related Matters | 121
    Final Reflections | 125

7   **God's Final Judgment** | 130
    Summary concerning the Final Judgment | 130
    The Necessity and Purpose of the Final Judgment | 132
    The Judgment of God's People | 136
    The Judgment of Unbelievers | 144
    Final Reflections | 154

8   **Conclusion** | 157

Bibliography | 161
Modern Authors Index | 169
Subject Index | 173
Scripture Index | 179

Foreword

THE SUBJECT OF DIVINE judgment is not a pleasant one or a popular one to discourse about. There are I suspect several reasons for this. First, most people, whether religious or not, have probably imbibed the idea of the final judgment as a type of heavenly court with God simultaneously acting as judge, jury, prosecutor, and executioner. Or else they have a cartoonish idea of "hell" as a subterranean cavern filled with fire, burning lakes, and devils armed with pitched forks. That is to say, things like judgment, perdition, hell, and punishment often conjure up images somewhere between mythical to surreal and thus appear less than real to us. Second, the idea of a God who judges people, other than the most truly wicked, has never been terribly popular. It is far more satisfying to imagine God as a kind of benign old grandfather who is not easily agitated by anything and can all too easily have the wool pulled over his eyes. Third, alternatively the idea of judgment is thought to imply vengeance and retribution, dispositions which cannot allegedly be squared with a God of love, mercy, and grace. So it is no wonder that in theology and preaching there has always been a propensity to gloss over divine judgment, to blunt the force of biblical warnings that threaten judgment, or even to deny that God really does judge. Maybe God threatens judgment but doesn't really mean it. Maybe there is a hell, but perhaps it has an exit door built into it.

It is very helpful then that my good friend and former colleague John Coulson, takes us on a tour of the theme of divine judgment in Paul's letters. In this short but learned book, he shows how deeply connected biblical notions of divine justice and divine mercy are to the theme of divine judgment in Paul's letters. These are not blights on God's character, rather, they show forth his character, and buttress God's claims to rule in righteousness and to vindicate the faithful. Coulson's exposition of key texts in the Pauline corpus shows over and over how it is not just the wicked or unbelievers who fall under the remit of divine judgment, but ministers and all God's people have an experience of judgment, of sorts, as well. He takes time to

Foreword

wisely expound and expand on such salient points. Beyond a quick survey of key texts, he explains why people come under judgment, he examines temporal judgments, God's judgment against evil and wickedness at the cross, and explains Paul's account of the final judgment.

Coulson has provided a readable, informed, and stimulating account of the place of divine judgment in Paul's letters and suggests ways in which we can learn from it. It is a book I hope pastors and students from all parts of the Christian fold will take up and read, and learn to appreciate, with Coulson's guidance, the manifold wisdom and glory of God as revealed in his judgments.

Michael Bird

Ridley College, Melbourne, Australia
18 July 2016

Preface

> If only we knew the power of your anger!
> Your wrath is as great as the fear that is your due. (Ps 90:11)

GOD'S JUDGMENT, THAT IS, his judgment of the character and conduct of human beings, has never been a popular subject. This is not surprising. Who wants to hear "the bad news"? And yet if there is bad news that involves us, we really do need to hear it. This is why the Bible declares the message about God's judgment together with the message about salvation.

As Christians we have a responsibility: to be faithful in declaring to our generation the whole truth of God's Word. And yet with respect to proclaiming the message about God's judgment, for many decades now the church in the western world generally has failed to be faithful. In his 1951 Tyndale Fellowship Lecture Professor R. V. G. Tasker lamented:

> In more recent years, however, there has been widespread neglect and indeed denial of the doctrine of the divine wrath; and emphasis has been placed almost exclusively upon the love of God revealed in Jesus Christ. In consequence the severity of Biblical Christianity has largely been lost sight of, with far-reaching and disastrous results in many spheres of life . . . It is surely time that the balance was redressed, and that a generation which has little or no fear of God should be faced with the reality of His wrath as well as with His loving-kindness.[1]

If such was the case in Professor Tasker's time, how much more is it true in the western church of the early twenty-first century? The "balance" has not been "redressed." We have continued down the road of neglect concerning the message about God's judgment, with even less fear of God in

---

1. Tasker, *Biblical Doctrine*, vii. Note also the arresting comment by Professor Büchsel in his theological article on God's judgment: "The very proclamation of God's love presupposes that without God's saving work we are moving hopelessly to judgment. To excise or restrict the thought of divine judgment is thus to destroy the gospel" ("*krinō*," 473).

the church and our society. We see the fruit of it all around us. It is now even more urgent that our generation be presented with the reality of God's judgment. As the Christian church it is our responsibility.

My purpose in this book is to contribute to the recovery in the church today of the biblical message concerning God's judgment. There are numerous good books on the topic.[2] This book will focus on what Paul the apostle says in his letters about God's judgment.[3] The book title, *The Righteous Judgment of God*, comes from Paul's description of the final judgment in Romans 2:5: "in the day of wrath and of revelation of the righteous judgment of God." Paul was an outstanding theologian and missionary of the early church. Divine judgment was integral to his worldview and indispensable to his message. If we can grasp something of his understanding about God's judgment, and of his commitment to live accordingly and to communicate it to others, we will be part of the urgently needed recovery of this truth among God's people today.

I have written this book for God's people, including and especially for Christian leaders. It is a serious biblical study that seeks to help us "get into" God's Word and then think about some of the implications of the truth about God's judgment. It is not an exhaustive or overly technical study. While it pursues some controversial issues, others are mentioned only briefly; footnotes guide the reader to helpful sources for such matters. It uses some theological terms that are helpful in understanding Paul and the Christian worldview. In particular, "eschatology" and the "eschatological judgment" are used regularly. We need to understand these terms, even if we use them only in particular contexts. Eschatology is the study of the *eschata*, the "last things." The eschatological judgment is the "last" judgment, the final judgment at the end of history. The benefit in calling it the eschatological judgment is that it evokes the broader New Testament understanding of eschatology, of "the kingdom of God," both "now"—God's rule present through the coming of Jesus and the Holy Spirit—and "not yet"—the consummation of God's rule that will come when the Lord Jesus comes again. A basic understanding of New Testament eschatology helps us to appreciate the final judgment in connection with the full outworking

---

2. For example, Tasker, *Biblical Doctrine*; Morris, *Biblical Doctrine*; Milne, *Message of Heaven and Hell*; Morgan and Peterson, *Hell under Fire*.

3. We will draw from all thirteen of Paul's letters, on the assumption that Paul was the author of them all.

Preface

of God's purpose, not as an isolated event. The book seeks to paint something of this glorious picture.

While we are dealing with definitions, I will very briefly define God's judgment as it is presented in the Bible.[4] God's judgment is his evaluation of people, his assessment of their character and conduct against a standard of righteousness that he has set and given to humans. His judgment also involves his verdict, and where this is negative, his sentence and the execution of the sentence. Because people are sinful, the biblical presentation of judgment is largely negative: of the consequences of human failure to acknowledge God and to seek to do his will. Thus, wrath, condemnation, and death are close companions of divine judgment. But because of the mercy of God and his provision of forgiveness and renewal through Jesus Christ to those who come to him in repentance and faith, God's judgment can also involve a favorable verdict and resulting blessings from God. There is much more to be said—read the book!

Regarding the structure of the book, chapter 1 lays a biblical foundation for the study of Paul by providing a very brief overview of God's judgment in the Old Testament and in the teaching of Jesus. Chapters 2 and 3 work through each of Paul's letters and give an overview of his teaching on God's judgment. From this overview four main aspects of Paul's teaching are identified; these are discussed in chapters 4–7. Chapter 8 is a final challenge to action. I wish to comment on chapters 2 and 3 in particular. These are not a "light read." I encourage you to read carefully through them. They are the foundation of the book, and provide the opportunity to engage with Paul and to gain a sense of the big picture and impact of his understanding. The many quotations from Paul's letters in these chapters seek to facilitate the process. One way of working through these chapters that my wife and I have found helpful is to read one section at a sitting, focusing on just one Pauline letter. We have used this as the basis for reflection and prayer, focusing on particular truths or Scriptures. The book contains a short reflection at the end of each Pauline letter (except for Philemon).

I wish to acknowledge the kind support of the Board of Brisbane School of Theology in providing a period of study leave in 2010 that allowed me to write this book. I also thank the many people who have encouraged me along the way, especially those who read and commented on

---

4. See articles on judgment in Bible and theological dictionaries and encyclopedias (e.g. Elwell, *Evangelical Dictionary of Biblical Theology*; Alexander and Rosner, *New Dictionary of Biblical Theology*).

the manuscript. My heartfelt thanks go to Dr Denise Austin, Garry Austin, Vicki Binnie, Dr Mike Bird, Jesse Caulfield, Lisa Caulfield, Dr Johan Ferreira, Rev Dr Richard Gibson, Paul Grant (deceased), Dr Elizabeth Guntrip, Sue Ilich, Ann Schluter, Joe Schluter, Alan Shanks, Dave Smith, and Dr Alan Stanley, whose comments and constructive criticism have helped me to improve the book in many ways. I also thank the staff at Wipf and Stock for their kind assistance throughout the publication process. Any remaining errors and weaknesses are entirely my own. Finally, I wish to express my appreciation to my wife Rowena, who has encouraged me in this project, just as she does in everything I do.

May the Lord help us to grasp and to be faithful to his truth.

Abbreviations

AB	Anchor Bible
ACUTE	Evangelical Alliance Commission on Unity and Truth among Evangelicals
BBR	*Bulletin for Biblical Research*
BDAG	Walter Bauer, Frederick W. Danker, William F. Arndt, and Felix W. Gingrich. *A Greek-English Lexicon of the New Testament and Other Early Christian Literature*. 3rd ed. Chicago: University of Chicago Press, 2000.
BECNT	Baker Exegetical Commentary on the New Testament
BNTC	Black's New Testament Commentary
EQ	*Evangelical Quarterly*
ERT	*Evangelical Review of Theology*
HTR	*Harvard Theological Review*
ICC	International Critical Commentary
Int	*Interpretation*
JBL	*Journal of Biblical Literature*
JETS	*Journal of the Evangelical Theological Society*
JSNT	*Journal for the Study of the New Testament*
JSNTSup	Journal for the Study of the New Testament Supplement Series
JTS	*Journal of Theological Studies*
KJV	King James Version (Authorized Version) of the Holy Bible
MNTC	Moffatt New Testament Commentary

Abbreviations

NASB	New American Standard Bible
NIBC	New International Biblical Commentary
NICNT	New International Commentary on the New Testament
NIDNTT	*New International Dictionary of New Testament Theology.* Edited by Colin Brown. 4 vols. Rev. ed. Carlisle, UK: Paternoster, 1992.
NIGTC	New International Greek Testament Commentary
NovTSup	Supplements to *Novum Testamentum*
NSBT	New Studies in Biblical Theology
NTS	*New Testament Studies*
PNTC	Pillar New Testament Commentary
SBLMS	Society of Biblical Literature Monograph Series
SNTSMS	Society for New Testament Studies Monograph Series
TDNT	*Theological Dictionary of the New Testament: Abridged in One Volume.* Edited by Gerhard Kittel and Gerhard Friedrich. Translated and abridged by Geoffrey W. Bromiley. Grand Rapids: Eerdmans, 1985.
TNIV	Today's New International Version
TynBul	*Tyndale Bulletin*
WBC	Word Biblical Commentary
WTJ	*Westminster Theological Journal*
WUNT	Wissenschaftliche Untersuchungen zum Neuen Testament
ZECNT	Zondervan Exegetical Commentary on the New Testament

1

Judgment in the Old Testament and in the Teaching of Jesus

MOST OF US READ the Bible to find good news, and in our reading, meditation, and conversation, we focus on the message of God's grace that we find. But the reason we focus on grace is because we need it. We are a race under God's judgment and we live with the effects of that judgment. God's grace is his loving response to our predicament. However, if we are to appreciate his grace we must understand that predicament. We need to look carefully at what the Bible says about God's judgment. We will find that the Bible has much to say, all the way through, from Genesis to Revelation.

The purpose of this chapter is modest: to overview very briefly what the Old Testament[1] and the Gospels[2]—about eighty-seven percent of the Bible—say about God's judgment. This will provide us with a basic biblical description of what God's judgment is. It will help us to see judgment as a fundamental issue in God's relationship with humanity. It will prepare us for our study of Paul and help us to appreciate that his view of judgment is consistent with that of God's people throughout history.

Judgment in the Old Testament

The book of Genesis provides the framework within which God's judgment is understood in the Bible:

---

1. For a more detailed study that focuses on key Hebrew words, see Morris, *Biblical Doctrine*, 7–43. For an overview of God's wrath in the Old Testament, see Morris, *Apostolic Preaching*, 147–54. On judgment in the Writing Prophets, see Roetzel, *Judgement in the Community*, 15–27. On the social functions of judgment teaching in the Old Testament, see Kuck, *Judgment and Community Conflict*, 38–53. On judgment according to deeds in the Old Testament, see Yinger, *Paul, Judaism and Judgment*, 19–63.

2. While the Gospels were generally written after Paul's letters, Jesus taught before Paul wrote. We are assuming that Paul knew and was influenced by the Jesus tradition.

The Righteous Judgment of God

> ¹⁶ And the LORD God commanded the man, "You are free to eat from any tree in the garden; ¹⁷ but you must not eat from the tree of the knowledge of good and evil, for when you eat of it you will certainly die." (Gen 2:16–17)

When the first human couple disobeyed God (Gen 3:1–7), they began to experience the "death" that God had spoken about. This death affected every aspect of life: their relationship with God, with self, with each other, and with creation (Gen 3:8–24). Death is the judgment of God on their sin. God declared beforehand that if they disobeyed him death would be the consequence; and the consequence followed under the sovereignty of God. The death that came to the first humans and that spread to all their descendants (Rom 5:12) is traditionally called "the Fall" in Christian theology.

However, Genesis makes it clear that God is not only a God of judgment, but also a God of grace who acts to alleviate the effects of his judgment (e.g., Gen 3:21). He promises to eventually reverse these effects (Gen 3:15). He begins to work toward this purpose, especially in the calling of Abram (Gen 12:1–3) and the establishing of the nation of Israel.

God's grace and his judgment coexist throughout Genesis (and the Bible). Humans are under judgment generally. They all die physically (e.g., Gen 5:5, 8, 11, 14) and experience other aspects of the "curses" in Genesis 3. Humans continue to come under specific judgment because of their rebellion against God, as seen especially in the Flood (Gen 6:5—7:24) and at the tower of Babel (Gen 11:1–9). God's grace is his loving response to the plight of humanity, enabling people to have a relationship with him (Gen 4:26b), and choosing individuals through whom he will continue the human line (Gen 6:8) and eventually save humanity from his judgment (Gen 12:3). But God's grace is not simply a matter of his "clicking his fingers" and "everything is okay." God's judgment is not so easily removed. It remains as long as human sin remains. God's grace operates to deal with human sin and restore people to a relationship with himself. But God's ultimate solution to sin and judgment is beyond the Old Testament.

Judgment continues to loom large throughout the Old Testament story, which focuses on the history of Israel as God's people, chosen to bring God's blessing to all the peoples of the earth (Gen 12:3). God saves Israel from Egypt through judging Egypt (Exod 6:6; 12:12). God judges a generation of his own people in the wilderness because of their unbelief (Num 14:26–35). He judges the nations east of the Jordan River and within the land of Canaan, in order to bring his people into the land he has given them

(Ps 135:10–12). From the time of the Judges, God uses surrounding nations as instruments of judgment on his people because of their unfaithfulness to him (Judg 2:13–14; Ps 78:56–64). This climaxes in the exiles of the northern tribes (721 BC) (2 Kgs 17:5–18) and Judah in the south (586 BC) (2 Kgs 25:1–11). God also continues to judge the surrounding nations because of their sinfulness, including their sins against Israel (Amos 1:3—2:3; Ezek 25:1—32:32).

The Old Testament focuses on God's judgment as his periodic actions that deal with prolonged or worsening sin among his people or other nations. These judgments may come in the form of natural disaster or military attack that result in loss of life, livelihood and land, and great physical and emotional suffering. These judgments are punitive, that is, punishments for evil (e.g., Exod 4:23; Jer 34:17; Joel 3:4–8).[3] People get what they deserve:

> The one who sins is the one who will die. (Ezek 18:4, 20)

> "You reward everyone according to what they have done." (Ps 62:12b)

> According to what they have done, so will he repay wrath to his enemies and retribution to his foes; he will repay the islands their due. (Isa 59:18)

> The day of the LORD is near for all nations. As you have done, it will be done to you; your deeds will return upon your own head. (Obad 1:15)

However, God takes no "pleasure in the death of the wicked" (Ezek 18:23, 32), which is why he is "slow to anger" (Exod 34:6). He desires that people "repent and live" (Ezek 18:32). His judgments also have a redemptive purpose: to turn the hearts of his people back to him. This was a major purpose in the exiles of his people (Deut 4:25–31; Jer 46:28; Ezek 6:8–10). Having suffered the loss of loved ones, the loss of their land, and the shame of exile, there was a degree of repentance in God's people (Zech 1:6). Those who returned to Judea were generally more faithful to God than earlier generations (see Ezra; Nehemiah). Finally, God's judgments also bring justice for his faithful remnant. The judgment of the wicked brings relief for the poor and afflicted (Deut 10:18; Ps 9:7–10, 12, 18–20; 34:15–22; 146:7–9;

---

3. For a discussion of divine retribution in the Old Testament, see Miller, *Sin and Judgment in the Prophets*, 121–39; Yinger, *Paul, Judaism and Judgment*, 26–29; Travis, *Christ and the Judgement of God*, 13–25.

Isa 61:1–2; Ezek 34:16). Thus, God's grace works together with his judgment to bring repentance, restoration, and justice.

But there is no ultimate historical solution to sin and judgment in the Old Testament. While God's grace continues to provide forgiveness of sins to his believing people under the Mosaic covenant, they continue to struggle to be faithful to him. They also struggle with difficult physical circumstances. The presence of sin and its effects—the "curse" that afflicts all humanity (Gen 3), the judgment of God—is very much in evidence. But there is hope. The prophets speak about a future when Israel's transgressions will be "wiped out" and its sins no longer remembered (Isa 43:25), when Yahweh's suffering servant will bear the sins of God's people to heal the nation (Isa 53), and when God's people will enter a "new covenant" in which they will have hearts to obey the LORD (Jer 31:31–34; Ezek 36:24–27). A solution to sin is coming. But what about judgment? The prophets speak about "the day of Yahweh," when he will judge the nations and save Israel (Isa 66:15–24; Ezek 38–39; Joel 3; Obad 15–17; Zech 14; cf. Ps 59:5, 13; 79:6; 96:13). This is a general description of the future. More specifically, it seems that those who accept the new covenant will be saved from judgment, and those who reject it will be condemned. Not all Israelites will enter; there will be a separation of obedient from disobedient (Ezek 20:33–38). But neither will all the Gentiles be condemned. God's salvation of Israel will also be offered to the nations: "Turn to me and be saved, all the ends of the earth" (Isa 45:22; cf. Isa 42:1–4; 51:4–5). Presumably, as with Israel, those Gentiles who accept the new covenant will be saved from judgment and those who reject it will be condemned. Thus, the promise to Abraham that in him "all the families of the earth shall be blessed" (Gen 12:3), will be fulfilled.

It is significant that the Old Testament promise of a solution to human sin does not dispense with God's judgment of humanity. The reason is that people must choose whether they will receive God's gracious provision. Those who do are saved from God's judgment. Those who do not are condemned. Those who hold on to their sin are inevitably condemned.

> [22] "As the new heavens and the new earth that I make will endure before me," declares the LORD, "so will your name and descendants endure. [23] From one New Moon to another and from one Sabbath to another, all people will come and bow down before me," says the LORD. [24] "And they will go out and look on the dead bodies of those who rebelled against me; their worm will not die,

nor will their fire be quenched, and they will be loathsome to the whole human race." (Isa 66:22–24)

Judgment in the Teaching of Jesus

The expectation of coming salvation and judgment, and the separation of humanity according to their response to God's saving action, is very evident in the message of John the Baptist and of Jesus.[4] The essential message of both is: "Repent, because the kingdom of heaven has come near" (Matt 3:2; 4:17). John spoke about the separation to be performed by the Coming One:

> [12] "His winnowing fork is in his hand, and he will clear his threshing floor, gathering his wheat into the barn and burning up the chaff with unquenchable fire." (Matt 3:12)

Jesus spoke about future salvation and judgment on many occasions in various ways.[5] His parable of the wheat and tares (Matt 13:24–30) powerfully presents the separation of people at the end of the age:

> [40] "As the weeds are pulled up and burned in the fire, so it will be at the end of the age. [41] The Son of Man will send out his angels, and they will weed out of his kingdom everything that causes sin and all who do evil. [42] They will throw them into the blazing furnace, where there will be weeping and gnashing of teeth. [43] Then the righteous will shine like the sun in the kingdom of their Father. Whoever has ears, let them hear." (Matt 13:40–43)

Jesus believed in and proclaimed an eschatological[6] judgment that would result in many people being condemned (Matt 7:13). He spoke on numerous occasions about "hell" (Gr. *Gehenna*), the place of eternal judgment (Matt 5:22, 29, 30; 10:28; 18:9; Mark 9:43, 45, 47; Luke 12:5).[7] He also

---

4. On eschatological judgment in the proclamation of John the Baptist and of Jesus, see Reiser, *Jesus and Judgment*. See also Travis, "Judgment," 408–11.

5. For example, in Matthew's Gospel alone, see Matt 7:1–2, 21–23; 8:11–12; 10:14–15; 11:21–24; 12:36–37, 41–42; 13:24–30, 36–43, 47–50; 18:21–35; 19:28; 22:2–14; 24:37–41, 45–51; 25:1–13, 14–30, 31–46.

6. See the definition in the Preface. "Eschatological" is derived from the Greek *eschatos*: "last." The eschatological judgment is the last or final judgment, the judgment at the end of history as we know it.

7. *Gehenna* is the Greek equivalent of the Hebrew *gê-hinnōm*, the "Valley of Hinnom" south of Jerusalem. From Josiah's time it was a dumping place for rubbish and the corpses of criminals (2 Kgs 23:10). Its decomposition and smoldering fires provided a

called it "eternal punishment" (Matt 25:46). He spoke about the judgment of both Israel and the nations, resulting in salvation or condemnation (Matt 8:11–12; 25:31–46).[8] He spoke about his own role in the final judgment (Matt 7:21–23; 10:32–33; 16:27; John 5:25–27). He affirmed judgment according to a person's works (Matt 7:21–23; 12:36–37; 16:27; 25:31–46; John 5:28–29), with allegiance and obedience to him as the crucial factor (Matt 7:24–27; 10:32–33; John 5:24).

Jesus also spoke about the coming judgment of Israel that would result from its rejection of him (Matt 23:34–39; Luke 19:41–44; 21:20–24; 23:27–31). While some scholars would see this as Jesus' expectation of eschatological judgment, it seems more likely that he saw it as a severe, temporal judgment of Israel, in some ways similar to previous judgments of the nation for rejecting God's word through his prophets. But the rejection of God's Son is even more serious and will result in Israel's suffering until the end of the present age.

In John's Gospel, Jesus also speaks about the judgment of the world and of Satan that will occur in his death on the cross:

> [31] "Now is the time for judgment on this world; now the prince of this world will be driven out. [32] And I, when I am lifted up from the earth, will draw all people to myself." (John 12:31–32)

The cross of Jesus reveals God's judgment on a sinful world that rejects his Son. There can be no question that the world stands under God's judgment. Its rebellion and guilt are supremely revealed in its rejection of God's Son. At the same time the death of Jesus provides salvation for those who believe in him (John 12:32; 3:14–16). In other words, his death provides escape from condemnation for believers (John 5:24). Through the cross Satan is also judged (John 16:11) and dethroned. His power over humanity is broken.

I am very conscious of the brevity, selectivity and inadequacy of this overview. However, two observations can be made concerning Jesus' understanding of judgment. Firstly, it is fairly clear that Jesus holds the Old Testament view of God's judgment. In particular, he believes in and emphasizes eschatological judgment, incorporating some contemporary Jewish beliefs,[9] and also relating final judgment to himself. Secondly, Jesus sees

powerful symbol of eschatological judgment.

8. "Jesus' concept of judgment is crucial. If it is wrong, his ministry has no relevance for our relationship with God. If it is right, our situation is hopeless and intolerable apart from his forgiving word" (Büchsel, "*krinō*," 472).

9. On eschatological judgment in early Jewish literature, see Travis, *Christ and the*

his imminent death as related to God's judgment. His death demonstrates the judgment of the world, breaking Satan's power and providing salvation for those who trust in him. The prophetic hope of God's suffering servant, a new covenant, and forgiveness of sins, comes together in him, through his death and resurrection. The Gospels show us that this is the case (Mark 10:45; Luke 22:37; cf. Isa 53; Matt 26:28; cf. Jer 31:31–34). Jesus sees himself as the fulfillment of the Old Testament hope for a solution to the problem of human sin and divine judgment.

Summary of Main Points

We will briefly summarize what we have found in our overview of God's judgment in the Old Testament and Jesus' teaching:

1. The Fall of humanity as a result of disobedience is the primary manifestation of the judgment of God. Humanity continues to live under this judgment.
2. People and nations are judged, often through physical calamities, for their persistent sin against God or people. As God's chosen people, Israel is not exempt from such judgment.
3. God's judgment has various purposes: to punish evildoers; to bring people to repentance and salvation; to restore justice.
4. It is God's grace that provides salvation through, and ultimately from, God's judgment. People must repent in order to receive God's salvation.
5. There will be a judgment of all nations at the end of history, an "eschatological" judgment to finally deal with human sin. The result of this judgment will be salvation for some and condemnation for others.
6. Jesus' death involves God's judgment on the world and on Satan. It provides salvation from God's judgment for those who believe in Jesus. He is the fulfillment of the prophetic hope for salvation from sin and divine judgment.

Judgement of God, 26–49. For a broader study of judgment in this literature, see Roetzel, *Judgement in the Community*, 28–67. For a study of the social functions of judgment teaching, see Kuck, *Judgment and Community Conflict*, 53–95. For a study of judgment according to deeds, see Yinger, *Paul, Judaism and Judgment*, 64–140.

2

Overview of God's Judgment in Paul's Letters, Part 1

THE PREVIOUS CHAPTER HAS shown that God's judgment is a major element in the worldview of the Old Testament writers and of Jesus. They see the fundamental human problem in terms of being under God's judgment, which is what humanity needs to be saved from. The good news is that God has graciously provided salvation from his judgment through his Son, Jesus Christ.

We now come to the focus of our study, namely, the apostle Paul's understanding of God's judgment. This is very important for us as Christians, because in his letters to the churches Paul is a major contributor to the New Testament. He builds on the foundation of the Old Testament and of the life, teaching, death, and resurrection of Jesus Christ, in bringing a Christian theology, ethic, and way of mission to God's people. Our main question is: *Is God's judgment a major issue for Paul?* Beyond this, we wish to discover the various aspects of his understanding of God's judgment and how these relate to other major themes in his theology. Our purpose is to learn and to be challenged about our theology, life, and mission.

While there are different ways to approach our topic,[1] I have chosen to do a "reconnaissance" of Paul's letters, working through each letter from Romans to Philemon to see the big picture of God's judgment.[2] This chap-

---

1. For more focused studies of God's judgment in Paul, see Roetzel, "Judgment Form," 305–12; Roetzel, *Judgement in the Community*, 68–180 (eschatology and the church); Kuck, *Judgment and Community Conflict*, 150–239 (1 Cor 3:5—4:5); Yinger, *Paul, Judaism and Judgment*, 143–291 (judgment according to deeds); Travis, *Christ and the Judgement of God*, 53–213 (focus on the limits of divine retribution); McFadden, *Judgment* (judgment according to deeds in Romans).

2. There will not be time to stop and discuss some details; these will be pursued in later chapters of the book. Other possible approaches include a chronological study of Paul's letters concerned with the development of his thought on judgment, or a thematic study that highlights major judgment themes in each letter or across letters. While the latter would be useful, it begins with a structure, rather than allowing a structure

ter will cover Romans to Galatians; the next chapter will cover Ephesians to Philemon. There will be reflections along the way, and a final section that draws together key findings.

Romans

The Wrath of God

We encounter God's judgment early in Romans, immediately after the introduction (Rom 1:1–15) and Paul's theme statement (1:16–17). In verse 18 Paul begins to describe "the wrath of God" which is being revealed against the sin of humanity:

> The wrath of God is being revealed from heaven against all the godlessness and wickedness of human beings who suppress the truth by their wickedness (Rom 1:18)

This verse begins a substantial section of Paul's letter (Rom 1:18—3:20) in which he describes human sinfulness and God's judgment. Paul sees the wrath of God as a major issue in the divine-human relationship that must be dealt with if people are to be in right relationship with God and to escape condemnation. The revelation of "God's righteousness" (Rom 1:17) in Jesus Christ is the answer to the human predicament. Salvation is God's gracious provision to the human race living under the sentence of God's judgment.

Thus, the early chapters of Romans indicate that God's wrath is a fundamental element in Paul's theology of salvation. Salvation is first and foremost salvation from the wrath of God. But what is God's wrath and why is God wrathful? What is it about him that causes his wrath? What is it about humans that they are deserving of his wrath? We will keep these questions in mind as we proceed.

Paul's description of human sinfulness in Romans 1:18–32 begins to give an answer concerning why people deserve God's wrath. Basically, they have dishonored God and chosen a way of living that is contrary to his will. Paul also describes how God's wrath has been manifested in human history. With his three statements, "God gave them over" (vv. 24, 26, 28), Paul spells out specific ways in which the judgment of God has come upon people. Paul explains that the human decline into sexual impurity (vv. 24–25), sexual

---

to emerge more inductively. I have chosen a more inductive approach, in the hope of helping the reader to engage more closely with Paul and to discern the structure of his theology of divine judgment.

perversion (vv. 26–27), and corrupted thinking that leads to all manner of sins (vv. 28–32), is a manifestation of the wrath of God. God gives people over to these things. Paul is evidently describing an aspect of God's temporal judgment on humans. While this could be classified under the "Fall" of humanity,[3] it is not simply Paul's description of original sin, but of the sin of humans subsequent to the Fall. It is a description of the fallen condition of humans resulting from the Fall, a condition that involves ongoing sinful activity and the ongoing judgment of God on humans throughout history. We will consider temporal judgment in chapter 5 of the book.

In Romans 2 Paul comes to the eschatological judgment:

> [5] But because of your stubbornness and your unrepentant heart, you are storing up wrath against yourself for the day of God's wrath, when his righteous judgment will be revealed. [6] God "will repay everyone according to what they have done." [7] To those who by persistence in doing good seek glory, honor and immortality, he will give eternal life. [8] But for those who are self-seeking and who reject the truth and follow evil, there will be wrath and anger. [9] There will be trouble and distress for every human being who does evil: first for the Jew, then for the Gentile; [10] but glory, honor and peace for everyone who does good: first for the Jew, then for the Gentile. [11] For God does not show favoritism. (Rom 2:5–11)

This is a very important passage in Paul's letters in which he summarizes the basic elements of his understanding of the future judgment of all humans. That future judgment is fundamental to Paul's worldview. It is based on the Old Testament teaching about the "day of Yahweh," here described as "the day of God's wrath" (v. 5). It sees God as a righteous, moral being, judging between those who have sought to live according to his will and purpose, and those who have rejected him and his way. The outcome for those who have "reject[ed] the truth and follow[ed] evil" will be "wrath and anger . . . trouble and distress" (vv. 8–9). The outcome for those who throughout their lives have sought "glory, honor and immortality" will be "eternal life" (v. 7). God's righteous judgment is a moral judgment of human behavior (v. 6 cf. Ps 62:12; Prov 24:12)—behavior that expresses a person's fundamental attitude toward God—honoring him, wanting to be with him and please him; or dishonoring him and living for oneself, not for God and according to his will. While Paul does not elaborate on the outcomes of

---

3. Hooker argues that this passage is very dependent on the Adam narratives in Genesis 1–3, describing the human predicament in terms of the fall of Adam. Thus, the passage describes the Fall as well as its aftermath (Hooker, "Adam in Romans 1," 73–84).

God's judgment, it is apparent that the final destiny of each person will be consistent with how they have lived. "Eternal life" is life with God. "Wrath and anger" is a destiny separated from God and his life. While there are various questions about this passage that we will not seek to answer here,[4] Paul makes it clear that the eschatological judgment is coming, will be righteous, and will determine the eternal destiny of every person. We will see what Paul adds to the picture throughout his letters.

But what is God's wrath? Is it an outburst of anger similar to human outbursts of anger? Certainly not! Paul puts God's wrath in context in Romans 2:4:

> Or do you show contempt for the riches of his kindness, forbearance and patience, not realizing that God's kindness is intended to lead you to repentance? (Rom 2:4)

God's wrath is not like human anger that is so often self-seeking, uncontrolled, malicious, and vindictive. It is not "a passionate state of non-reflective self-assertion."[5] God's wrath is his settled disposition against evil that judges evil and removes it from his world, for the ultimate benefit of the world. It involves "a decision taken deliberately and based on righteous grounds."[6] God's wrath coexists with his deep compassion toward his creatures: "his kindness, forbearance and patience" that lead people to repentance. In other words, God is at work to enable people to recognize their sin, forsake it, and come to him for forgiveness and restoration of relationship with him. Then they will be separated from their sin and will not incur his judgment. God takes "no pleasure in the death of the wicked" (Ezek 18:23, 32). All of this presupposes that God has made a way of escape from sin and judgment, which Paul describes in Romans 3:21–26, and to which we will come shortly.

Paul also says concerning the eschatological judgment:

> This will take place on the day when God judges everyone's secrets through Jesus Christ, as my gospel declares. (Rom 2:16)

---

4. These include whether the description of those living for God is a theoretical but not an actual possibility, or whether Paul is describing the people of God who have received his grace through faith. See the discussions in Schreiner, *Romans*, 141–45; McFadden, *Judgment*, 139–53.

5. Vos, *Pauline Eschatology*, 263.

6. Ibid., 263–64. It is a "strong and settled opposition to all that is evil[,] arising out of God's very nature" (Morris, *Apostolic Preaching*, 180). For studies of God's wrath in the Bible, see Schönweiss and Hahn, "Anger, Wrath," 105–13; Stählin et al., "*orgē*," 716–26.

This is a powerful statement. We note firstly that Paul's gospel includes the announcement of the eschatological judgment. In his preaching Paul spoke about God's judgment (cf. Acts 17:30–31; 24:24–25).[7] Also, Paul incorporates Jesus Christ into the final judgment. Christ is the one who will judge humanity on God's behalf. Paul is consistent with Jesus' anticipation of his involvement in the eschatological judgment, as seen in the Gospels. Evidently, Paul sees Christ through his life, death, and resurrection as having the right to judge humanity, for whom judgment will be in the light of the saving work of Christ. Those who trust in him will be saved on the basis of his death and resurrection. For them the final judgment will be "a salvific judgment."[8]

In Romans 2:12 Paul introduces the law of Moses as the standard by which those who are under the law, that is, Jews, will be judged:

> All who sin apart from the law will also perish apart from the law, and all who sin under the law will be judged by the law. (Rom 2:12)

Paul's argument in the second half of Romans 2 concerning Jews, Gentiles, keeping the law, and right relationship with God has generated much scholarly discussion.[9] This is not our immediate concern. What is significant for our purpose is that Paul sees the law of Moses as God's revelation of his will to Israel. While this is God's gracious provision and a great privilege (Rom 3:2), it also brings the responsibility of obeying the law, and it establishes a standard for judging the conduct of God's people. Israel's history shows its general failure to obey God's law (cf. Rom 2:21–25). Paul comes to several conclusions:

> Therefore no one will be declared righteous in God's sight by observing the law; rather, through the law we become conscious of our sin. (Rom 3:20)

> because the law brings wrath. (Rom 4:15a)

The law makes Israel conscious of its sin. No person is justified before God by keeping the law. In fact, the law "brings wrath." In short, when

---

7. Lincoln argues that Paul is reminding his readers of his main point thus far, "namely, that it is precisely his gospel which takes the righteousness of God in the sense of his righteous judgment seriously and that it is because it takes it seriously that this gospel is necessary for all" ("From Wrath to Justification," 143).

8. Fitzmyer, *Romans*, 312.

9. See Moo, *Romans*, 144–77; Dunn, *Romans 1–8*, 93–128; Gathercole, "Law unto Themselves," 27–49; McFadden, *Judgment*, 139–53.

people are judged by God's law, they end up being condemned as law-breakers, under the wrath of God.

If people today struggle with the doctrine of God and his judgment, we note that it was no different in Paul's time. In Romans 3:3–8 Paul has to defend God's faithfulness and righteousness against those who would seek to excuse their unfaithfulness to God (v. 3) and their unrighteous behavior (vv. 5, 7):

> ⁵ But if our unrighteousness brings out God's righteousness more clearly, what shall we say? That God is unjust in bringing his wrath on us? (I am using a human argument.) ⁶ Certainly not! If that were so, how could God judge the world? (Rom 3:5–6)

In the process Paul states what for him is a fundamental assumption: "God [will] judge the world" (v. 6). Paul believes in universal eschatological judgment. In the light of universal human sinfulness that Paul seeks to demonstrate in Romans 1:18—3:20, it is clear that all humanity is "held accountable to God" (3:19), liable to punishment.[10] We note also that Paul explicitly includes God's wrath and judgment in the concept of God's righteousness. Some scholars have argued that the righteousness of God is his covenant faithfulness, his faithfulness to his covenant promises to Israel.[11] While there is truth in this, it falls well short of explaining the whole concept. God's judgment and wrath are also fundamental to Paul's idea of God's righteousness.[12]

Having described the human predicament under the power of sin (Rom 3:9) and liable to God's judgment, Paul goes on to describe God's gracious solution:

> ²¹ But now apart from the law the righteousness of God has been made known, to which the Law and the Prophets testify. ²² This righteousness is given through faith in Jesus Christ to all who believe. There is no difference between Jew and Gentile, ²³ for all have sinned and fall short of the glory of God, ²⁴ and all are justified freely by his grace through the redemption that came by Christ Jesus. ²⁵ God presented Christ as a sacrifice of atonement, through the shedding of his blood—to be received by faith. He did this to

---

10. So Moo, *Romans*, 205; Dunn, *Romans 1–8*, 152.

11. See Wright, *Climax of the Covenant*, 231–57; Wright, *New Testament and the People of God*, 271–72, 457–58; Wright, *What St Paul Really Said*, 95–111.

12. See Lincoln, "From Wrath to Justification," 136–37; Moo, *Romans*, 189–90; McFadden, *Judgment*, 63–82.

> demonstrate his justice, because in his forbearance he had left the sins committed beforehand unpunished— ²⁶ he did it to demonstrate his justice at the present time, so as to be just and the one who justifies those who have faith in Jesus. (Rom 3:21–26)

God's righteous action flows from his righteous character, providing right relationship with himself through Jesus Christ. This is Paul's gospel. We note that the death of Christ (v. 25) is at the heart of the gospel. And while God's action was motivated by his love (Rom 5:8), what happened in Christ's death was not about God's love, as such. It was about righteousness. It is God's act of righteousness in Christ's death that allows guilty sinners to be put right with God and freed from condemnation.

We saw in John's Gospel that Jesus related his death to God's judgment (John 12:31). The question is whether Paul sees God's judgment at work in Christ's death. In particular, what does Paul mean by describing Christ as a "sacrifice of atonement" (Gr. *hilastērion*: propitiation) in verse 25? This is much disputed by scholars and we will return to it in chapter 6.

In Paul's enumeration of the blessings associated with being in right relationship with God through faith in Christ (Rom 5:1–11), he describes future salvation in the following way:

> ⁹ Since we have now been justified by his blood, how much more shall we be saved from God's wrath through him! ¹⁰ For if, while we were God's enemies, we were reconciled to him through the death of his Son, how much more, having been reconciled, shall we be saved through his life! (Rom 5:9–10)

Paul sees future salvation as being saved from the wrath of God at the eschatological judgment. Salvation is for those who were "God's enemies" (v. 10), which is Paul's description of the relationship and attitude of fallen humans to God. Salvation is through the death and resurrection of Jesus Christ: "his blood" (v. 9) and "his life" (v. 10). Those who are justified through faith in Christ can be confident that they will not be condemned at the final judgment. Evidently, present justification anticipates final justification/acquittal.

We see then that Paul's argument in Romans 1:18—5:11 is framed by the wrath of God (Rom 1:18; 5:9). God's judgment is one of the fundamental assumptions of Paul's theology. It is a key element within the larger topic of God's righteousness: his righteous activity in Jesus Christ that brings sinful humans into right relationship with God, no longer subject to the wrath of God.

Overview of God's Judgment in Paul's Letters, Part 1

Freedom from Condemnation in Relationship with Christ

In Romans 5:12–21 Paul goes back to Adam to explain what Christ has accomplished for us:

> [12] Therefore, just as sin entered the world through one man, and death through sin, and in this way death came to all people, because all sinned— [13] To be sure, sin was in the world before the law was given, but sin is not charged against anyone's account where there is no law. [14] Nevertheless, death reigned from the time of Adam to the time of Moses, even over those who did not sin by breaking a command, as did Adam, who is a pattern of the one to come. [15] But the gift is not like the trespass. For if the many died by the trespass of the one man, how much more did God's grace and the gift that came by the grace of the one man, Jesus Christ, overflow to the many! [16] Nor can the gift of God be compared with the result of one man's sin: The judgment followed one sin and brought condemnation, but the gift followed many trespasses and brought justification. [17] For if, by the trespass of the one man, death reigned through that one man, how much more will those who receive God's abundant provision of grace and of the gift of righteousness reign in life through the one man, Jesus Christ! [18] Consequently, just as one trespass resulted in condemnation for all people, so also one righteous act resulted in justification and life for all. [19] For just as through the disobedience of the one man the many were made sinners, so also through the obedience of the one man the many will be made righteous. (Rom 5:12–19)

Paul sees all humanity in relationship with Adam, united with him in sin, under the dominion of death, subject to God's judgment. Christ, through his "one act of righteousness" (v. 18), has secured righteousness and life for all who are united with him. It is clear that Paul shares the view of Genesis concerning the Fall of humanity.[13] He sees the human condition in sin and death as the judgment of God and the fundamental human problem. While there is also the problem of human sinning and God's temporal judgment throughout history (Rom 1:18–32), and the future problem of God's eschatological judgment (Rom 2:5–16), the basic problem is God's judgment in the fallen condition of humanity. God deals with it in Christ.

---

13. It is not so clear how Paul sees the relationship between Adam and humanity in relation to sin. For a discussion of the "natural headship" and "federal headship" of Adam, and another proposal, see Blocher, *Original Sin*, 63–81.

Paul then proceeds to explain the freedom of Christians from the power of sin (Rom 6) and from being under the law of Moses (Rom 7). Paul gives further insights into the fallen human condition. He describes humanity "under sin" (Rom 3:9) in terms of slavery to sin (6:16–17). Sin is a master that people serve; it pays death as its "wages" (6:23). In Romans 7 Paul goes on to explain that the law of Moses did not solve this problem for Israel. In fact, in some ways it exacerbated the problem because in defining sin the law had the effect of increasing sinning among people (vv. 7–11; cf. Rom 5:20). Paul explains that the problem is not God's law (v. 12), but sinful humans, who are "fleshly" (v. 14) and who in their "flesh" (Gr. *sarx*) find the power of sin to be very active (vv. 15–25). Sin is not an external power, but a principle that indwells fallen humans and that is the source of sinful acts.

Paul then addresses life in the Spirit (Rom 8). He sees God's Spirit as bringing the revelation of freedom from condemnation, sin, and death, that is, from the fallen human condition under the judgment of God (vv. 1–2). The Spirit also brings the revelation of righteousness and life in Christ (vv. 2, 10). Ultimately, God through his Spirit will raise the bodies of his people (v. 11), finally freeing them from physical death. Everything the Spirit does flows from the coming and sacrificial death of God's Son:

> For what the law was powerless to do because it was weakened by the sinful nature [lit. flesh; Gr. *sarx*], God did by sending his own Son in the likeness of sinful humanity [lit. flesh] to be a sin offering. And so he condemned sin in human flesh (Rom 8:3)

Paul thus returns to the heart of the gospel. His description of Christ's death and its effect—"he condemned sin in the flesh," that is, in the flesh of Jesus[14]—shows that Paul's understanding of Christ's death involves the judgment of God on human sin in Christ. Given the centrality of the cross in delivering humanity from God's judgment, seen here and in Romans 3:25, it would seem logical that the judgment of God which takes place in Christ's death is at the very heart of Paul's understanding of the gospel. But what does it mean? We will pursue it as we work through Paul's letters, and also in chapter 6.

Before proceeding we will take a moment to go back to Romans 6 to connect what Paul says there with Romans 8:3. Paul says:

---

14. See Moo, *Romans*, 480; Dunn, *Romans 1–8*, 422.

> ² By no means! We are those who have died to sin; how can we live in it any longer? ³ Or don't you know that all of us who were baptized into Christ Jesus were baptized into his death? ⁴ We were therefore buried with him through baptism into death in order that, just as Christ was raised from the dead through the glory of the Father, we too may live a new life. ⁵ If we have been united with him in a death like his, we will certainly also be united with him in a resurrection like his. ⁶ For we know that our old self was crucified with him so that the body ruled by sin might be done away with, that we should no longer be slaves to sin— (Rom 6:2–6)

Paul sees believers as participating in Christ's death and resurrection, which is the basis of the freedom and new life brought by the Spirit (Rom 8). Freedom from sin and condemnation comes from sharing in Christ's death to sin (Rom 6:10) and from the condemnation of sin in Christ (Rom 8:3). Christ's death means the sinner's death and the sinner's judgment: "our old self was crucified with him" (Rom 6:6).[15] For Paul the judgment of sin in Christ thus includes the judgment of sinful humanity in his death, whereby believers are freed from condemnation.

It is the Spirit who brings the experience of freedom from sin for Christians. Paul describes this in terms of no longer being "in the flesh" (Gr. *sarx*) but "in the Spirit" (Rom 8:9). In this connection Paul says more about fallen humanity:

> ⁶ For the mind set on the flesh is death, but the mind set on the Spirit is life and peace, ⁷ because the mind set on the flesh is hostile toward God; for it does not subject itself to the law of God, for it is not even able *to do so*; ⁸ and those who are in the flesh cannot please God. (Rom 8:6–8 NASB)

Paul thus elaborates on humans as enemies of God (cf. Rom 5:11). People's enmity toward God is innate to them, through the principle of sin within them. The good news is that God's Spirit is the new principle, or "law" (Rom 8:2),[16] that comes within us to free us from sin so that we become friends of God, willing and able to do his will. We are "in the Spirit" (Rom 8:9). Praise God.

---

15. "Our old man" (v. 6) means "the whole of our fallen human nature, the whole self in its fallenness. It is the whole man, not merely a part of him, that comes under God's condemnation, and that died in God's sight in Christ's death" (Cranfield, *Romans*, 1:308–9).

16. See discussion in Moo, *Romans*, 473–77.

The Righteous Judgment of God

As Paul looks to the future hope of God's people, he is reminded of the present state of humanity:

> [20] For the creation was subjected to frustration, not by its own choice, but by the will of the one who subjected it, in hope [21] that the creation itself will be liberated from its bondage to decay and brought into the freedom and glory of the children of God. (Rom 8:20–21)

Paul again describes the judgment of God at the Fall of humanity, involving "frustration" and "bondage to decay," a state that has continued to the present time and will continue until the "sons of God" are revealed (v. 19) with redeemed bodies (v. 23). While God's people have the "firstfruits of the Spirit," they "groan" along with the creation (vv. 22–23), that is, they still share in the effects of God's judgment; they are still part of fallen humanity. Also, because they live among fallen humans who oppose the rule of God, they also suffer with Christ and for Christ (vv. 17–18). Paul catalogues their sufferings in verses 36–37. Thus, while in Christ God's people are delivered from God's judgment on sin, they still experience the effects of judgment in the present age: in their own fallenness and through the hostility of other fallen humans.

Making sense of everything Paul says in Romans 5–8 is made easier if we are aware of his eschatology, that is, his understanding of the "last things." For Paul those last things are not merely final salvation and judgment. They are the things promised by God that have begun to be fulfilled with the coming of Jesus and the Spirit, and that will be consummated when Jesus comes again. Thus, everything we have in Christ is included in Paul's eschatology. There is the "now"—what we already have—union with Christ through God's Spirit, freedom from sin, death, and condemnation, and entry into new life and righteousness. There is also the "not yet"—what we will have at the Second Coming—ultimate freedom from sin and death in the resurrection of our bodies, and a new creation. Paul's eschatology helps us to understand the tension in the Christian life between what we presently experience and all that God has promised—between the "now" and the "not yet." God's kingdom does not come all at once: the "now" has come; the "not yet" is still to come. We will keep Paul's eschatology in mind as we continue to study what he says about God's judgment and salvation.

Overview of God's Judgment in Paul's Letters, Part 1

Unbelief as Judgment

The judgment of God is also very evident in Paul's discussion in Romans 9–11 of the unbelief of Israel. God "hardens" the heart of Pharaoh in order to display God's power on earth (9:17–18). God endures "with great patience the objects of his wrath—prepared for destruction" (9:22), that is, sinful humans who will be condemned at the eschatological judgment.[17] God has "hardened" many Israelites in their unbelief (11:7–10). Clearly, this is God's judgment on "a disobedient and obstinate people" (10:21). Gentile Christians are warned to "continue in [God's] kindness," lest they be "cut off" like unbelieving Israelites (11:22). However, Paul does not believe in God's rejection of Israel (11:11); he hopes for a great turning of Israelites to God in the future (11:25–27), so that "all Israel will be saved" (11:26).[18] Thus, Paul seems to see God's present judgment on unbelieving Israelites not just as punitive but also as redemptive, ultimately leading to repentance in a future generation(s).

In these chapters Paul speaks about temporal judgments. In the case of Pharaoh it was to further God's saving purpose for Israel, God's chosen people. In the case of unbelieving Jews (and Gentiles), God's judgment means leaving them in their unbelief. There are eschatological consequences: they will experience the wrath of God. Paul's particular interest is in why some people believe and others do not. He finds the answer in God's sovereign purpose (9:11, 14–23), whereby God hardens some but has mercy on others. Thus, the judgment and mercy of God operate within the sovereign purpose of God.

Ethical Implications of God's Judgment

In his practical exhortations to the church in Rome (Rom 12:1—15:13) Paul touches on three aspects of God's judgment. The first is in Paul's teaching about not taking personal revenge:

---

17. So Moo, *Romans*, 607. Both Cranfield and Dunn question this interpretation, arguing that while these people are presently objects of wrath, there is the possibility that they could become "objects of his mercy" (v. 23) through God's "great patience" (Cranfield, *Romans*, 2:492–97; Dunn, *Romans 9–16*, 558–60). While they may be correct, the point is that some people do remain "objects of wrath," and ultimately experience eschatological condemnation.

18. See Moo, *Romans*, 720–23; Dunn, *Romans 9–16*, 681–82.

The Righteous Judgment of God

> ¹⁷ Do not repay anyone evil for evil. Be careful to do what is right in the eyes of everyone. ¹⁸ If it is possible, as far as it depends on you, live at peace with everyone. ¹⁹ Do not take revenge, my dear friends, but leave room for God's wrath, for it is written: "It is mine to avenge; I will repay," says the Lord. (Rom 12:17-19)

People do not have the right to "repay . . . evil for evil" (v. 17). The right of retribution is God's: "It is mine to avenge; I will repay" (v. 19). No doubt Paul has in mind the eschatological judgment. But he may also be thinking of God's temporal wrath at work through earthly authorities (Rom 13:4),[19] which is a second aspect of judgment in this section of Romans:

> ¹ Let everyone be subject to the governing authorities, for there is no authority except that which God has established. The authorities that exist have been established by God. ² Consequently, whoever rebels against the authority is rebelling against what God has instituted, and those who do so will bring judgment on themselves. ³ For rulers hold no terror for those who do right, but for those who do wrong. Do you want to be free from fear of the one in authority? Then do what is right and you will be commended. ⁴ For the one in authority is God's servant for your good. But if you do wrong, be afraid, for rulers do not bear the sword for no reason. They are God's servants, agents of wrath to bring punishment on the wrongdoer. (Rom 13:1-4)

Paul sees earthly rulers as having God's authority to maintain righteousness in society. The punishment of wrongdoers is part of the maintenance of right order and an expression of God's wrath against evil.

The third aspect of God's judgment comes up in the context of Christians not judging each other (Rom 14). Again, Paul teaches that we do not have the right to judge each other (vv. 3-4, 10, 13), because each of us belongs to the Lord (vv. 4, 7-9) and is accountable to him:

> ¹⁰ You, then, why do you judge your brother or sister? Or why do you treat your brother or sister with contempt? For we will all stand before God's judgment seat. ¹¹ It is written: "'As surely as I live,' says the Lord, 'every knee will bow before me; every tongue will confess to God.'" ¹² So then, we will all give an account of ourselves to God. (Rom 14:10-12)

---

19. So Dunn, *Romans 9-16*, 749, 765; Morris, *Romans*, 454.

Here Paul is speaking about the eschatological judgment, when Christians will be accountable for the lives they have lived.[20] The influence of the Old Testament is evident in verse 11 (cf. Isa 45:23). This is an important text for us as Christians. It says that every believer in Jesus will ultimately stand before God and give an account for his or her life. There is still a judgment for us in the future. Our justification in Christ does not mean no future judgment. We will discuss the judgment of believers in chapter 7.

The clear teaching in these chapters is that we do not have the right to judge others. Paul is consistent with the teaching of Jesus in Matthew 7:1–2. God has given the right of temporal judgment in part to earthly rulers. The ultimate right to judge belongs to God alone.

Finally, we note Paul's warning against false teachers in Romans 16:17–19:

> [17] I urge you, brothers and sisters, to watch out for those who cause divisions and put obstacles in your way that are contrary to the teaching you have learned. Keep away from them. [18] For such people are not serving our Lord Christ, but their own appetites. By smooth talk and flattery they deceive the minds of naive people. [19] Everyone has heard about your obedience, so I rejoice because of you; but I want you to be wise about what is good, and innocent about what is evil. (Rom 16:17–19)

Paul does not speak about divine judgment in relation to the false teachers, but simply separation: "Keep away from them" (v. 17). Paul does not regard these people as Christians and so does not give instruction for correcting them. Paul concludes with the assurance:

> The God of peace will soon crush Satan under your feet. (Rom 16:20a)

In the context of Paul's instruction about false teachers it would seem that he is affirming the victory of the Roman church over such evil in the here and now.[21] But Paul is probably also looking to the eschatological judgment when all evil spiritual powers will finally be overcome.[22] In both cases God's judgment of evil powers is evident.

---

20. For a discussion of this judgment, see McFadden, *Judgment*, 103–19.
21. So Morris, *Romans*, 541; Moo, *Romans*, 932–33.
22. So Cranfield, *Romans*, 2:803; Moo, *Romans*, 932–33; Dunn, *Romans 9–16*, 905.

Conclusion

It is time to ask what we have found concerning God's judgment in the letter to the Romans. Perhaps we could answer in the words of Paul: "Much in every way!" (Rom 3:2). Judgment is a major theme running through and surfacing at times throughout the letter, and interacting with other themes such as righteousness, sin, the law of Moses, God's love, salvation, faith in Christ, God's Spirit, suffering, election, Israel, the people of God, Christian ethics, and spiritual powers. In various ways Paul's theology of divine judgment also corresponds with what we found in the Old Testament and Jesus' teaching, although Paul develops various aspects in the light of the coming of Christ and the Spirit. Paul sees the Fall of humanity into sin and death as the fundamental judgment, from which flow temporal and eschatological judgment. Christ's death and resurrection are central in saving humans from the judgment of God. Faith in Christ results in right relationship with God in the present, anticipating salvation from God's eschatological wrath. Paul's understanding of God's judgment sits within the larger framework of Paul's eschatology.

A Reflection from Romans

For us who live in a culture obsessed with self, pleasure, and "love," increasingly unable to cope with an absolute standard of righteousness and the consequences of wrongdoing, Romans is a loud worldview "wakeup call." Paul teaches us that we are not at the center of reality; God is. We do not determine what is right or wrong; God does. And how I live is not "my own business"; I am accountable to God to live for him according to his revealed will. Human-defined love is not "all you need"; the holy love of God that establishes God's righteousness is what we need, desperately. My problem is not a lack of money, friends, or self-esteem; it is that left to myself, I am under the wrath of God, headed for hell. Jesus Christ is not an irrelevant figure of history; he is our loving, powerful Savior, through whom we can now live a new life for God and his glory. As I put my trust in the Lord Jesus today, I will experience more of his love and saving righteousness.

Overview of God's Judgment in Paul's Letters, Part 1

First Corinthians

As we proceed through Paul's letters we will note aspects of Paul's teaching that reinforce what we have already found in Romans, as well as aspects that add to the picture we have seen so far.

The "World" Judged

God's judgment is a very strong theme in 1 Corinthians 1. After encouraging God's people that they will be "blameless in the day of our Lord Jesus Christ" (v. 8), that is, at the eschatological judgment, Paul comes to God's judgment of the world that has taken place in the death of Christ (vv. 18–31).

> [18] For the message of the cross is foolishness to those who are perishing, but to us who are being saved it is the power of God. [19] For it is written: "I will destroy the wisdom of the wise; the intelligence of the intelligent I will frustrate." [20] Where are the wise? Where is the teacher of the law? Where is the philosopher of this age? Has not God made foolish the wisdom of the world? [21] For since in the wisdom of God the world through its wisdom did not know him, God was pleased through the foolishness of what was preached to save those who believe. (1 Cor 1:18–21)

Christ is "the wisdom of God," because his crucifixion is the way in which God has brought salvation to the world (vv. 21–24, 30). Human wisdom and ways of salvation have therefore been judged as foolish and ineffective (vv. 20–21). Those who believe the message of the cross are "being saved"; those who reject the message "are perishing" (v. 18). Generally speaking, God's electing grace is coming to those of low worldly esteem, while God is "shaming" the highly esteemed (vv. 26–29).

Paul thus sees the eschatological judgment of "the world," that is, humanity alienated from and in opposition to God,[23] as already anticipated in the death of Christ. Christ's death demonstrates God's estimation of human wisdom that will apply in the Last Day. People are being given the opportunity to learn about it, respond in faith, and enter the process of salvation.

---

23. Fee notes that "world" (Gr. *kosmos*) and "age" (Gr. *aiōn*) have merged in Paul's thought. Both the *kosmos*, "the world order that has been under the domination of Satan, and the present age have been judged by God in Christ and are thus in the process of passing away" (*1 Corinthians*, 71–72).

God's judgment is at work through his election of people; those not chosen by God will perish.

Paul continues this theme in chapter 2 as he challenges the church to understand God's estimation of things: "the rulers of this age ... are coming to nothing" (v. 6).[24]

Eschatological Judgment of Leaders

Paul then comes to God's judgment of his people (cf. 1 Pet 4:17). Teaching the Corinthians about God's servants, Paul speaks about the eschatological judgment of the work of those who build the church (1 Cor 3:10-15).

> [12] If anyone builds on this foundation using gold, silver, costly stones, wood, hay or straw, [13] their work will be shown for what it is, because the Day will bring it to light. It will be revealed with fire, and the fire will test the quality of each person's work. [14] If what has been built survives, the builder will receive a reward. [15] If it is burned up, the builder will suffer loss but yet will be saved—even though only as one escaping through the flames. (1 Cor 3:12-15)

Paul says that each person's work will be judged (vv. 13, 14, 15). If their work is found to be of a quality that pleases God, they will be rewarded. If a leader's work fails God's test, they will suffer the loss of seeing their work "burned up," but they will be saved. Paul is issuing a serious warning about the necessity of building according to the "character of Christ [and] his gospel."[25] He is not encouraging leaders that they will be "saved by the skin of their teeth," even if they are poor gospel workers.

Paul goes further in verse 17:

> If anyone destroys God's temple, God will destroy that person; for God's temple is sacred, and you together are that temple. (1 Cor 3:17)

Paul is probably referring to eschatological judgment for those who work against God's purpose in the church. Such people will be condemned.[26] Paul is obviously not speaking about God's true servants. In the context he

---

24. On "the rulers of this age," see Fee, *1 Corinthians*, 103-4.

25. Ibid., 145.

26. For a discussion of the context and purpose of this warning, see Fee, *1 Corinthians*, 148-49; Käsemann, "Sentences of Holy Law," 66-68. See also Kuck, *Judgment and Community Conflict*, 186-88; Yinger, *Paul, Judaism and Judgment*, 222-28.

is challenging the Corinthians about their arrogance and divisiveness. Are some in danger of destroying God's church in Corinth?

Paul then goes on to consider God's future judgment of him and of all God's people (4:1–5). We note again that the eschatological judgment of Christians, including Christian leaders, is a fundamental assumption of Paul (Rom 14:12; 2 Cor 5:10). It is a major reason for care and faithfulness in service (1 Cor 3:10; 4:2). We will note it as we proceed through Paul's letters, and discuss it in chapter 7.

Temporal Judgment within the Church

The theme of judgment continues strongly as Paul addresses various sins in the Corinthian community. In the case of the man involved in incest (1 Cor 5), it is clear that Paul sees God's judgment as operating through discipline in the church:

> ³ For my part, even though I am not physically present, I am with you in spirit. As one who is present with you in this way, I have already passed judgment in the name of our Lord Jesus on the one who has been doing this. ⁴ So when you are assembled and I am with you in spirit, and the power of our Lord Jesus is present, ⁵ hand this man over to Satan for the destruction of the sinful nature so that his spirit may be saved on the day of the Lord. (1 Cor 5:3–5)

It would seem that Paul is speaking about God's temporal judgment of this person operating through the church in the form of (temporary) expulsion from the community (v. 13), in order to save him from condemnation at the eschatological judgment.[27] It is thus temporal judgment with the purpose of bringing the person to repentance. This is consistent with the general principles Paul states at the end of 1 Corinthians 5: the need to make judgments about behavior within the church (v. 12) and to be separate from sinning Christians (v. 11); and not making judgments about "outsiders," whom God will judge (vv. 12, 13). Paul therefore sees God's authority as operating within the church. God's people are to live in obedience to him; where they do not, his judgment may work through community discipline to correct sinning members. We will return to this passage in chapter 5.

---

27. See discussion in Fee, *1 Corinthians*, 196–228.

The Righteous Judgment of God

Eschatological Condemnation of Sinners

Paul extends the principle of community discipline in his instruction regarding litigation between the Christians in Corinth (1 Cor 6:1–11). We note in passing two of Paul's statements:

> Or do you not know that the Lord's people will judge the world? (1 Cor 6:2a)

> Do you not know that we will judge angels? (1 Cor 6:3a)

Paul sees a future role for God's people in the eschatological judgment,[28] which he uses in his argument to the church. At the end of his instruction Paul strongly affirms the eschatological judgment of sinful humans:

> ⁹ Or do you not know that wrongdoers will not inherit the kingdom of God? Do not be deceived: Neither the sexually immoral nor idolaters nor adulterers nor male prostitutes nor practicing homosexuals ¹⁰ nor thieves nor the greedy nor drunkards nor slanderers nor swindlers will inherit the kingdom of God. (1 Cor 6:9–10)

Judgment is here described as not "inherit[ing] God's kingdom." Evildoers will be shut out from what God has prepared for his people. Paul reminds the Corinthians of their way of life before believing in Christ:

> And that is what some of you were. But you were washed, you were sanctified, you were justified in the name of the Lord Jesus Christ and by the Spirit of our God. (1 Cor 6:11)

The work of Christ and of God's Spirit has changed the Corinthians. Paul is reminding them of God's gracious work in their lives. But they must continue in the grace of God, and live holy lives. He is warning them not to return to their old ways. Evildoers will be condemned.

More on the Judgment of Christians

In his instruction about eating meat sacrificed to idols (1 Cor 8:1—11:1), Paul uses himself as an example of one who gives up his rights for the sake of others (1 Cor 9). The last thing he says concerning himself is:

---

28. On the apocalyptic background to Paul's theology here, see Fee, *1 Corinthians*, 233–34.

> No, I strike a blow to my body and make it my slave so that after I have preached to others, I myself will not be disqualified for the prize. (1 Cor 9:27)

Paul's desire not to be "disqualified" would seem to refer to the eschatological judgment. The question is whether Paul sees final rejection as a possibility for himself.[29] We will pursue this in chapter 7. Presently, though, we note Paul's effort to live a life consistent with the righteous standing he has in Christ. It is not enough for someone to merely claim that they are "justified" (6:11). One's way of life must testify to the genuineness of one's relationship with God. Then a person will not be "disqualified" in the end.

Paul then describes the temporal judgment of Israel in the time of Moses because of their lust, idolatry, sexual immorality, unbelief, and complaining (1 Cor 10:5–10). Paul warns the Corinthians against idolatry by eating in an idol's temple (10:14–22). Those who do so are in danger of "falling" (v. 12), of "provoking the Lord to jealousy" (v. 22). Some see this as eschatological condemnation.[30] Others argue that in the light of 1 Corinthians 5:1–5 and 11:29–32, Paul is also speaking about possible temporal physical judgment in the form of suffering or death,[31] which would seem quite possible.

Temporal Judgment in Relation to the Lord's Supper

The problematic attitude of the Corinthians surfaces again in their celebration of the Lord's Supper during their meals together (1 Cor 11:17–34). They are divided (v. 18) and their behavior at meals is dishonoring both to God and to each other (vv. 21–22). After his instructions concerning proper eating of the Lord's Supper (vv. 23–28) Paul says:

> [29] For those who eat and drink without discerning the body of Christ eat and drink judgment on themselves. [30] That is why many among you are weak and sick, and a number of you have fallen asleep. [31] But if we were more discerning with regard to ourselves, we would not come under such judgment. [32] Nevertheless, when we are judged in this way by the Lord, we are being disciplined so that we will not be finally condemned with the world. (1 Cor 11:29–32)

---

29. See Fee, *1 Corinthians*, 440.
30. See ibid., 459–60, 473–74; Travis, *Christ and the Judgement of God*, 154–56.
31. For example, Gundry Volf, *Paul and Perseverance*, 120–30.

Clearly, Paul sees God's temporal judgment operating through the sickness and even death of some church members. Such judgment is disciplinary, apparently to keep God's people from greater sins that may lead to ultimate condemnation (v. 32). We will return to this passage in chapter 5.

Eschatological Condemnation of Opponents

In his teaching about the resurrection of Christ and the eschatological resurrection (1 Cor 15), Paul describes the eschatological judgment of cosmic powers:

> [24] Then the end will come, when he hands over the kingdom to God the Father after he has destroyed all dominion, authority and power. [25] For he must reign until he has put all his enemies under his feet. [26] The last enemy to be destroyed is death. (1 Cor 15:24–26)

Paul is referring to all powers hostile to God's rule.[32] Ultimately, these powers will be judged and will have no influence in the new creation. The power of death will be broken in the resurrection of the dead (vv. 54–55).

Finally, Paul makes a strong statement in the conclusion of his letter:

> If anyone does not love the Lord, let that person be cursed! Come, Lord! (1 Cor 16:22)

This does not seem to be a curse on unbelievers in general. Rather, it appears to be equivalent to 1 Corinthians 3:17, where Paul declares that God will destroy those who destroy his temple. It affirms the ultimate condemnation of false believers who oppose the work of God.[33]

Conclusion

While 1 Corinthians does not contain as complete a teaching about God's judgment as Romans, much of the "scaffolding" is still present: the eschatological judgment of believers to salvation and for rewards, and of unbelievers to condemnation; the temporal judgment of Israel in the past and the church in the present; the cross of Christ as a place of judgment, securing salvation for those who believe; present justification in Christ

---

32. See Fee, *1 Corinthians*, 754.
33. See Fee, *1 Corinthians*, 837–39; Roetzel, *Judgement in the Community*, 142–62.

as anticipating final justification for believers. Paul's larger eschatological framework is again evident. But more is added to our picture so far of God's judgment. Where Romans focuses on the judgment of sin through the cross (Rom 8:3), 1 Corinthians emphasizes the judgment of the world—in particular, human pride—through the cross. The cross reveals God's judgment on the idolatrous mentality that rejects him and exalts human wisdom. Paul's focus is thus on human complicity in sin (cf. Rom 1:18–32) more than on sin as a power over humanity (Rom 3:9). Connected with this Paul also emphasizes the judgment of the rulers of the world, whether earthly or spiritual (1 Cor 2:6, 8; 15:24). We are reminded again of Jesus' words concerning the judgment of the world and of Satan at the cross (John 12:31). Paul also focuses more in 1 Corinthians on the temporal judgment of the church. The issue is holiness (1 Cor 1:2; 3:16–17; 6:19–20; 10:21; 11:27). God works both directly and through the believing community to discipline his people, so that they live as his holy people. Paul addresses the tension involved in living as a "justified" person: it is not just a matter of status; one's life must conform to and confirm their status if they are to realize eschatological salvation (1 Cor 9:27; 10:11–13).[34] Finally, Paul also stresses the eschatological condemnation of those who oppose the work of God in his church (1 Cor 3:17; 16:22).

A Reflection from 1 Corinthians

First Corinthians is particularly relevant for the church today. Paul writes to people who seem quite ignorant of true spirituality, of God's holiness, and of what the church is called to be. Paul's answer to the problem includes a significant "dose" of teaching concerning God's judgment to wake up the Corinthians concerning how they must think and live as God's people. In our increasingly "post-Christian" society that morally is looking more and more like "pagan" ancient Corinth, we must not follow the world in its view of reality. We must cultivate a biblical worldview that pursues biblical holiness in God's church. We need to learn how God's judgment has worked in the past, is working at present, and will work in the future, to deal with sin and promote holiness. Daily, we need to open our lives to him to deal with sin in us and to promote holiness in and through us. Together we will discover what a holy life looks like in our society. May we see people "fall down and worship God, exclaiming, 'God is really among you!'" (1 Cor 14:25).

---

34. Jesus taught the same thing in Matt 7:21–23.

Second Corinthians

Various Themes

Paul begins his letter by focusing on the "trouble" (Gr. *thlipsis*: pressure, affliction) (vv. 4, 8) and "sufferings" (Gr. *pathēmata*) (vv. 5, 6, 7) experienced by him and his associates, and more generally, by God's people (2 Cor 1:3–11). We are reminded of the effects on God's people of living in a fallen world that is under God's judgment. Paul's message is that there is comfort and hope for the church in a troubled world.

Two aspects of judgment seen in 1 Corinthians then reemerge. Paul refers to the community discipline of a church member, calling it "punishment" by the church (2 Cor 2:6).[35] Evidently, the discipline has brought the person to repentance (2:7–8). Paul expects the church to be "obedient" in dealing with sinning church members (2:9). He also contrasts "those who are being saved" with "those who are perishing" (2:15). The eschatological verdict has already been pronounced in Christ's death and resurrection. Those who believe will be saved at the Last Day; those who do not believe will perish, that is, be condemned.

In his contrast of the old and new covenants (2 Cor 3) Paul calls the old covenant "the ministry that brought death" (v. 7), "the ministry that brought condemnation" (v. 9). We are reminded of Romans 4:15: "the law brings wrath." Again, Paul points out the effect of the law of Moses: it condemns people as sinners. Paul thus highlights God's judgment through the law.

Spiritual Blindness of Unbelievers

In his description of his ministry Paul points out the situation of unbelievers:

> [3] And even if our gospel is veiled, it is veiled to those who are perishing. [4] The god of this age has blinded the minds of unbelievers, so that they cannot see the light of the gospel that displays the glory of Christ, who is the image of God. (2 Cor 4:3–4)

This is a significant element in Paul's understanding of fallen humanity. People are influenced by Satan and evil powers, and hindered from coming to faith in Christ. Spiritual blindness is part of the judgment of God on humans. But by the grace of God, through the preaching of the gospel

---

35. See Barnett, *2 Corinthians*, 125–26.

(v. 5), people are enabled to see the light "of the knowledge of God's glory displayed in the face of Christ" (v. 6), and then to "turn to the Lord" (3:16).

God's People: Suffering, Decay, Eschatological Judgment

Paul then explains more about the suffering involved in being an apostle of Christ (4:8–9). Paul understands it as follows:

> ¹⁰ We always carry around in our body the death of Jesus, so that the life of Jesus may also be revealed in our body. ¹¹ For we who are alive are always being given over to death for Jesus' sake, so that his life may also be revealed in our mortal body. ¹² So then, death is at work in us, but life is at work in you. (2 Cor 4:10–12)

In the background is a world under God's judgment, hostile to God, that killed Christ and that continues to persecute and even kill his disciples. But out of Christ's death came his life and the life of his people. Paul sees his own life as one of contrast and tension:

> Therefore we do not lose heart. Though outwardly we are wasting away, yet inwardly we are being renewed day by day. (2 Cor 4:16)

Paul still shares in a world "wasting away" under God's judgment, but within himself he also has new life from God that renews him day by day. He is looking forward to the full realization of eternal life (4:17—5:4).

The future will also involve the eschatological judgment of God's people:

> For we must all appear before the judgment seat of Christ, that everyone may receive what is due them for the things done while in the body, whether good or bad. (2 Cor 5:10)

Paul expects to give an account of his life to Christ as his judge. Judgment will be according to one's actions; a just recompense will be given.[36] Some see the judgment as universal, not just for believers.[37]

---

36. See ibid., 273–77.
37. So Travis, *Christ and the Judgement of God*, 162–67.

The Righteous Judgment of God

Judgment at the Cross

Paul returns to describing his ministry, focusing again on the death and resurrection of Christ as the way in which God has reconciled people to himself (2 Cor 5:11–21). Second Corinthians 5:21 is the gospel "in a nutshell":

> God made him who had no sin to be sin for us, so that in him we might become the righteousness of God. (2 Cor 5:21)

While Paul does not mention God's judgment directly in relation to the death of Christ, this verse and its context imply it strongly. Clearly, people's trespasses did count against them (v. 19) and they were liable to God's judgment. But in Christ, that is, in his death (vv. 14, 15), God was "not counting people's sins against them" (v. 19). Paul connects our sin with Christ's death: "He made him who knew no sin [to be] sin for us." While there has been much debate about what it means for Christ to be "made sin,"[38] Paul's basic meaning seems fairly clear. Christ the sinless one was not under the sentence of death like other humans. However, he identified with sinful humans and submitted himself to the death to which they were liable. Given that death is God's judgment for sin (Rom 5:12–18), Christ's death logically means that he entered into and experienced God's judgment of human sin. This does not mean that God judged Christ; he was sinless and not liable to judgment. It was sin that God judged (Rom 8:3); Christ experienced that judgment in his death. With sin condemned in Christ's death, humans who identify with him through faith are freed from sin and death, and enter into his righteousness and life.

Thus, we see more evidence of a strong connection in Paul's thought between the cross and God's judgment. The cross is at the center of Paul's understanding of how people are saved from God's judgment on sin. The reason is that human sin is judged in the death of Christ.

Holiness and Community Discipline

As Paul continues to describe his ministry (2 Cor 6:1–10) he again lists the sufferings of God's servants in the present age (vv. 4–5, 8–10). He also challenges the Corinthians to live holy lives:

---

38. See Barnett, *2 Corinthians*, 312–15.

Overview of God's Judgment in Paul's Letters, Part 1

> Therefore, since we have these promises, dear friends, let us purify ourselves from everything that contaminates body and spirit, perfecting holiness out of reverence for God. (2 Cor 7:1)

Paul goes on to describe the repentance of the Corinthians in relation to the sinning brother (cf. 2:5–11):

> ⁹ yet now I am happy, not because you were made sorry, but because your sorrow led you to repentance. For you became sorrowful as God intended and so were not harmed in any way by us. ¹⁰ Godly sorrow brings repentance that leads to salvation and leaves no regret, but worldly sorrow brings death. ¹¹ See what this godly sorrow has produced in you: what earnestness, what eagerness to clear yourselves, what indignation, what alarm, what longing, what concern, what readiness to see justice done. At every point you have proved yourselves to be innocent in this matter. (2 Cor 7:9–11)

Again, the truth of God's judgment underlies Paul's instruction here. Paul has reminded the Corinthians that they will stand before Christ as judge (5:10). They are to live holy lives in the fear of God (7:1). When they sin they must repent and continue on the path to salvation (7:9–10); the alternative is "death," under the judgment of God (7:10). Christian ethics is a serious business (7:11). It is about pleasing the one (5:9) we both love (5:14) and fear (5:11).

Paul continues the theme of holiness in his later description of his apostolic ministry and authority:

> ⁴ The weapons we fight with are not the weapons of the world. On the contrary, they have divine power to demolish strongholds. ⁵ We demolish arguments and every pretension that sets itself up against the knowledge of God, and we take captive every thought to make it obedient to Christ. ⁶ And we will be ready to punish every act of disobedience, once your obedience is complete. (2 Cor 10:4–6)

Paul expects the Corinthians to be obedient to Christ. Paul sees himself as authorized by the Lord to discipline the church to bring about obedience. Again, God's judgment is at work through community discipline to correct sinning members and promote holy living.

Paul's "Thorn"

As Paul continues to describe his ministry he contrasts himself with "false apostles" (2 Cor 11:13), whose "end will be what their actions deserve" (11:15). Again, Paul affirms the eschatological condemnation of those who destroy the church (cf. 1 Cor 3:17). Paul then lists his sufferings for Christ (11:23–27). He also describes his "thorn in the flesh":[39]

> 7 . . . Therefore, in order to keep me from becoming conceited, I was given a thorn in my flesh, a messenger of Satan, to torment me. 8 Three times I pleaded with the Lord to take it away from me. 9 But he said to me, "My grace is sufficient for you, for my power is made perfect in weakness." Therefore I will boast all the more gladly about my weaknesses, so that Christ's power may rest on me. 10 That is why, for Christ's sake, I delight in weaknesses, in insults, in hardships, in persecutions, in difficulties. For when I am weak, then I am strong. (2 Cor 12:7b–10)

Paul's "thorn" is not a judgment of God upon him. Rather, it is a reminder that Paul still belongs to a fallen creation that continues to experience the effects of God's judgment on human sin, including the activity and influence of Satan. Here the purpose is to keep Paul from pride and to make him more dependent on the grace of God.

Paul finishes his letter with a warning that he may need to discipline unholy behavior in the church on his next visit (2 Cor 13:2, 10).

Conclusion

Second Corinthians reiterates various elements of Paul's doctrine of divine judgment that we have already seen: the eschatological judgment of believers and unbelievers; the law of Moses as leading to condemnation; the cross as a place of judgment on human sin, leading to salvation for believers. Paul expands on his teaching in Romans 8 concerning the effects on God's people of his judgment in the Fall of humanity. Believers share in that fallenness and also suffer at the hands of fallen humans who oppose the gospel. This is a strong theme in 2 Corinthians. So also is community discipline for the purpose of holiness. Paul sees the Lord's discipline as operating through Paul and the church to address sinful behavior and bring about repentance. But in 2 Corinthians there is not the element of direct temporal judgment

---

39. On the nature of the "thorn," see ibid., 568–70.

by God (cf. 1 Cor 11:29–32). Finally, we see another dimension of God's judgment in the Fall of humanity, namely, spiritual blindness caused by Satan (2 Cor 4:3–4).

A Reflection from 2 Corinthians

As humans we seek comfort: escape from conflict, war, poverty, hunger, sickness, and environmental danger and extremes; and life in a situation of peace, prosperity, and health. In the twenty-first-century western world the pursuit of comfort has become an obsession. To some extent this pursuit is a flight from the reality of living in a fallen world that is under God's judgment. Our comfort may make us feel better, but it does not change the fact that we are sinners against God: weak, mortal, and facing the final judgment. The apostle Paul reminds us that while God is the giver of physical comforts, we are called to suffer for the gospel (Rom 8:17; Phil 1:29). There is comfort in Christ, both now and in the future, that far surpasses present physical comfort (2 Cor 1:3–7; 4:16–18). Suffering keeps us in contact with reality—the reality of a fallen, hostile, and lost world under God's judgment. Will we seek to escape this reality, or will we face it, get involved with it, and seek to be part of God's answer to it?

Galatians

Eschatological Condemnation of Opponents

The judgment of God emerges early in Galatians as Paul expresses his extreme displeasure with those who would pervert the gospel of Christ:

> [8] But even if we or an angel from heaven should preach a gospel other than the one we preached to you, let that person be under God's curse! [9] As we have already said, so now I say again: If anybody is preaching to you a gospel other than what you accepted, let that person be under God's curse! (Gal 1:8–9)

Paul's strong language regarding false teachers being "accursed" (Gr. *anathema*) means that they will come under the wrath of God.[40] If they

---

40. Longenecker, *Galatians*, 16–18. Both Dunn and Martyn see Paul's meaning more in terms of such false teachers being separated from the church so as not to influence it (Dunn, *Galatians*, 46–47; Martyn, *Galatians*, 114).

persist in their error then their end will be eschatological condemnation (cf. 1 Cor 3:17; 16:22; 2 Cor 11:15).

The Fallen State of Humanity

Paul's teaching concerning justification by faith in Christ is consistent with that in Romans:

> [15] "We who are Jews by birth and not sinful Gentiles [16] know that a person is not justified by observing the law, but by faith in Jesus Christ. So we, too, have put our faith in Christ Jesus that we may be justified by faith in Christ and not by observing the law, because by observing the law no one will be justified.... [21] I do not set aside the grace of God, for if righteousness could be gained through the law, Christ died for nothing!" (Gal 2:15, 16, 21)

The need to be justified by God presupposes that people are not in right relationship with him. Paul goes on to describe that predicament:

> All who rely on observing the law are under a curse, for it is written: "Cursed is everyone who does not continue to do everything written in the Book of the Law." (Gal 3:10)

> But Scripture has locked up everything under the control of sin, so that what was promised, being given through faith in Jesus Christ, might be given to those who believe. (Gal 3:22)

> [3] So also, when we were underage, we were in slavery under the elemental spiritual forces of the world. [4] But when the set time had fully come, God sent his Son, born of a woman, born under the law, [5] to redeem those under the law, that we might receive adoption to sonship. [6] Because you are his sons, God sent the Spirit of his Son into our hearts, the Spirit who calls out, "*Abba*, Father." [7] So you are no longer slaves, but God's children; and since you are his children, he has made you also heirs. [8] Formerly, when you did not know God, you were slaves to those who by nature are not gods. [9] But now that you know God—or rather are known by God—how is it that you are turning back to those weak and miserable forces? Do you wish to be enslaved by them all over again? (Gal 4:3–9)

Paul is writing to a predominantly Gentile church which is being pressured by Judaizers to come under the law of Moses.[41] Paul points out that

---

41. See Longenecker, *Galatians*, xciv–xcviii; Martyn, *Galatians*, 117–26.

the situation of Israel under the law is not to be desired. The reason is that all who fail "to do everything written in the Book of the Law" are "under a curse" (Gal 3:10), or as Paul describes it later, "under the control of sin" (3:22), "in slavery under the elemental spiritual forces of the world" (4:3). This is true for Israel, and while Gentiles are technically not under Moses' law, their situation is basically the same. Israel under the law shows the situation of all humanity under the power of sin. Paul's teaching here is thus consistent with what we have found in Romans and 2 Corinthians: the law brings wrath (Rom 4:15), condemnation, and death (2 Cor 3).

Paul is describing the human situation under the judgment of God, in particular, the fallen situation of humanity in slavery to sin and spiritual forces, subject to God's wrath. Clearly, there are eschatological consequences, but Paul does not draw attention to that here. Neither does he speak about God's temporal judgment on disobedience, which is the focus of Deuteronomy 28:15–68 in its description of the curse in Deuteronomy 27:26, which Paul quotes in Galatians 3:10.

Paul is saying that those who are seeking right relationship with God through keeping the law of Moses will get nowhere. They will remain in slavery under God's judgment with the rest of humanity. It is those who trust in Jesus Christ who are redeemed from such slavery and blessed with right relationship with God and the indwelling of God's Spirit.

Judgment at the Cross

Again, Paul sees the death and resurrection of Christ as the way in which people are freed from "the curse of the law," that is, God's judgment and its effects, and brought into the blessing of righteousness and life:

> [13] Christ redeemed us from the curse of the law by becoming a curse for us, for it is written: "Cursed is everyone who is hung on a pole." [14] He redeemed us in order that the blessing given to Abraham might come to the Gentiles through Christ Jesus, so that by faith we might receive the promise of the Spirit. (Gal 3:13–14)

Verse 13 virtually repeats 2 Corinthians 5:21, but uses the language of "curse" rather than "sin":

> He made him . . . sin for us (2 Cor 5:21)
>
> by becoming a curse for us (Gal 3:13)

As seen previously, there is a strong implication here of God's judgment at work in Christ's death. Christ was "cursed," that is, in his death he experienced the judgment of God on human sin. He did this "for us," "on our behalf" (Gr. *huper hēmōn*), that is, as our representative and for our benefit.[42] The effect was redemption, freedom from "the curse," from God's judgment on human sin. The cross stands in the center of Paul's theology of salvation from God's judgment.

In this connection, we will return for a moment to Galatians 2:

> [19] For through the law I died to the law so that I might live for God. [20] I have been crucified with Christ and I no longer live, but Christ lives in me. The life I now live in the body, I live by faith in the Son of God, who loved me and gave himself for me. (Gal 2:19-20)

Here Paul affirms his identification and union with Christ in death and resurrection. While Paul's focus is on death to the law of Moses, and living for God (v. 19), judgment is implied; but now it is the judgment of Paul, who has been "crucified with Christ." Believers participate in the judgment of human sin that took place in Christ (Rom 8:3). They were judged and died in Christ. Now they are alive in him, free from condemnation and in right relationship with God.

Eschatological Salvation or Condemnation, and Ethical Implications

In the application section of his letter (Gal 5-6) Paul touches on several matters related to God's judgment. He speaks about "the righteousness for which we hope" (5:5), that is, the hope of final acquittal in God's presence at the end of the age,[43] which the present status of righteousness in Christ anticipates. Paul affirms the eschatological condemnation of those who practice "the acts of the sinful nature" (5:19): they "will not inherit the kingdom of God" (5:21); they will be shut out from the future rule of God over his people. Paul elaborates concerning the eschatological judgment of both unbelievers and believers:

> [8] Those who sow to please their sinful nature [lit. flesh; Gr. *sarx*], from that nature [lit. the flesh] will reap destruction; those who

---

42. See Dunn, *Galatians*, 177. The meaning and suitability of "substitution" to describe the work of Christ will be discussed in chapter 6.

43. See Dunn, *Galatians*, 269-70.

sow to please the Spirit, from the Spirit will reap eternal life. ⁹ Let us not become weary in doing good, for at the proper time we will reap a harvest if we do not give up. (Gal 6:8–9)

Paul affirms the principle of judgment according to deeds, as in Romans 2:6–8. Here he uses the metaphor of sowing and reaping, contrasting two different kinds of ground and their harvest. For unbelievers the harvest is "destruction" or "corruption" (Gr. *phthora*), complete ruin and loss; for believers it is "eternal life," life in the presence of God.

Paul's contrast of "flesh" and "Spirit" in relation to final judgment is in the context of encouraging God's people to "walk by the Spirit" and not "carry out the desire of the flesh" (5:16). As in Romans Paul describes fallen humanity in terms of "flesh," opposed to God (5:17), with sinful desires (5:17, 24), and engaged in evil actions (5:19–21, 26). It is not surprising that those who live that way will be condemned in the end. Their life has been lived in opposition to God and his will. Their end will correspond to their way of life. For believers in Jesus the Spirit brings freedom from indwelling sin; those who "walk by" (5:16), are "led by" (5:18), and who "live by" the Spirit (5:25), bear "the fruit of the Spirit" (5:22–23) and will ultimately "reap eternal life" (6:8). A life lived for God is lived by the power of his Spirit and leads to the presence of God.[44]

The "World" Judged

Paul also implies God's judgment of "the world," in the sense of a rival system with its values:[45]

> May I never boast except in the cross of our Lord Jesus Christ, through which the world has been crucified to me, and I to the world. (Gal 6:14)

Here the focus is on Paul's relationship with the world: it has been "crucified" to him and he has been "crucified" to it.[46] This is a corollary

---

44. "Paul's gospel of grace in Galatians does not countenance moral laxity. Righteousness is not based on works, but those who do not practice good works will not receive the final inheritance. The Pauline gospel of grace does not provide a foundation for license" (Schreiner, *Galatians*, 369).

45. Quoting Burton, Longenecker argues that "world" in this context means "the mode of life which is characterized by earthly advantages, viewed as obstacles to righteousness" (*Galatians*, 295).

46. For the significance of this within Paul's broader theology, see Dunn, *Galatians*,

of what Paul says in Galatians 2:20. But God's verdict on the world is also implied: it is condemned and its condemnation has been declared at the cross. This is consistent with Paul's teaching in 1 Corinthians 1. There is no future for a system—a mindset, a way of life—that is opposed to the Creator. It stands condemned and will be condemned. God's people must understand this and live accordingly.

Finally, Paul touches on the theme of suffering for Christ (Gal 5:11; 6:12, 17), a very real aspect of living in a world that is fallen and under God's judgment.

Conclusion

It is becoming apparent from the letters we have considered so far that particular elements in Paul's doctrine of divine judgment keep surfacing. I will no longer list all of these as we briefly "wrap up" each letter, but simply note the distinctive features of the letter. The feature that stands out in Galatians is "the curse," the judgment of God under which fallen humanity lives. Paul goes to considerable length to describe it and to urge his readers to hold fast to the salvation that Christ in his grace has secured for them. In so doing Paul explains the positive and negative role of the law of Moses and the centrality of the cross in redemption from "the curse." He also explains the role of God's Spirit in the lives of those who are "waiting for the hope of righteousness" (Gal 5:5).

A Reflection from Galatians

We need to keep returning to the message of freedom in Galatians. In a society that defines and seeks freedom in ways quite different from what Paul teaches, it is relatively easy for Christians to misunderstand true freedom and to pursue fruitless goals. There are other "gospels" that would lead us astray: the "gospel" of personal fulfillment; the "prosperity gospel" that defines curse and blessing in more material and physical terms;[47] "gospels" involving an externally regulated spirituality. Paul teaches us what true free-

---

341–42.

47. While people have many physical needs that are important to God (Matt 6:31–33), and while the gospel obviously does have many physical implications, these are not the main thrust of the gospel message. The "prosperity" gospel puts the emphasis in the wrong place. See ACUTE, *Faith, Health and Prosperity*.

dom is: freedom from "the curse" of slavery to sin and condemnation; and freedom to live a new life in which God's Spirit produces his precious fruit in our lives. Understanding God's judgment helps us to better understand and appreciate our freedom in Christ and to live fruitfully for him.

3
Overview of God's Judgment in Paul's Letters, Part 2

Having overviewed Paul's letters to the Romans, Corinthians, and Galatians, we are part-way in our "reconnaissance" of Paul to see the "big picture" of his understanding of God's judgment. The picture is not yet complete or clear. Parts of the picture have begun to be sketched, but there is more to be added, and the parts need to be joined together into a whole. That is the task of this chapter.

Ephesians

In Paul's great exposition of God's gracious purpose for his people there are two descriptions of fallen humanity that highlight the transformation that takes place in people's lives through the grace of God. The first description is a reminder to Paul's audience of their situation before coming to faith in Christ:

> [1] As for you, you were dead in your transgressions and sins, [2] in which you used to live when you followed the ways of this world and of the ruler of the kingdom of the air, the spirit who is now at work in those who are disobedient. [3] All of us also lived among them at one time, gratifying the cravings of our sinful nature and following its desires and thoughts. Like the rest, we were by nature deserving of wrath. (Eph 2:1–3)

Paul provides a brief but graphic description of humanity engaged in sinful actions, under the sway of evil spiritual powers, spiritually "dead" and "deserving of wrath." It is a description of humanity under the judgment of God.

The second description is of "the Gentiles," whom Paul urges the believers not to emulate:

Overview of God's Judgment in Paul's Letters, Part 2

> ¹⁷ So I tell you this, and insist on it in the Lord, that you must no longer live as the Gentiles do, in the futility of their thinking. ¹⁸ They are darkened in their understanding and separated from the life of God because of the ignorance that is in them due to the hardening of their hearts. ¹⁹ Having lost all sensitivity, they have given themselves over to sensuality so as to indulge in every kind of impurity, and they are full of greed. (Eph 4:17–19)

This is a summary of Paul's teaching in Romans 1:18–32. While Paul does not refer to God's judgment, clearly it is presupposed. People are in this sad state because fallen humanity is under the judgment of God. Paul does not highlight God's ongoing temporal judgment here; Paul says that the Gentiles "have given themselves over" (v. 19), rather than saying that "God gave them over" (Rom 1:24, 26, 28).

In Paul's exhortation to the believers to live a holy life he warns them about the consequences of living a sinful life:

> ⁵ For of this you can be sure: No immoral, impure or greedy person—such a person is an idolater—has any inheritance in the kingdom of Christ and of God. ⁶ Let no one deceive you with empty words, for because of such things God's wrath comes on those who are disobedient. ⁷ Therefore do not be partners with them. (Eph 5:5–7)

Paul strongly affirms the eschatological condemnation of sinners. The reason is that people are "disobedient" to God; they reject his holy laws regarding human behavior (cf. Rom 1:32). Therefore the wrath of God comes upon them. Some scholars see the present tense ("comes") as also referring to the present manifestation of God's wrath as in Romans 1:18–32.[1]

In his later exhortations to various groups in the church Paul focuses on the eschatological judgment of believers as he instructs slaves and their masters:

> ⁷ Serve wholeheartedly, as if you were serving the Lord, not people, ⁸ because you know that the Lord will reward each one of you for whatever good you do, whether you are slave or free. ⁹ And masters, treat your slaves in the same way. Do not threaten them, since you know that he who is both their Master and yours is in heaven, and there is no favoritism with him. (Eph 6:7–9)

---

1. O'Brien, *Ephesians*, 365.

Consistent with Paul's teaching in other letters, God's judgment will be impartial, in accordance with people's actions, and for reward.

While Paul says nothing more about God's judgment in Ephesians, his teaching on spiritual powers provides further insight into God's judgment of these powers.[2] We note several passages:

> [19] . . . That power is the same as the mighty strength [20] he exerted when he raised Christ from the dead and seated him at his right hand in the heavenly realms, [21] far above all rule and authority, power and dominion, and every name that can be invoked, not only in the present age but also in the one to come. [22] And God placed all things under his feet and appointed him to be head over everything for the church, [23] which is his body, the fullness of him who fills everything in every way. (Eph 1:19b–23)

> His intent was that now, through the church, the manifold wisdom of God should be made known to the rulers and authorities in the heavenly realms (Eph 3:10)

> For our struggle is not against flesh and blood, but against the rulers, against the authorities, against the powers of this dark world and against the spiritual forces of evil in the heavenly realms. (Eph 6:12)

We have already seen that subjection to evil spiritual powers is an aspect of God's judgment on fallen humanity (Eph 2:2; 2 Cor 4:3–4). Paul teaches that in Christ's resurrection he has been exalted over all spiritual powers, both in the present age and in the age to come (1:20–22). The church shares in his exaltation (1:22–23; 2:6; 3:10). But this does not mean that the church is no longer troubled by evil powers. The church is engaged in an ongoing struggle with such powers and is able to overcome only through the superior power of God (6:10–18).

How does this contribute to Paul's doctrine of divine judgment? It teaches that through Christ's resurrection God has judged evil spiritual powers. Christ is "far above" them, and God's people have victory over them in Christ. Admittedly, Paul does not speak about Christ's exaltation above the powers in terms of judgment, but it is implied by their loss of authority over humanity, specifically, over believers in Christ. In this sense the powers have been judged by God. While Ephesians does not spell out the final abolition of evil powers at Christ's second coming, as does 1 Corinthians 15:24, it does affirm his supremacy "in the [age] to come" (1:21).

2. For a study on the spiritual powers in Ephesians, see Arnold, *Power and Magic*.

Conclusion

Besides reinforcing a number of aspects of Paul's teaching concerning God's judgment, Ephesians highlights the present judgment of evil spiritual powers through the death and resurrection of Christ. While sinful humanity is still subject to these powers, the church has been delivered from them. Though there is still a struggle for God's people, they can withstand these powers in all aspects of life and gospel service.

A Reflection from Ephesians

The church in the west often functions as though there were no hostile spiritual powers. The truth is that there are and that to be effective, we must have a biblical understanding of these powers and know how to engage and overcome them through the power of Christ. An important component of a biblical understanding is the judgment of God. We need to understand that apart from God's grace we are subject to evil powers and that this is part of God's judgment on fallen humanity. Our problem is not just the effects of evil powers, but the judgment of God that has allowed them to influence our lives. Our main problem is with God, not with the devil. In this light Paul's "but God" in Ephesians 2:4 is wonderful news, because God's saving work gets to the heart of our problem: our sin and his wrath on our sin. In delivering us from his wrath God has also delivered us from subjection to evil powers that was part of his judgment upon us. In dealing with our sin God has broken the power of the evil one over our lives. We are free because God has set us free. But understanding and walking in our freedom in Christ requires an understanding of the various aspects of God's judgment. The judgment of God is broader and deeper than we think it is. We need to know what we have been saved from.

Philippians

Paul's letter to the Philippians has a strong future focus on "the day of Christ (Jesus)" (Phil 1:6, 10; 2:16). For believers in Jesus this will be the day when God's good work in them will have been "perfected" (1:6), when they will be "sincere and blameless" (1:10) and "filled with the fruit of righteousness" (1:11), when Paul will have cause to "boast" in God's work in the lives of his people (2:16), when their "Savior, the Lord Jesus Christ," will exert his power to raise their bodies (3:20–21). Accordingly, Paul's letter is an encouragement to "work out your salvation with fear and trembling" (2:12).

There are three places in the letter where eschatological judgment is either described or alluded to. In chapter 1 Paul raises the matter of God's judgment in the context of the church's suffering for the gospel:

> ²⁷ Whatever happens, as citizens of heaven live in a manner worthy of the gospel of Christ. Then, whether I come and see you or only hear about you in my absence, I will know that you stand firm in the one Spirit, striving together with one accord for the faith of the gospel ²⁸ without being frightened in any way by those who oppose you. This is a sign to them that they will be destroyed, but that you will be saved—and that by God. ²⁹ For it has been granted to you on behalf of Christ not only to believe on him, but also to suffer for him, ³⁰ since you are going through the same struggle you saw I had, and now hear that I still have. (Phil 1:27–30)

Paul speaks about the eschatological condemnation of those who oppose God's people: "they will be destroyed." God's people will be saved at the end of the age (v. 28).³ Again, we note the struggle and suffering of God's people in a fallen world that is under God's judgment (see also 1:13; 3:10). Paul calls the opposition of unbelievers a "sign" (Gr. *endeixis*: proof, evidence) of their ultimate destruction. In opposing God they are in effect "signing their own death warrant." God in his love and grace is presenting them with a way out of condemnation. The church proclaims the good news of what Christ has done. But those who do not believe not only reject the message but persecute the messengers, thus showing their rejection of Christ and God.

Eschatological judgment is alluded to at the end of Paul's "Christ hymn" (2:5–11):

> ⁹ Therefore God exalted him to the highest place and gave him the name that is above every name, ¹⁰ that at the name of Jesus every knee should bow, in heaven and on earth and under the earth, ¹¹ and every tongue acknowledge that Jesus Christ is Lord, to the glory of God the Father. (Phil 2:9–11)

---

3. On this verse, see Fee, *Philippians*, 167–70. Fee argues (131–32) that salvation here means both eschatological salvation as well as present vindication, in the sense of being able to testify for Christ.

There is a strong parallel here with Romans 14:

> [10] . . . For we will all stand before God's judgment seat. [11] It is written: "'As surely as I live,' says the Lord, 'every knee will bow before me; every tongue will confess to God.'" [12] So then, we will all give an account of ourselves to God. (Rom 14:10c–12)

In both passages Paul is quoting Isaiah 45:23:

> By myself I have sworn, my mouth has uttered in all integrity a word that will not be revoked: Before me every knee will bow; by me every tongue will swear. (Isa 45:23)

In Romans 14 Paul uses Isaiah to teach about the eschatological judgment: we will each stand before God and "give an account of ourselves." In Philippians 2 Paul focuses on worship toward God in the day of God. He sees Isaiah's prophecy fulfilled through Jesus Christ, whom God raised from the dead. Christ has been given the highest "name," and in his name "every knee will bow . . . and every tongue will confess" that he is Lord. Clearly, this will occur on "the day of Christ" (1:6, 10; 2:16), the day of judgment and salvation. Paul is again pointing to Jesus Christ as God's appointed Judge and Savior (Rom 2:16; 2 Cor 5:10), whom everyone will acknowledge, both believers and unbelievers. Paul is not teaching universal salvation, but universal submission to Christ's lordship. Believers will be saved on that day (1:28; 3:20–21); unbelievers will be "destroyed" (1:28). Christ's lordship will be acknowledged by those "in heaven and on earth and under the earth"—"heavenly beings, angels and demons"; and humans, both alive and dead.[4] As in Ephesians Christ's authority over spiritual powers is affirmed.

Later, in encouraging the church to follow his example, Paul says:

> [18] For, as I have often told you before and now tell you again even with tears, many live as enemies of the cross of Christ. [19] Their destiny is destruction, their god is their stomach, and their glory is in their shame. Their mind is set on earthly things. (Phil 3:18–19)

Again, Paul affirms the eschatological condemnation of those who oppose the gospel.[5]

---

4. Ibid., 224–25.
5. See ibid., 370–71.

Conclusion

Philippians presents God's judgment in the context of the ministry of the gospel. The church is a testimony to the grace of God: believers are to "shine among them like stars in the sky as you hold firmly to the word of life" (Phil 2:15–16). There is no mention of temporal judgment of unbelievers. The emphasis in the present is on the opportunity to receive the grace of God. But if people reject the gospel and inflict suffering on the church, there can be only one end for them: "destruction" on the day of Christ. Believers are encouraged to be faithful, knowing that we are privileged not only to believe in Christ, but also to suffer for him (1:29), eagerly waiting for our Savior (3:20).

A Reflection from Philippians

God's gift to his people of suffering for Christ (Phil 1:29) is a challenging truth for those of us in the comfortable west, where many Christians are not actively "shining" for God. We know so little about opposition and suffering, partly because we say so little about the great truths of judgment and salvation that call people to make a decision and that inevitably arouse strong opposition in some people. But can we afford to be quiet? What is the church if it does not actively proclaim and live by the truth? How otherwise will people know about hell and heaven and the two different "roads" that lead to them? How will we ever truly know Christ if we do not suffer for him (Phil 3:10)?

> "You are the salt of the earth. But if the salt loses its saltiness, how can it be made salty again? It is no longer good for anything, except to be thrown out and trampled underfoot." (Matt 5:13)

Colossians

God's judgment is largely presupposed in Colossians, coming clearly to the surface only in the second half of the letter. But the effects of God's judgment are evident from the beginning of the letter, as Paul touches on the situation from which believers have been delivered, and as he encourages the church to live in the freedom they have in Christ. Paul summarizes the human situation under God's judgment as follows:

Overview of God's Judgment in Paul's Letters, Part 2

> For he has rescued us from the dominion of darkness and brought us into the kingdom of the Son he loves (Col 1:13)

Fallen humanity under God's judgment is enslaved by spiritual powers in spiritual darkness. In the darkness people are God's enemies:

> Once you were alienated from God and were enemies in your minds because of your evil behavior. (Col 1:21)

Paul thus repeats aspects of his description of fallen humanity (cf. Rom 1:18–32; Eph 2:1–3; 4:17–19). To people in this hopeless situation the good news about Jesus Christ is indeed the gospel of hope, something that Paul emphasizes in his letter (Col 1:5, 23, 27). Paul reminds the Colossians of the gospel:

> But now he has reconciled you by Christ's physical body through death to present you holy in his sight, without blemish and free from accusation (Col 1:22)

Paul affirms the truth we have seen in previous letters: reconciliation of God's enemies to himself through the death of Jesus (cf. Rom 5:10), and the right standing with God enjoyed by those who trust in Jesus (cf. Rom 5:1). Through Christ believers are "free from accusation" (Gr. *anenklētos*: blameless), free from God's condemnation, and with the hope of salvation from God's eschatological wrath (cf. Rom 5:9).[6] While Paul does not elaborate here on the death of Christ, we note again how central it is in deliverance from God's judgment. We are also reminded of the judgment on human sin, in Christ's death, seen in other letters (Rom 8:3; 2 Cor 5:21; Gal 3:13).

While believers have been rescued from "the dominion of darkness" (Col 1:13), it does not mean that they are immune from the effects of the Fall, including the influence of evil powers. The Christian life is not easy: it is a struggle against the ways of the world; Paul is an outstanding example in his hard work and suffering for Christ (Col 1:24, 29; 2:1; 4:3, 18). Paul thus focuses on a number of areas where the Colossians need to live in freedom:

> [8] See to it that no one takes you captive through hollow and deceptive philosophy, which depends on human tradition and the elemental spiritual forces of this world rather than on Christ. [9] For

---

6. O'Brien highlights the eschatological meaning (O'Brien, *Colossians, Philemon*, 68–69).

> in Christ all the fullness of the Deity lives in bodily form, [10] and in Christ you have been brought to fullness. He is the head over every power and authority. (Col 2:8–10)

> [13] When you were dead in your sins and in the uncircumcision of your sinful nature, God made you alive with Christ. He forgave us all our sins, [14] having canceled the charge of our legal indebtedness, which stood against us and condemned us; he has taken it away, nailing it to the cross. [15] And having disarmed the powers and authorities, he made a public spectacle of them, triumphing over them by the cross. (Col 2:13–15)

> [20] Since you died with Christ to the elemental spiritual forces of this world, why, as though you still belonged to the world, do you submit to its rules: [21] "Do not handle! Do not taste! Do not touch!"? (Col 2:20–21)

Various aspects of God's judgment can be seen here: his judgment of evil powers (vv. 10, 15), the judgment of sinners in Christ's death (v. 20), the judgment of "the world," in the sense of the whole human worldview and way of life apart from God (v. 20),[7] and the removal of his condemnation for those who are in Christ (vv. 13–14). Therefore, believers can be free from deception (v. 8) and human regulations (vv. 20–21).

Paul then focuses on the risen life of believers with Christ (Col 3:1–4), which means putting to death a sinful way of life:

> [5] Put to death, therefore, whatever belongs to your earthly nature: sexual immorality, impurity, lust, evil desires and greed, which is idolatry. [6] Because of these, the wrath of God is coming. (Col 3:5–6)

Talk about various sins leads Paul to their consequence: eschatological condemnation.[8] As in Ephesians 5:6 he declares that such sinful practices will incur God's wrath. But the command to "put to death" such sins shows that God has already condemned them in the death of Jesus (cf. Rom 8:3). Christians are to live in the light of Christ's death and resurrection. God's condemnation of sin at the cross points to his eschatological condemnation of those who remain in their sin.

In his instruction to various groups Paul returns to the eschatological judgment:

---

7. O'Brien sees the sense as being "the old way of life" (ibid., 149).
8. For a concise overview of God's wrath in the Bible, see ibid., 184–85.

> ²² Slaves, obey your earthly masters in everything; and do it, not only when their eye is on you and to curry their favor, but with sincerity of heart and reverence for the Lord. ²³ Whatever you do, work at it with all your heart, as working for the Lord, not for human masters, ²⁴ since you know that you will receive an inheritance from the Lord as a reward. It is the Lord Christ you are serving. ²⁵ Those who do wrong will be repaid for their wrongs, and there is no favoritism. ¹ Masters, provide your slaves with what is right and fair, because you know that you also have a Master in heaven. (Col 3:22—4:1)

Again, the principles of God's just recompense and impartiality are evident. Some regard the judgment as applying only to Christians;[9] others see it as the judgment of all people, with verse 24 applying to Christians and verse 25 to unbelievers.[10]

Conclusion

Colossians focuses on the freedom of God's people from the effects of God's judgment in the Fall of humanity. Besides being free from condemnation, believers are free from the "dominion of darkness" that would enslave them in deception, fear and human regulations. This freedom is through the death and resurrection of Jesus Christ, who is preeminent over all things and all powers.

A Reflection from Colossians

Both Galatians and Colossians show us how easily we can be led astray from the gospel of Christ. We think we already know the gospel and then seek to add something to it or substitute something for it, in order to find freedom or fulfillment. We must regularly check ourselves to see in whom or in what we are trusting to live our lives with purpose and joy. Substitutes for faith in Christ tend to creep into our lives. Paul's message in Colossians is that Jesus Christ is incomparable. When we look again at who he is and what he has done for us, there is no one and nothing that even comes close to him. Who else can save us from the effects of God's judgment? Who else can bring us into the love and life of God? We need to stay in touch with

---

9. So O'Brien, *Colossians, Philemon*, 228–31.
10. So Travis, *Christ and the Judgement of God*, 167–69.

our real need before God. Then the Lord Jesus will remain the First Love in our lives.

First Thessalonians

In 1 Thessalonians salvation from God's eschatological wrath is a key component of the gospel that Paul preached to the Thessalonians. Thus, he reminds them:

> ⁹ for they themselves report what happened when we visited you. They tell how you turned to God from idols to serve the living and true God, ¹⁰ and to wait for his Son from heaven, whom he raised from the dead—Jesus, who rescues us from the coming wrath. (1 Thess 1:9–10)

Paul believes that the wrath of God is coming on humanity. Here it is connected with human idolatry, the worship of false gods rather than "the living and true God" (v. 9), as in Romans 1:21–23. Later in 1 Thessalonians Paul associates God's wrath with sinful practices, in particular, sexual immorality:

> ³ It is God's will that you should be sanctified: that you should avoid sexual immorality; ⁴ that each of you should learn to control your own body in a way that is holy and honorable, ⁵ not in passionate lust like the pagans, who do not know God; ⁶ and that in this matter no one should wrong or take advantage of a brother or sister. The Lord will punish all those who commit such sins, as we told you and warned you before. (1 Thess 4:3–6)

Paul warns the believers to avoid the sins that will draw the wrath of God on humans (v. 6; cf. Eph 5:6; Col 3:6). Paul may be thinking of temporal judgment such as that described in Romans 1:18–32.[11] More likely, the eschatological judgment is foremost in his mind.[12] Shortly after, he refers to it explicitly:

> ³ While people are saying, "Peace and safety," destruction will come on them suddenly, as labor pains on a pregnant woman, and they will not escape.... ⁹ For God did not appoint us to suffer wrath but to receive salvation through our Lord Jesus Christ. (1 Thess 5:3, 9)

---

11. Morris, *1 and 2 Thessalonians*, 124–25.
12. Wanamaker, *Thessalonians*, 156.

Overview of God's Judgment in Paul's Letters, Part 2

It is clear that salvation from eschatological wrath is fundamental to Paul's gospel. Presumably, it is an aspect of the gospel that the Thessalonians responded to as they repented and believed (1:9–10).[13] They wanted to come into right relationship with the true God and escape the coming wrath. Presumably also, they passed the message on to others as the gospel "rang out" from them so widely (1:8).

We note also that while Paul does not speak in the letter about the justification of believers, he does see them as having a standing before God—being "blameless and holy"—that will continue to the eschatological judgment and will result in salvation:

> May he strengthen your hearts so that you will be blameless and holy in the presence of our God and Father when our Lord Jesus comes with all his holy ones. (1 Thess 3:13)

> May God himself, the God of peace, sanctify you through and through. May your whole spirit, soul and body be kept blameless at the coming of our Lord Jesus Christ. (1 Thess 5:23)

While Paul refers to the death and resurrection of Christ in his letter (1 Thess 4:14), his focus is not on Christ's death as the basis for salvation from God's judgment, but on the second coming of the Lord for eschatological salvation. It is God's "Son from heaven . . . who rescues us" (1:10). Salvation will involve meeting "the Lord in the air. And so we will be with the Lord forever" (4:17).

As in other letters Paul associates suffering with preaching the gospel, both his suffering (1 Thess 2:2; 3:7) and the Thessalonians' suffering (1:6; 3:2–5). Suffering is an inevitable part of living for the true God among those "who do not know God" (4:5) and in a world where Satan is active (2:18; 3:5). Paul sees suffering as something for which God's people are "destined" (3:3–4). But suffering also comes from those who should know better, that is, the Jewish people, who claim to know God. Evidently, some of them do not:

> [14] For you, brothers and sisters, became imitators of God's churches in Judea, which are in Christ Jesus: You suffered from your fellow citizens the same things those churches suffered from the Jews, [15] who killed the Lord Jesus and the prophets and also drove us out. They displease God and are hostile to everyone [16] in their effort to keep us from speaking to the Gentiles so that they may be saved.

---

13. Ibid., 85, 87.

The Righteous Judgment of God

> In this way they always heap up their sins to the limit. The wrath of God has come upon them at last. (1 Thess 2:14–16)

Paul's final statement regarding God's wrath on the Jews (v. 16) has puzzled commentators. The Greek text says literally, "But the wrath [of God] has come upon them to the end (*eis telos*)." *Eis telos* can also mean "finally" (= "at last," TNIV), "fully" or "forever."[14] Some argue that Paul is referring to the future eschatological judgment of these Jews, with the past tense of the verb ("has come") indicating the certainty of it.[15] Others argue that it refers to recent events in Judea—military action by the Romans, or famines—whereby God is seen to have judged the Jews.[16] If so, Paul sees God's natural judgments on Israel as still occurring. Others see it as God's "hardening" of unbelieving Jews in their unbelief, which will continue "until the end," that is, the eschatological judgment.[17] Thus, it is a spiritual temporal judgment with eschatological consequences. We cannot be certain about what Paul means. Perhaps the third interpretation is more likely. It involves a straightforward interpretation of the past tense of the verb and is consistent with Paul's teaching in Romans 11:7–10 concerning the hardening of the Jews.

In this connection we note that Paul says nothing about God's temporal wrath against Gentiles who persecute God's people. While the Gentiles face God's eschatological wrath, for the time being they have the opportunity of hearing and responding to the gospel of salvation. The mercy of God is toward them, despite their sin in persecuting Christians.

Finally, Paul teaches the church that they do not have the right to avenge wrongdoing:

> Make sure that nobody pays back wrong for wrong, but always strive to do what is good for each other and for everyone else. (1 Thess 5:15)

Paul's instruction is consistent with his teaching in Romans 12:17–19, where he adds that God will avenge wrongdoing. Christians who are

---

14. BDAG, s.v. τέλος, 2γ.

15. Morris, *1 and 2 Thessalonians*, 85; Fee, *1 and 2 Thessalonians*, 101–2. Fee sees it as future, but is ambiguous as to whether it is the eschatological judgment.

16. Caird and Hurst, *New Testament Theology*, 83–84; Bockmuehl, "1 Thessalonians 2:14–16," 1–31.

17. Donfried, "1 Thessalonians 2:13–16," 242–53; Travis, *Christ and the Judgement of God*, 57–60.

suffering for the gospel are to do good, not evil, to their persecutors, which is consistent with Jesus' teaching (Matt 5:44–45).

Conclusion

First Thessalonians emphasizes the eschatological judgment. It shows us that escape from God's eschatological wrath is an integral part of the gospel message. It challenges us to have strong convictions about the final judgment and to communicate salvation from God's wrath as we preach the gospel. This will help people to understand what salvation is and to truly repent.

A Reflection from 1 Thessalonians

The Second Coming of the Lord must be more than simply a truth to which we give mental assent. It must be a hope that we nurture day by day. This is not easy in a culture that lives for the present. As we meditate on the Lord's Second Coming we need to remember that judgment will be at the center of his coming. Every person who has ever lived will stand before the Lord and be judged by him. This is one thing about the future that we know, that the Bible affirms consistently. It will be *the* Day of Judgment, an awesome day when the Holy One will give his final verdict and sentence on all human behavior. Why am I confident that I will be saved from his wrath on that day? How does my confidence affect the way I live today? Why do I believe that people who do not know or trust Christ will be condemned on that day? What am I doing to warn them and to win them to faith in the only Savior?

Second Thessalonians

Second Thessalonians follows 1 Thessalonians in its emphasis on eschatological judgment and salvation. Paul's instruction is prompted by the suffering of the church:

> [4] Therefore, among God's churches we boast about your perseverance and faith in all the persecutions and trials you are enduring. [5] All this is evidence that God's judgment is right, and as a result you will be counted worthy of the kingdom of God, for which you are suffering. [6] God is just: He will pay back trouble to those who

> trouble you ⁷ and give relief to you who are troubled, and to us as well. This will happen when the Lord Jesus is revealed from heaven in blazing fire with his powerful angels. ⁸ He will punish those who do not know God and do not obey the gospel of our Lord Jesus. ⁹ They will be punished with everlasting destruction and shut out from the presence of the Lord and from the glory of his might ¹⁰ on the day he comes to be glorified in his holy people and to be marveled at among all those who have believed. This includes you, because you believed our testimony to you. (2 Thess 1:4–10)

Again, we note the suffering of God's people in a fallen world that is under God's judgment. Paul says that the faithful suffering of the Thessalonians is "evidence" (Gr. *endeigma*: evidence, plain indication) that "God's judgment is right" (v. 5), or more literally, "of God's righteous judgment." Paul goes on to describe the outcome of that judgment as salvation for God's people (vv. 5, 7, 10) and condemnation for unbelievers (vv. 6, 8, 9). God's people are suffering for his kingdom and will be "counted worthy" of it (v. 5). Those who persecute them are opposing God and his kingdom as announced in the gospel (v. 8).

In relation to the suffering church there is a similar thought here to that in Philippians 1:28. The faithful suffering of the church in its gospel witness is "evidence" of the coming eschatological judgment that will bring salvation to believers and condemnation to unbelievers. Is there a message in the suffering of God's people for the gospel? Yes! It is that God is righteous and that his righteous judgment is coming. God will do the right thing for those who faithfully represent him in suffering: he will sustain them now and save them in the Last Day. And he will condemn those who reject and oppose him now through rejecting and opposing his message and his messengers. The stakes are high, much higher than they seem.

As in 1 Thessalonians Paul presents salvation in relation to the coming of the Lord. The Lord's people will share in his glory (v. 10; 2:14). It is also the Lord Jesus who will judge unbelievers (vv. 7–8).

Paul gives the most graphic description of eschatological judgment in his letters. He says unbelievers will be "punished with everlasting destruction" (v. 9). These are very strong words, highlighting the righteously punitive, eternal and desolating aspects of God's judgment.[18] The punishment will consist of being excluded from the Lord's presence and glory (v. 9). This gets to the heart of the matter: condemnation is permanent exclusion from

---

18. See Morris, *1 and 2 Thessalonians*, 204–05.

the presence of God, who is the source of life and all that is good. It is death and desolation. It is the inevitable outcome of a decision to reject God and the truth of the gospel. We will consider this further in chapter 7.

Paul goes on to describe the future judgment in relation to the revelation of "the man of lawlessness" (2 Thess 2:3), whose self-idolatry will result in his "destruction" when the Lord Jesus appears (2:3–8). Satan will be very active in the lawless one (2:9) and will also work to deceive many people:

> [9] . . . He will use all sorts of displays of power through signs and wonders that serve the lie, [10] and all the ways that wickedness deceives those who are perishing. They perish because they refused to love the truth and so be saved. [11] For this reason God sends them a powerful delusion so that they will believe the lie [12] and so that all will be condemned who have not believed the truth but have delighted in wickedness. (2 Thess 2:9b–12)

The temporal judgment of God can be seen in hardening people in their unbelief. Their eschatological condemnation will be righteous, because they reject the truth and delight in doing what God opposes.

Paul's description of God's people is in complete contrast:

> But we ought always to thank God for you, brothers and sisters loved by the Lord, because God chose you as firstfruits to be saved through the sanctifying work of the Spirit and through belief in the truth. (2 Thess 2:13)

Believers will be saved from God's eschatological wrath because of God's electing love, the sanctifying work of the Spirit in them, and their faith in the truth of the gospel.

In the last part of his letter Paul requests prayer to be "delivered from wicked and evil people" in his gospel ministry (2 Thess 3:2). It does not appear that Paul is asking for God to judge Paul's opponents. Paul also issues instructions for disciplining undisciplined members of the church (3:6–15). While Paul does not mention divine judgment, we note this passage for later consideration in chapter 5.

Conclusion

Second Thessalonians focuses on eschatological judgment and salvation. It is a person's response to the gospel that determines whether that person will be condemned or saved. God's judgment and grace are at work in people's responses. God's people are gospel witnesses who suffer in a fallen world that is under God's judgment. Their suffering is a sign of God's righteous judgment that will issue in eschatological salvation or condemnation.

A Reflection from 2 Thessalonians

We have seen in both Philippians and 2 Thessalonians the truth of the suffering church as a witness to the gospel and as a sign of final judgment and salvation, a truth that is fundamental to Paul's view of the church (cf. Acts 14:22). It is a truth known by today's suffering church. But generally the western church knows little about it. How will we recover it? Let us learn from our suffering brothers and sisters. Let us help them. Let us obey the instructions of our Lord to the church in Laodicea (Rev 3:14–22).

First Timothy

The first verse of Paul's letter reveals the "big picture" in his mind that governs the instruction he gives Timothy for the church:

> Paul, an apostle of Christ Jesus by the command of God our Savior and of Christ Jesus our hope (1 Tim 1:1)

Paul is concerned with matters related to the salvation provided by God to his people, a salvation focused on the future hope found in Christ Jesus. In his letter Paul considers various aspects of salvation in relation to God and his people. Along the way he touches on aspects of God's judgment.

The judgment that is large in Paul's mind throughout the letter is the eschatological judgment. But it is mainly assumed, coming to the surface only at one point:

> The sins of some are obvious, reaching the place of judgment ahead of them; the sins of others trail behind them. (1 Tim 5:24)

The solemnity of Paul's commands to Timothy reflects the awesome majesty of God, which clearly includes his sovereignty in the coming judgment when Christ will appear:

> I charge you, in the sight of God and Christ Jesus and the elect angels, to keep these instructions without partiality, and to do nothing out of favoritism. (1 Tim 5:21)

Overview of God's Judgment in Paul's Letters, Part 2

> ¹³ In the sight of God, who gives life to everything, and of Christ Jesus, who while testifying before Pontius Pilate made the good confession, I charge you ¹⁴ to keep this command without spot or blame until the appearing of our Lord Jesus Christ, ¹⁵ which God will bring about in his own time—God, the blessed and only Ruler, the King of kings and Lord of lords, ¹⁶ who alone is immortal and who lives in unapproachable light, whom no one has seen or can see. To him be honor and might forever. Amen. (1 Tim 6:13–16)

It is only in the light of the eschatological judgment that Paul's teaching about salvation makes sense:

> Here is a trustworthy saying that deserves full acceptance: Christ Jesus came into the world to save sinners—of whom I am the worst. (1 Tim 1:15)

> ⁵ For there is one God and one mediator between God and human beings, Christ Jesus, himself human, ⁶ who gave himself as a ransom for all people. This has now been witnessed to at the proper time. (1 Tim 2:5–6)

Paul sees Christ's death as securing salvation for people from God's wrath (Rom 5:9). But it is those who believe the gospel who will be saved, and Paul sees himself and the church as having a key role in prayer and witness, both in word and conduct, in bringing people to faith in Jesus:

> But for that very reason I was shown mercy so that in me, the worst of sinners, Christ Jesus might display his immense patience as an example for those who would believe in him and receive eternal life. (1 Tim 1:16)

> ¹ I urge, then, first of all, that petitions, prayers, intercession and thanksgiving be made for everyone— ² for kings and all those in authority, that we may live peaceful and quiet lives in all godliness and holiness. ³ This is good, and pleases God our Savior, ⁴ who wants all people to be saved and to come to a knowledge of the truth. (1 Tim 2:1–4)

> And for this purpose I was appointed a herald and an apostle— I am telling the truth, I am not lying—and a true and faithful teacher of the Gentiles. (1 Tim 2:7)

> if I am delayed, you will know how people ought to conduct themselves in God's household, which is the church of the living God, the pillar and foundation of the truth. (1 Tim 3:15)

Also, God's people must continue in the grace of God they have already received in order to enter into eschatological salvation:[19]

> But women will be saved through childbearing—if they continue in faith, love and holiness with propriety. (1 Tim 2:15)

> Watch your life and doctrine closely. Persevere in them, because if you do, you will save both yourself and your hearers. (1 Tim 4:16)

Paul addresses various situations where professing Christians fail to live in accordance with God's will for his people:

> [19] holding on to faith and a good conscience, which some have rejected and so have suffered shipwreck with regard to the faith. [20] Among them are Hymenaeus and Alexander, whom I have handed over to Satan to be taught not to blaspheme. (1 Tim 1:19-20)

Verse 20 recalls the Corinthian situation where Paul instructed the church to "hand over to Satan" the incestuous man (1 Cor 5:5). Here again it would seem that Paul sees God's temporal judgment working in these men. They are exposed to the working of Satan. The purpose is that they may learn a lesson. But it is not clear what hope Paul has concerning their return to faith.[20] Paul may have such men in mind when he says:

> Those who want to get rich fall into temptation and a trap and into many foolish and harmful desires that plunge people into ruin and destruction. (1 Tim 6:9)

Such people are associated with the church but do not have a heart for godliness. They are not truly converted; their future will be eschatological condemnation.

Paul is also concerned with the conduct of some young widows:

> [11] As for younger widows, do not put them on such a list. For when their sensual desires overcome their dedication to Christ, they want to marry. [12] Thus they bring judgment on themselves, because they have broken their first pledge. [13] Besides, they get into the habit of being idle and going about from house to house. And not only do they become idlers, but also busybodies who talk

---

19. While some commentators have come to understand salvation in these texts in a non-spiritual sense, the spiritual sense fits well within Paul's theology. See Fee, *1 and 2 Timothy, Titus*, 74–77, 109; Mounce, *Pastoral Epistles*, 143–48, 264–65.

20. Mounce points out the remedial purpose of Paul's action, but does not address the question of Paul's expectation (ibid., 66–70).

> nonsense, saying things they ought not to. ¹⁴ So I counsel younger widows to marry, to have children, to manage their homes and to give the enemy no opportunity for slander. ¹⁵ Some have in fact already turned away to follow Satan. (1 Tim 5:11–15)

The interpretation of this passage depends on understanding the situation Paul is describing, which is not easy. Paul's strong language in verses 11–12 may suggest that these women want to marry non-Christian men. If so, the judgment Paul refers to (v. 12) may be God's temporal judgment of allowing these women to do as they please, and so effectively deny their faith in Christ.[21] Verse 15 indicates such a denial in its description of some Ephesian women who have turned from the Lord "to follow Satan." To prevent this, Paul instructs younger widows to marry Christian men and live a godly life (v. 14; cf. 1 Cor 7:39). Thus, they will remain faithful to Christ.

In his instruction on the selection of overseers Paul says:

> He must not be a recent convert, or he may become conceited and fall under the same judgment as the devil. (1 Tim 3:6)

It is not clear what Paul means here concerning judgment. The Greek text says simply "the judgment of the devil," meaning either "the [same] judgment as the devil" (so TNIV) or "the judgment/condemnation inflicted by the devil." If it is the latter, then the devil's role as "the accuser of the brothers" may be referred to (cf. Rev 12:10). More likely, Paul means the former, with God's judgment being the conceited state into which the person falls, thus following the devil's fall into pride (cf. Isa 14:12–15).[22]

Finally, Paul gives instruction regarding elders who sin:

> But those elders who are sinning you are to reprove before everyone, so that the others may take warning. (1 Tim 5:20)

Paul requires community discipline, but with no reference to God's judgment. Again, we note it for later discussion in chapter 5.

---

21. So Fee, *1 and 2 Timothy, Titus*, 121–22; Mounce, *Pastoral Epistles*, 290–92, 297; Marshall, *Pastoral Epistles*, 598–601.

22. See discussion in Fee, *1 and 2 Timothy, Titus*, 83; Mounce, *Pastoral Epistles*, 182; Marshall, *Pastoral Epistles*, 482–83.

Conclusion

The focus of 1 Timothy is salvation from God's eschatological judgment. Paul wants the church to live a godly life that will honor God and testify to the truth of the gospel. Thus God's people will continue on their way to salvation and make it possible for others to join them. But it is not all "smooth sailing" in the church. The challenges of fallen humanity are very apparent, in the sins of its adherents, both true and false believers. Paul sees God's temporal judgment at work in various ways.

A Reflection from 1 Timothy

Our overviews of Paul's letters so far have shown that he sees salvation as a process with a strong future focus. People are being saved and will be saved when Christ appears. Paul's understanding contrasts with the view of many contemporary Christians that we are already saved. The problem with this is that it neglects the "not yet" aspect of salvation. It weakens the link between Christian conduct and eschatological salvation. Christian conduct is not seen as an integral part of ongoing salvation leading to final salvation. A direct line is drawn between the gift of righteousness and final acquittal before God, neglecting righteous living in the middle. Paul does not draw such a line. He holds gift, conduct and future salvation together in a holistic view of the grace of God. This is why he concentrates on Christian conduct. In his view it is indispensable in the big picture of salvation. If we do not live as Christians now, we are denying the grace of God in our lives and will not be saved in the end. We need to recover Paul's view of salvation.[23]

Second Timothy

Suffering for the gospel is a major theme in Paul's letter in which he urges Timothy to follow his example in preaching the gospel and persevering in godly ministry in the church (2 Tim 1:6–8, 12–14; 2:1–13; 3:10–12; 4:1–2, 5–8, 16–18). The reason why God's people, especially leaders like Paul and Timothy, suffer is because of a sinful world outside the church and because of troublemakers in the church:

---

23. For an excellent study of the Christian doctrine of salvation, see Hoekema, *Saved by Grace*.

Overview of God's Judgment in Paul's Letters, Part 2

> ¹ But mark this: There will be terrible times in the last days. ² People will be lovers of themselves, lovers of money, boastful, proud, abusive, disobedient to their parents, ungrateful, unholy, ³ without love, unforgiving, slanderous, without self-control, brutal, not lovers of the good, ⁴ treacherous, rash, conceited, lovers of pleasure rather than lovers of God— ⁵ having a form of godliness but denying its power. Have nothing to do with such people. (2 Tim 3:1–5)

> ¹⁶ Avoid godless chatter, because those who indulge in it will become more and more ungodly. ¹⁷ Their teaching will spread like gangrene. Among them are Hymenaeus and Philetus, ¹⁸ who have departed from the truth. They say that the resurrection has already taken place, and they destroy the faith of some. (2 Tim 2:16–18)

The evidences of fallen humanity under God's judgment are very apparent here. Christian ministry is therefore hard work and involves suffering. God's servants must persevere.

Paul comes quickly to the gospel for which he is suffering:

> ⁸ So do not be ashamed of the testimony about our Lord or of me his prisoner. But join with me in suffering for the gospel, by the power of God, ⁹ who has saved us and called us to a holy life—not because of anything we have done but because of his own purpose and grace. This grace was given us in Christ Jesus before the beginning of time, ¹⁰ but it has now been revealed through the appearing of our Savior, Christ Jesus, who has destroyed death and has brought life and immortality to light through the gospel. (2 Tim 1:8–10)

In verse 10 Paul alludes to the death and resurrection of Christ, in whom death has been destroyed and life has been made available. We have seen that Christ's death speaks of judgment on human sin (Rom 8:3), the judgment he entered into to bring life to humanity. Again, in 2 Timothy Christ is central in Paul's view of salvation.

Paul's words, "who has saved us and called us to a holy life" (v. 9), introduce what he has to say about salvation and judgment in the letter. He touches on various aspects of salvation:

> Therefore I endure everything for the sake of the elect, that they too may obtain the salvation that is in Christ Jesus, with eternal glory. (2 Tim 2:10)

> and how from infancy you have known the Holy Scriptures, which are able to make you wise for salvation through faith in Christ Jesus. (2 Tim 3:15)

> Nevertheless, God's solid foundation stands firm, sealed with this inscription: "The Lord knows those who are his," and, "Everyone who confesses the name of the Lord must turn away from wickedness." (2 Tim 2:19)

> Now there is in store for me the crown of righteousness, which the Lord, the righteous Judge, will award to me on that day—and not only to me, but also to all who have longed for his appearing. (2 Tim 4:8)

Those who have entered into salvation are those graciously chosen by God, who believe the gospel and live a holy life, and who will be saved at the eschatological judgment (see also 2 Tim 1:16–18). On the matter of election, we have seen in Romans 9 that it involves the mercy and judgment of God. God's judgment "hardens" some in their unbelief. His mercy enables others to believe (Rom 9:18, 22–24). Paul endures in his ministry for the sake of the elect (2 Tim 2:10).

Those who do not believe the gospel, especially those who oppose it and cause trouble for the church, are destined for eschatological condemnation:

> [14] Alexander the metalworker did me a great deal of harm. The Lord will repay him for what he has done. [15] You too should be on your guard against him, because he strongly opposed our message. (2 Tim 4:14–15)

It seems that Paul does not now expect Alexander (cf. 1 Tim 1:20) to come to repentance. Paul affirms a just recompense to him from the Lord at the final judgment.[24]

But not all opponents are beyond repentance:

> [25] Opponents must be gently instructed, in the hope that God will grant them repentance leading them to a knowledge of the truth, [26] and that they will come to their senses and escape from the trap

---

24. This assumes that Alexander is the person whom Paul previously excommunicated (1 Tim 1:20). Paul's language is very strong, indicating that Alexander is a firm opponent of the gospel. Numerous commentators see him as involved in having Paul arrested ("did me a great deal of harm"). See Fee, *1 and 2 Timothy, Titus*, 295–96; Mounce, *Pastoral Epistles*, 592–94.

of the devil, who has taken them captive to do his will. (2 Tim 2:25–26)

Perhaps Paul is reflecting on his own opposition to the gospel and how the Lord had mercy on him (1 Tim 1:12–16). Only God knows whether an opponent will eventually repent. The task of God's servants is to be patient, gentle, and prayerful with respect to such people. Once again, the activity of Satan is apparent in hindering people from believing in Christ (cf. 2 Cor 4:3–4). By the grace of God people can escape his control.

The prominence of the eschatological judgment in Paul's thought as he writes is seen in his solemn charge to Timothy:

> In the presence of God and of Christ Jesus, who will judge the living and the dead, and in view of his appearing and his kingdom, I give you this charge: (2 Tim 4:1)

The final judgment is the great event to which all of history is moving. It will determine the eternal destiny of every person. In the light of it every person is called to believe in and be faithful to Jesus Christ, who is the Judge of all people and the Savior of those who trust in him.

Conclusion

Thus we see again the importance of the eschatological judgment for Paul. In 2 Timothy he stresses the necessity of endurance in gospel ministry and holy living for the sake of those who will "obtain the salvation that is in Christ Jesus, with eternal glory" (2:10).

A Reflection from 2 Timothy

Why do we or should we persevere in serving God in the church and in Christian mission? One obvious answer is our love for God and for people. Where does this love come from? It comes from our experience of God's love in forgiving our sins and bringing us into his family. It comes from our experience of salvation so far. Paul would add a dimension to love: our love for "his appearing" (2 Tim 4:8). Paul's service is future-oriented. He is thankful for what the Lord has done for him (1 Tim 1:12–15), but Paul's focus in his service is on the day of the Lord's "appearing," when his "kingdom" will come, when he will judge all people (2 Tim 4:1), and when God's people will be "crowned" with the righteousness secured for them by Jesus Christ (2 Tim 4:8; cf. Gal 5:5; Phil 3:9). Paul longs for and labors toward that day of glorious consummation. How about us? Do we have the same vision and passion? Let's ask the Lord to give us understanding of and desire for his appearing.

Titus

Paul's particular emphasis in his letter to Titus is the good works of God's people. Paul sees these as accompanying salvation. Besides describing the good works, he seeks to explain their origin and purpose. While he does not refer to God's judgment, aspects of it can be seen in the background.

Good works are an integral part of the salvation that God has provided by his grace:

> ¹¹ For the grace of God has appeared that offers salvation to all people. ¹² It teaches us to say "No" to ungodliness and worldly passions, and to live self-controlled, upright and godly lives in this present age, ¹³ while we wait for the blessed hope—the appearing of the glory of our great God and Savior, Jesus Christ, ¹⁴ who gave himself for us to redeem us from all wickedness and to purify for himself a people that are his very own, eager to do what is good. (Titus 2:11–14)

The death of Christ secures salvation (v. 14). The aspect of salvation Paul highlights here is freedom from a sinful life in order to live a holy life. As we have seen in other letters, the sinful condition from which people are redeemed is part of the judgment of God on fallen humanity (cf. Rom 5:18–19). Paul is thus speaking about salvation from the judgment of God in the sense of slavery to sin.

The appearing of the risen Lord consummates salvation (v. 13). Again, we know from other Pauline letters that salvation includes escape from the eschatological wrath of God (cf. Rom 5:9). Judgment is in the background.

Paul elaborates on how sinful people are transformed so as to do good works:

> ³ At one time we too were foolish, disobedient, deceived and enslaved by all kinds of passions and pleasures. We lived in malice and envy, being hated and hating one another. ⁴ But when the kindness and love of God our Savior appeared, ⁵ he saved us, not because of righteous things we had done, but because of his mercy. He saved us through the washing of rebirth and renewal by the

> Holy Spirit, ⁶ whom he poured out on us generously through Jesus Christ our Savior, ⁷ so that, having been justified by his grace, we might become heirs having the hope of eternal life. (Titus 3:3–7)

Transformation occurs through the inner washing and renewing by the Holy Spirit (v. 5), which is in conjunction with being brought into right relationship with God, with the hope of eternal life (v. 6). Christians thus have a new ability and desire to live for God. We note that justification in the present anticipates eternal life in the future. In the time between these, there is a life of good works (cf. Eph 2:10).

Paul does not speak about the judgment of non-Christians, which is assumed. He sees the church as a witness for the gospel to unbelievers through good works:

> ... so that in every way they will make the teaching about God our Savior attractive. (Titus 2:10b)

Paul desires others to enter into salvation through the church's witness.[25]

Finally, Paul gives instructions for the disciplining of divisive church members:

> ¹⁰ Warn divisive people once, and then warn them a second time. After that, have nothing to do with them. ¹¹ You may be sure that such people are warped and sinful; they are self-condemned. (Titus 3:10–11)

Those who continue to sin are to be ostracized, but not necessarily excommunicated.[26] Such community judgment reflects the dangerous position of the persons concerned. They are not living in God's way or showing evidence of salvation. Paul's strong words in verse 11 suggest the danger of eschatological condemnation for them.

Conclusion

The distinctive feature of Titus is its strong emphasis on good works in relation to salvation. These good works are not just human effort but flow from the redemptive work of Christ that frees people from slavery to sin. Good

---

25. For a presentation of the various practical aspects of Christian witness, see Dickson, *Promoting the Gospel*.

26. See Fee, *1 and 2 Timothy, Titus*, 211–12; Mounce, *Pastoral Epistles*, 454–55.

works are a way of life for God's people on their way to eschatological salvation. Paul thus builds on a similar emphasis in 1 Timothy and challenges us to have a more complete understanding of salvation.

A Reflection from Titus

"Good deeds, good works"—how much do we think about them—what they are and how we can do them? And how zealous are we to do them (Titus 2:14), and for what reasons? "Good" presupposes judgment: judgment of the moral quality and value of an attitude or action. Everyone makes such judgments. Everyone has their definitions of "good" and "evil" attitudes and actions. The definition that ultimately counts is God's. The Bible is full of God's definition of good and evil works. God loves good works and will reward them. He opposes evil works and will punish them. If this is so plain, why are we so often so complacent about doing good works? The Bible is correct in its description of our fallen human nature: "we too were foolish, disobedient, deceived and enslaved by all kinds of passions and pleasures. We lived in malice and envy, being hated and hating one another" (Titus 3:3). How desperately we need to be renewed! The good news is that the process began at our conversion: "rebirth and renewal by the Holy Spirit" (Titus 3:5). But then day by day we must cry out to God for ongoing renewal, learning the difference between good and evil (Heb 5:14), earnestly desiring to do good works (Titus 2:14), walking in the good works that God has prepared for us (Eph 2:10), and bringing glory to our Father in heaven (Matt 5:16). It is his grace—and his grace alone—that empowers us to live a godly life, working in us "to will and to work for his good pleasure" (Phil 2:13).

Philemon

There is nothing in Philemon specifically about God's judgment. However, as in all of Paul's other letters he refers to Christian suffering, in this case, his own (Phlm 1:1, 9, 10). We are reminded that God's people live in a fallen world that is under God's judgment.

Concluding Observations

I will not attempt to summarize all the findings from our reconnaissance of Paul's letters. Rather, I wish to make a number of observations concerning the significance and the general "shape" of God's judgment in Paul's thought. This will prepare the way for later chapters, where we will pursue the main aspects of Paul's thought and consider their implications for us today.

God's Judgment Fundamental

One thing that has become obvious from our study of Paul's letters is that God's judgment is a fundamental presupposition of Paul's theology. He never argues for it; he argues from it; often he assumes it. But it comes to the surface again and again, and from the places where it does we are able to discern a theology that is broad, deep, coherent, and held with conviction. What have we found?

1. Paul is not afraid to speak about God's judgment. He makes no excuses for it. The reason is that for him, the good news of salvation makes no sense apart from God's judgment. The human predicament is fundamentally one under God's judgment, and unless salvation addresses the judgment of God, it is no real salvation at all. Thus, in his preaching Paul proclaimed repentance for salvation from God's wrath (1 Thess 1:9–10; Rom 2:16; cf. Acts 17:30–31; 24:24–25). Evidently, he thought people must know what they need to be saved from before they can repent and be saved.

2. Paul's doctrine of judgment is a corollary of his doctrine of God. It is because God is the holy and righteous one that he is the Judge of humanity. God is in the center of Paul's doctrine of judgment. Paul does not allow human-centered thinking to determine, cloud or diminish in any way his theology of divine judgment.

3. And yet, because God is in the center for Paul, judgment itself is not central. Paul is not enthusiastic about judgment; it is not a preoccupation for him. Rather, he is preoccupied with what God has done to deliver people from his judgment. Paul is preoccupied with the salvation that God has provided through Jesus Christ. As John says, "For God did not send his Son into the world to condemn the world, but to save the world through him" (John 3:17). This is the truth that Paul

seeks to live in, proclaim, and teach. It is salvation from the wrath of God into life in Christ.

4. While the eschatological, or final, judgment is the major event on Paul's future horizon, his view of judgment is not restricted to this end point. His view is much broader and deeper. He sees God's judgment as extending from the Fall of humanity, throughout history, to the consummation of creation at the second coming of the Lord. Every human being is affected and every aspect of human life as we know it is impacted by God's judgment. It is true also for those graciously called by God to be his people. Paul wants God's people to understand the big picture of God's judgment.

5. Just as the death and resurrection of Jesus are at the center of Paul's theology of salvation, so they are at the center of his theology of judgment. We have seen repeatedly in Paul's letters that the death of Jesus delivers us from condemnation. We have seen, especially in Romans 8:3, that Jesus' death involved an act of judgment, namely, God's judgment on human sin. God's act of judgment at the cross of Christ is at the center of Paul's broad view of judgment, stretching from creation-Fall to consummation.

God's Judgment Historical

Our study has also shown that Paul's theology of divine judgment is consistent with the theology of the Old Testament and of Jesus. But not surprisingly, Paul's theology goes further, in the light of the coming of Christ and the Spirit, and with a view to the second coming of Christ. Paul's theology is historical, seeing God's judgment as an historical phenomenon, commencing at humanity's Fall into sin and continuing throughout history in temporal judgments on Israel and the nations. Similarly, Paul's view of judgment at the cross of Christ is historical. While it is a theological conviction, it is a conviction about something that took place in history, namely, the death of Christ. Paul's view of eschatological judgment is also historical. While it has not yet happened, it is something that Paul is convinced will happen at the consummation of history. Jesus Christ is at the center of Paul's historical view of God's judgment. This is because Jesus fulfills the Old Testament hopes for salvation from sin and judgment. In Jesus' death human sin is judged (Rom 8:3). Jesus' death and resurrection have also inaugurated the

Overview of God's Judgment in Paul's Letters, Part 2

new age of God's kingdom, in which God's life-giving Spirit is given to humanity. People who believe in Jesus are therefore freed from condemnation and experience the life of the Spirit that begins to set them free from the effects of God's judgment at the Fall (Rom 8:1–2). When Jesus comes again he will be the Judge of all humanity (Rom 2:16). He will save his people from God's eschatological wrath (Rom 5:9). In their resurrection they will finally be saved from the power of death (Rom 8:11) and will enter into their eternal inheritance in Christ (Rom 8:17). Those who do not believe in Jesus continue to live as slaves of sin and will ultimately be condemned at the final judgment (Rom 6:20–21).

Four Aspects of God's Judgment

From an historical perspective four main aspects of Paul's theology of judgment can be identified:

1. There is God's judgment at the Fall of humanity, when through the disobedience of the first human couple, humanity was plunged into slavery to sin, with all its terrible effects. For Paul this is the fundamental judgment, which "snowballs" into other kinds of judgment. Paul gives rich insights into the fundamental judgment. He also explains how the work of Christ deals with the judgment at the Fall (Rom 5:12–21).

2. There is judgment that takes place throughout human history after the Fall of humanity. For the sake of simplicity I have called it "temporal" judgment. While the Fall is also temporal, its significance in Paul's theology is such that it needs to be distinguished from sinful behavior and divine judgment that occur subsequent to the Fall. Paul speaks about temporal judgment in relation to humanity in general (Rom 1:18–32), Pharaoh (Rom 9:17), Israel (Rom 11:7–10; 1 Cor 10:5–10), earthly rulers (Rom 13:1–7), those who do not believe the gospel (2 Thess 2:11), and the church (1 Cor 11:28–32). Temporal judgment occurs throughout the whole of human history, past, present and future. It does not stop with the first coming of Christ.

3. There is the judgment that occurs in the death of Christ (see comments above).

4. There is the eschatological judgment at the end of history as we know it, through which God's creation is finally put right. All who remain in

rebellion to God are banished from his presence forever. All who have been reconciled to God through Christ will live with him forever in righteousness and peace.

Our purpose in the next four chapters of this book will be to pursue each of these four aspects of judgment, for greater understanding of Paul's theology and to consider what they mean for Christian life and ministry today. But before we look at these, I will make two final observations from our overview of Paul.

God's Righteousness, Sovereignty, and Grace

The first observation relates to the relationship between the different aspects/elements of judgment in Paul's theology. These elements do not stand alone, but are part of Paul's larger vision of the righteousness of God. God judges because he is righteous. Each aspect of judgment is a manifestation of God's righteousness. Each points to human sin and to the "rightness" of God's judgment on sinful humanity. The first three elements (i.e., Fall, temporal, cross) all anticipate the final judgment where justice finally prevails.[27] Thus, God's judgment is apparent and consistent throughout history, pointing to a final judgment, whilst giving humanity the opportunity to understand and to turn to God for a remedy which only he can provide through his grace. God's remedy is also within Paul's vision of God's righteousness, because righteousness does not mean only judgment that leads to condemnation, but also God's saving righteousness that saves through judgment, which is what the cross is all about. The sin of humanity is judged in Christ so that people can be saved from God's righteous wrath. Thus the righteousness of God judges and saves; in fact, it saves through judgment.[28] For Paul, judgment is a major and necessary element of God's

---

27. Vos says concerning the eschatological judgment: "This indeed is the finest note in Paul's manifold pursuit of the idea of the righteousness of God" (*Pauline Eschatology*, 285).

28. This is true not only within Paul's theology. The theme of salvation through judgment runs strongly through the whole Bible. Hamilton argues that "the glory of God in salvation through judgment" is the central theme of the Bible (Hamilton, "Glory of God in Salvation through Judgment," 57–84; Hamilton, *God's Glory in Salvation through Judgment*).

righteousness. While apart from Christ this is bad news for humanity,[29] with him it becomes good news.

Finally, Paul's clear vision of God's judgment magnifies the sovereignty and grace of God. For Paul the presence of evil in the world does not call into question God's power or goodness. It does not suggest that things are out of control or that Satan is a threat to God's sovereignty. It does not mean that God is not loving or good. Rather, while sin is present through human rebellion against God's sovereignty, God remains sovereign in his righteous judgment and gracious salvation. The effects of sin are not evidence of a world out of control; rather, they testify to the righteous judgment of the holy God. Paul begins here. In this clear light the awful truth of humanity's predicament can be appreciated. Our sinfulness and hopelessness can be seen. Our desperate need for God's mercy can be acknowledged. Then the gospel of Christ makes sense. Then the love of God cannot be denied. Then the grace of God can be received.

---

29. "The wrath of God is the righteousness of God—apart from and without Christ" (Barth, *Romans*, 43).

4

The Fallen Human Condition as God's Judgment

PAUL'S UNDERSTANDING OF GOD'S judgment is deeply challenging. If we accept it, there is no way our lives will not be radically changed. Our view of the world will be very different from that of the prevailing culture. Our purpose in life will be different, as will be the way we live our lives. These are the things we will now reflect on, as we consider the four aspects of God's judgment in Paul's theology. Our main question will be: *As people who believe in the judgment of God, how will we live?* Our attempts to answer the question will lead us back to Paul, and also to the whole Bible. We will also reflect on a number of contemporary issues.

Before we come to the topic of this chapter it is worth stopping to consider our basic attitude as God's people in the light of the truth about God's judgment. As people who are no longer under the sentence of condemnation (Rom 8:1), who are God's children (Rom 8:14–16), and who have the hope of eternal life (Rom 5:21; 6:23), what is our basic feeling, thought, inclination, or desire? The first word that comes to my mind is thankfulness, a deep sense of appreciation to God for all he has done for me. But it cannot stop here; it overflows into a new way of living, which Paul describes as follows:

> [1] Therefore, I urge you, brothers and sisters, in view of God's mercy, to offer your bodies as a living sacrifice, holy and pleasing to God—this is true worship. [2] Do not conform to the pattern of this world, but be transformed by the renewing of your mind. Then you will be able to test and approve what God's will is—his good, pleasing and perfect will. (Rom 12:1–2)

> [6] So then, just as you received Christ Jesus as Lord, continue to live your lives in him, [7] rooted and built up in him, strengthened in the faith as you were taught, and overflowing with thankfulness. (Col 2:6–7)

The Fallen Human Condition as God's Judgment

Let us cultivate this attitude in our lives. With it we are well set to learn how to live in the light of God's truth and for his honor.

Summary concerning the Fallen Condition of Humanity

We will begin with a brief summary of what we found concerning the human condition in chapters 2 and 3:

1. Humans have fallen out of right relationship with God. While God is still their Creator and Sustainer, there is an estrangement, involving:

    a. Hostility of humans toward God (Rom 5:10; 8:6–8; Gal 5:17; Col 1:21)

    b. Alienation from God's life, that is, spiritual death (Eph 2:1, 12; 4:18; Col 1:21; 2:13)

    c. God's wrath (Rom 1:18) and judgment (Rom 5:16) toward humans. People are condemned (Rom 5:16, 18) and under God's "curse" (Gal 3:10). In a word, the judgment is "death" (Rom 5:12–21).

2. Humans have become slaves of sin (Rom 3:9; 6:16–17), involving:

    a. Darkened and futile thinking, and "hardness of heart" toward God (Rom 1:21; Eph 4:17–18; Titus 3:3)

    b. Evil actions of all kinds, described as "godlessness and wickedness" (Rom 1:18), disobedience (Rom 2:8; Eph 5:6; Titus 3:3), idolatry (Rom 1:22–23, 25); and including sins of thought, word, and action, toward God and people, drawing the wrath of God (Rom 1:18–32; 1 Cor 6:9–10; Gal 5:19–21; Eph 5:5–6; Col 3:5–6).

    c. Sin as something that indwells humans, who are "fleshly" (Rom 7:14), "in the flesh" (Rom 7:5; 8:9), pursuing evil desires and performing evil actions (Rom 7:5, 15–25; Gal 5:16–21, 24; Eph 2:3)

3. Humans are enslaved by spiritual powers that bring spiritual darkness (Col 1:13), blindness (2 Cor 4:3–4), and futile religion (Gal 4:8–9), and that influence people toward a sinful way of life (Eph 2:2; 2 Tim 2:26).

4. Human existence involves frustration or futility (Rom 8:20), the inability to achieve God's intended purpose. It is "slavery to corruption" (Rom 8:21), involving physical death (Rom 5:12) and without eternal hope (Eph 2:12).

God's people, while beginning to experience freedom from these things, still live as fallen humans among other fallen humans in a fallen creation. There is the tension between the "now" and "not yet" of God's kingdom, between the "present evil age" (Gal 1:4) and the age to come (Eph 1:21). This involves the following:

1. Suffering at the hands of fallen humans who oppose God, the gospel, and the church. This is a major theme in Paul (Rom 8:17–18, 36–37; 2 Cor 1:3–11; 4:8–12; 6:4–5, 8–10; 11:23–27; Gal 5:11; 6:12, 17; Eph 3:1, 13; 6:20; Phil 1:29–30; Col 1:24; 2:1; 4:3, 18; 1 Thess 1:6; 2:2; 3:2–5, 7; 2 Thess 1:4–7; 2 Tim 1:8, 12; 2:3–13; 3:10–12; 4:5–8; Phlm 1:1, 9, 10).

2. The "flesh" versus "Spirit" tension: learning to overcome the indwelling principle of sin and to live instead by God's Spirit (Rom 8:1–16; Gal 5:13—6:10)

3. A struggle against evil spiritual powers (Rom 16:20; Eph 6:10–18; 1 Thess 2:18; 3:5)

4. The ongoing experience of corruption (Rom 8:21), including physical decline (2 Cor 4:16) and death (Rom 8:10)

5. A longing for the final redemption of creation (Rom 8:23–25).

Reflections

For Christians who know Paul's letters, the points here concerning fallen humanity and God's judgment are not new. What we need to see is that everything in the above summary is connected with God's judgment; all these things are in some way a result and an expression of judgment. When we realize this we gain a better appreciation of the reality of God's judgment upon humanity. We can see the various serious consequences of our rebellion. We can see the holiness and power of the righteous God who deals with all unrighteousness. We realize that we live in a universe where God is sovereign, where we are accountable to him, where sin has consequences, and where we are dependent on him. When we begin to understand the depth of our problem, we realize that only he can provide the answer. And of course, he has, in Jesus Christ. The more we appreciate the problem, the more we appreciate what Jesus has done for us. We can open our lives more fully to his grace, and do our part in bringing that grace to others.

The Fallen Human Condition as God's Judgment

Developing a Christian Worldview

We are talking about developing a worldview that includes the various aspects of the truth of God's judgment, here, God's judgment in the Fall. We will now explore some of the challenges that we have in developing such a worldview.

The first challenge is ignorance. The irony of our fallenness is that we are ignorant of our human situation, which we interpret in ways other than according to God's truth. Western thinking certainly does not see it as God's judgment; such thought denies the idea of "original sin"[1] and is still working hard at developing an atheistic evolutionary interpretation of humanity. While it acknowledges a "dark side" to humans, it hopes that humans can overcome this through education, opportunity, and effort. At the level of individual thought, many people know intuitively that there is something wrong with humans. They may even identify it as "sin," but they prefer to think about more positive and uplifting things, and so never come to grips with the human condition. It is easy for us as Christians not to come to grips with it either. While we may know some biblical truth regarding God's judgment, unless we make an effort to integrate this truth into our worldview and to apply it in our lives, we will end up being little different from our society. We will tend to see things as it does, to simply accept things as they are without understanding why, or to live in denial of our condition before God. There is work for us to do in coming to grips with the truth of God's judgment. We need to seek God for understanding through prayer, study, and meditation, and then finds ways to put it into practice in our daily lives (cf. Rom 12:1–2).

Another challenge to developing a worldview that includes the truth of God's judgment is human ability. It is obvious that the summary of the human condition at the beginning of this chapter is far from complete. It is very negative, leaving out the many positive aspects of human life and ability, and the many blessings of God. Another irony of our fallenness is that the positive aspects, rather than leading people to acknowledge God and give thanks to him, lead to self-sufficiency and unthankfulness. This is seen particularly in the relentless human attempt throughout history to break free from and overcome the effects of God's judgment in the Fall. We have developed human culture and technology to limit sinful behavior and

---

1. For an explanation and defense of the doctrine of original sin, see Blocher, *Original Sin*. For a broader study of the Fall and sin, see Shuster, *Fall and Sin*.

its effects, to reduce physical pain, to heal sickness and lengthen life, and to promote safety, comfort, and joy. We have had mixed success because human sinfulness expressed in various ways (including war), and natural disasters, have hindered progress. But gradually we have progressed to where we are in today's developed world, with prosperity, comfort, and great opportunity. The result is that we have a greatly reduced sense of our fallenness. Generally, we are not conscious of God's judgment, and we do not acknowledge him as our Creator. We "pat ourselves on the back" for all we have been able to achieve.

We need to realize that our culture and way of thinking have a great effect on us as Christians. We are beneficiaries of human achievement, and with the rest of society, like to enjoy the benefits. But as the people of God we must not be deceived by human success. We must develop and maintain a biblical understanding of the world and humanity, realizing that we are still a race under God's judgment. Human achievement has not changed the fundamentals of the human condition: we still sin against God and each other in a whole host of ways; we experience physical and emotional pain, weakness, and limitation; we struggle for a sense of identity and purpose; we are mortal. Judgment is still with us. This remains true for us as Christians, although hopefully less so with regard to sin. We must not be fooled into thinking that we have escaped God's judgment through human effort. We must be humble and dependent on God. Further, while we are encouraged by the apostle Paul to enjoy the good things in the world (1 Tim 6:17), we must not be fooled into thinking that this is what life is about, and thus to live a self-indulgent life. The purpose of our life is to give thanks to God and glorify him (cf. Rom 1:21).

An important key for us is our understanding of freedom. Human attempts to break free from the effects of the Fall and to achieve in various ways are one form of freedom. While there are good aspects to this, it does not solve the basic human problem of slavery to sin and death. Only the gospel of Jesus Christ is the answer to the human situation. This is where real freedom is found: freedom from the stranglehold of sin and death, into the righteousness and life of God through Jesus Christ. We need to be convinced of it and to spend our lives with our brothers and sisters in Christ pursuing true freedom, and helping other people to find it.

A dear friend of mine—to whose memory this book is dedicated—used to talk about "mortality memos" from God, short messages that remind us of our mortality. In his latter years my friend became more conscious of these "memos" as he struggled in various ways with the decline of his physical body. These messages come to us all through our own bodies; they also come through the physical illness, weakness, and struggles of others, especially our loved ones. The clearest "memo" we can receive is when someone close to us dies. Funeral services are a strong message and "wakeup call" from God to us about the reality, not only of death, but also of his judgment, which is what death is. We need to "get the message" and live differently. My friend did. His awareness of his own mortality caused him to keep hoping in the true life and freedom God has provided, and to declare it to others. He had a strong sense of the shortness of our present life, which he called an "apprenticeship" for the coming life of the ages. I believe that my friend is now experiencing what he hoped for in the presence of his Lord. His death was another "mortality memo" to those of us who remain.

Eschatology

Another key to building the truth of God's judgment into our worldview is Christian eschatology. Eschatology is not only about the expectation of the Lord's coming, but is a way of seeing both the present and the future in relation to God's kingdom, that is, his rule. We have already begun to consider Paul's eschatology. It is important to note that his eschatology is consistent with that of the other New Testament writers, all of whom follow Jesus in holding to a "now" and "not yet" eschatology—Christian eschatology. The kingdom of God is "now," and God's people can begin to experience freedom from the fallen human condition and to enter into new life in Christ, with a new relationship with God and people, a new desire, new purpose, new strength, and new hope (Rom 8). But the kingdom is also "not yet," and God's people will not experience their full eternal inheritance in Christ until his second coming (Rom 8:17–30). In the "now" Paul sought to experience new life in Christ as far as possible in the present age (Phil 3:7–14). He believed that Christians could experience freedom from sin's power in the present life (Rom 6).[2] He did not make excuses for sin. But he was also very much in touch with the reality of living in a fallen world. He knew human weakness, struggle, and much suffering for the gospel (2 Cor 4:7–12; 6:4–5, 8–10; 11:23–30; 12:9–10). He expected Christians to suffer

---

2. But Paul did not believe in "sinless perfection" in this life; perfection is in the age to come (Phil 3:12–14).

in the present world (Rom 8:17–18). He did not pursue the things of the world, but fixed his eyes on the age to come, the "not yet" (2 Cor 4:16–18).

The challenge for us is not just to understand Paul's eschatology, but to live it out. As western Christians we are generally doing quite poorly in this regard. Our view of the "now" tends to be quite different from Paul's. We are less passionate than Paul in our pursuit of Christ and life in the Spirit. We have a lower expectation concerning victory over sin; we make excuses for sin; we have invented many euphemisms for it: "weakness, failings, foibles, peccadillos, affairs," etc. We are less in touch with the realities of living in a fallen world; we feel stronger and more sufficient, and know little about suffering for Christ. We pursue the things of the world and often do not have our eyes fixed on the "not yet." Clearly, we have been deeply affected and "infected" by the culture in which we live.

What is the answer? In a word, we need to repent. We have been fooled by our culture. We struggle with the blindness of our own sinfulness. We have lost touch with the reality of our fallenness. As the Lord's people we need to seek him and ask him to forgive us and renew us to live fully for him and the gospel. We need renewal and revival.

Suffering for Christ

Part of the renewal we need is in our view of Christian suffering for the gospel. Again, Paul can help us. We have seen in chapters 2 and 3 that he says much about suffering for the gospel (Rom 8:17–18; 2 Cor 1:5–7; Gal 3:4; Phil 1:29; 3:10; Col 1:24; 1 Thess 2:14; 2 Thess 1:5). This is not because he enjoys suffering of itself, but because he sees suffering as inevitable for a church that is a living testimony to Jesus Christ among fallen humanity at enmity with God.[3] Accordingly, Paul sees the suffering church as a "sign" of eschatological judgment and salvation: of salvation to those who believe the gospel, and of judgment to those who reject it (Phil 1:27–30; 2 Thess 1:5–10). It is the church's calling, privilege, and responsibility to proclaim the gospel in word and deed, so that people have the opportunity of being saved from God's wrath. Apart from Christ we are lost.

We must recover the truth of suffering for Christ (Rom 8:17). Our western culture of religious freedom, while a blessing in some ways, has caused the church to become complacent and not to expect suffering. Very

---

3. On the significance of Paul's suffering in his apostolic mission, see Schreiner, *Paul*, 87–102.

few sermons are preached about suffering. Very few Christians see clearly the calling of the church to be a "sign" of salvation and judgment, and take it seriously enough to be passionate witnesses for Christ. We suffer little, in part because we do not challenge sinful humanity or the spiritual powers of the world. Thus, we are somewhat detached from the realities of fallen humanity and God's judgment. What is the answer? To begin with, we should not set out to suffer; it is not our goal. But at the same time we should expect to suffer, because suffering is an inevitable result of Christian witness in a fallen world. The answer is to take our calling more seriously, and with God's help, to be more passionate and faithful witnesses for Christ. Suffering will come, especially in the future as the west becomes more secularized and religiously pluralistic. We will be more in touch with the reality of fallen humanity, and will know the joy of being God's "sign." The other thing we must do is support our brothers and sisters who are suffering for their faith; at the present time these brothers and sisters are mainly overseas. We are one with them in the gospel: "Remember those in prison as if you were their fellow prisoners" (Heb. 13:3); "Remember my chains" (Col 4:18).[4]

Expectations concerning the "Now"

Another challenge faced by some Christians and Christian groups in developing a biblical worldview that includes God's judgment, is a tendency toward triumphalism. In part this usually reflects an eschatology that expects more in the "now" than what the Bible promises. It also reflects a failure to understand adequately the many ways in which the effects of the Fall continue for God's people in the present age. There is a tendency either to be unaware of some of these effects or to strive for freedom from them. There is a tendency to attribute the effects to Satan, without seeing the bigger picture of God's judgment. There are various forms of Christian triumphalism. One that I have encountered is the so-called "prosperity" or "health and wealth" gospel.[5] In my view it has some commendable features: a belief that God desires to bless his people; a desire to live by faith in every area of life; a desire to overcome sin and Satan, and to live in the reality of the salvation that Jesus has secured for us. I would say "Amen" to all of these. We need to enter into the life of the Spirit as fully as we can. There are far

4. For a description of persecution of Christians in the world today, and a call for action to address this injustice, see Marshall, *Their Blood Cries Out*.

5. For an evaluation of this movement, see ACUTE, *Faith, Health and Prosperity*.

too many Christians who do not, who expect far too little and do not live in the victory of Christ. But there is a problem with this "gospel." It overemphasizes material blessing and physical healing, and expects that these should always be forthcoming. Many people end up disappointed. Part of the problem is the failure to recognize that all people, including Christians, continue to live with the effects of God's judgment in the Fall. There is no escaping some of these, including sickness, and especially death. We should pray and trust God for healing (e.g., Jas 5:14–16; 1 Cor 12:9); God still heals today. But healing may not come as expected, and the grace of God can sustain, teach, and work through us in the midst of weakness and disappointment (e.g., 2 Cor 12:9–10). Our struggles in the present life help us to appreciate the reality of our fallen estate. They help us to understand God's judgment and his grace, to have compassion for others, and to nurture a biblical hope that looks to the age to come, rather than the present, for the fulfillment of our deepest desires (Rom 8:18–25).

As I have already commented, while some Christians have unrealistic expectations regarding the present, others expect too little, especially with respect to victory over sin and evil spiritual powers. While slavery to sin and evil powers is an effect of God's judgment in the Fall, the Lord has freed us from such slavery in the present age. This does not mean "sinless perfection" or no influence from Satan's power; it means victory in and through struggle, and learning how to walk in greater victory as we grow in Christ. There are two problems that are fairly widespread in the western church. One is taking sin lightly and making excuses for it. Connected with this is a wrong view of Paul's teaching on "flesh versus Spirit," which many see as a battle between two natures in which "the flesh" often wins. Paul would not agree. While sin is an indwelling principle that we must still deal with, Paul strongly teaches the sufficiency of the power of God's Spirit to overcome sin and to lead us in righteousness.[6] We need to get serious about holiness, and learn how to walk by the Spirit. He will teach us. Another problem is our ignorance of spiritual powers. We are too affected by a naturalist worldview. We need to learn from the Bible and from experience about spiritual powers, and then resist them in prayer and in our daily life and service. As we do we find new freedom in Christ, and we are also able to help others find true freedom.[7] Christ has set us free from the power of sin and of Satan.

---

6. See Fee, *God's Empowering Presence*, 876–83.

7. See the helpful practical instruction in Steadman, *Spiritual Warfare*; Bubeck, *Overcoming the Adversary*; Anderson, *The Bondage Breaker*.

The Fallen Human Condition as God's Judgment

Finally, the more we understand the fallen human condition under God's judgment, and integrate our understanding into the way we see people, the more compassionate we will become. When we see other people struggling with life, failing and sinning, we see ourselves. We should never see ourselves as being better than another person. It is only because of the grace of God that we are forgiven and that we have begun to find freedom and transformation. We must remember that the fallen human condition is not the last word. God has stepped in to save humanity. And what he has done for us, he desires to do for others. We need to remember his mercy to us and to catch more of his heart for people, both for our brothers and sisters in Christ, and for those who do not know the Lord. As Paul says in Philippians 1:9, our love for people needs to "abound more and more in knowledge and depth of insight." We need to reach out to others with friendship and practical help. As we do, we appreciate more both the glorious image of God in people and the awful damage that sin has done. God will continue to restore and equip us to bring his saving grace into people's lives.

5

God's Temporal Judgment

WE COME TO AN important and difficult topic: the question of God's judgment on people throughout history. Clearly, to some extent God's judgment throughout history is simply the continuing application of his judgment on humanity at the Fall, whose effects every human generation experiences. But this original judgment does not account for everything that Paul or the Bible says about God's judgment throughout history. There is clearly also a sense in which God is active in judging individuals and groups for what they have done. We have seen some aspects of Paul's understanding of this in chapters 2 and 3.

Our goal in this chapter is to gain a better understanding of God's temporal judgment, with the help of Paul. We will begin with a brief summary of what we found in chapters 2 and 3. Then we will reflect on the main elements of Paul's understanding and their implications for us today.

Summary of Paul's Teaching on Temporal Judgment

1. *The ongoing decline of humanity*: In Romans 1:18–32 Paul describes God's "handing over" of humans to their desires, so that they are corrupted further in their sin. This is evidently a process that occurs during the whole history of humanity. It has happened in the past and continues in the present. It would seem to be Paul's basic understanding of how God's temporal judgment works in sinful humanity. It is the post-Fall judgment of God. Other passages that may have such judgment in mind are Ephesians 5:6 and 1 Thessalonians 4:6.[1]

2. *The judgment of Israel*: In 1 Corinthians 10:5–10 Paul describes the judgment of Israel in the times of Moses because of their sin, resulting in the death of many Israelites in the desert. Paul sees God's judgment of Israel as also operating in the "hardening" of many Israelites

---

1. Both these passages refer mainly to the eschatological judgment.

in unbelief with respect to the gospel (Rom 11:7–10). Such hardening in unbelief may be the "wrath" that Paul speaks about in relation to Judean Jews who opposed the gospel (1 Thess 2:14–16).

3. *The "hardening" of people in unbelief:* Paul sees God's hardening of people in unbelief as also occurring outside the Old Covenant people of God. God hardened the heart of Pharaoh in order to work out his saving purpose for Israel (Rom 9:17). Paul also describes God as sending upon unbelievers "a powerful delusion so that they will believe the lie" (2 Thess 2:11). Usually, though, Paul describes people as being left in their unbelief, as not being chosen to believe in Christ (Rom 9:22–24; 1 Cor 1:26–29).

4. *The judgment of evil spiritual powers:* While Paul sees evil spiritual powers as being judged in the death and resurrection of Christ (Col 2:15; Eph 1:20–22) and at the end of the age (1 Cor 15:24), there is also a sense in which God's judgment works against Satan at the present time. As people are set free from the powers of darkness (Col 1:13) and as the church withstands these powers in its life and mission (2 Cor 10:3–5; Eph 6:10–20), Satan's power is overcome. In this sense he is being judged. Paul's encouragement to the Romans may apply here: "The God of peace will soon crush Satan under your feet" (Rom 16:20).[2]

5. *The judgment of citizens by civil authorities:* In Romans 13:1–7 Paul describes judgment as being dispensed by earthly authorities against evildoers.[3] Clearly, he sees such judgment as a major way in which God's temporal judgment operates within a society. The purpose is the good order of society for the benefit of its citizens. God's concern for the well-being of people is evident here. His "common grace" includes the justice systems of human societies.

6. *The judgment of church members:* Paul sees God's temporal judgment as working in various ways in the church. Sometimes the Lord works directly to discipline his people, through sickness and even death (1 Cor 11:28–32).[4] At other times Paul is involved in "handing over" people to Satan for discipline (1 Cor 5:1–5; 1 Tim 1:19–20), which would seem to be a way in which God's judgment operates. Most of

---

2. This verse probably also has an eschatological meaning.
3. Romans 12:19 may allude to this form of judgment.
4. It may also be the case in 1 Cor 10:12, 22; 1 Thess 4:6.

the time Paul apparently sees God's judgment as working indirectly through church discipline, with God's judgment not mentioned (1 Cor 6:1–8; 2 Cor 2:5–11; 7:8–12; 10:5–6; 13:2, 10; 2 Thess 3:6–15; 1 Tim 5:20; 2 Tim 2:24–26; Titus 3:10–11). Sometimes people experience the inherent consequences of their actions (1 Tim 3:6; 5:11–15). The purpose of judgment in the church is restorative, not punitive. The key issue for Paul is the holiness of the church. God's people must live in righteousness, love, and truth. Where they do not, God's disciplinary judgment works to deal with sin and promote holiness. The temporal judgment of Christians is a significant element in Paul's theology of divine judgment.

Romans 1:18–32: Increasing Sinfulness as Judgment

While there are various interpretations of the wrath Paul is describing in this passage and how it is revealed,[5] it seems that by and large Paul is describing how the wrath of God has operated and continues to operate during human history.[6] People with a biblical worldview can relate what Paul says to today's world. We still see the same pattern of human sin at work.

What is Paul teaching in Romans 1? Let us begin with a quotation:

> Paul diagnoses the moral disorder of the Greco-Roman world by means of announcement rather than persuasion: the ills of society are the result of the divine wrath upon idolatry. All sins are

---

5. Because Paul says God's wrath is "being revealed" (Gr. *apokaluptetai*) (v. 18) and then goes on to describe how God "hands people over" to sins (vv. 24, 26, 28), many commentators conclude that this historical manifestation of wrath is what Paul is describing. See Moo, *Romans*, 100–102; Seifrid, "Unrighteous by Faith," 110–11; Travis, *Christ and the Judgement of God*, 60; Caird and Hurst, *New Testament Theology*, 84–87. Others argue for a parallel between the revealing of God's righteousness in the gospel (vv. 16–17) and the revealing of his wrath; thus, just as God's righteousness is revealed in the gospel, so his wrath is revealed in the gospel, both in the death of Christ and in the preaching of it. See Cranfield, *Romans*, 1:109–10; Bockmuehl, *Revelation and Mystery*, 140–41; Finamore, "Gospel and the Wrath of God in Romans 1," 137–45. Others argue that the wrath in verse 18 is God's eschatological wrath that will be revealed, to which human sinfulness in verses 19–31 points. See Bell, *No One Seeks for God*, 14–18.

6. While Paul would have the Fall of humanity in mind, this is not specifically what he is describing. "Paul does not deal with the origin of sin in Romans 1:18–32, but with its real presence in the world of human beings" (Seifrid, "Unrighteous by Faith," 118). See also Fitzmyer, *Romans*, 274.

punishments, divine judgments upon the primal sin of exchanging the true God for idols.[7]

Paul gives fundamental insights into the nature of sin as human rejection of what God has revealed concerning himself (vv. 19–21, 28). Such rejection is followed by the decline into spiritual darkness and idolatry (vv. 21–23, 25), the pursuit of various sinful desires, especially sexual immorality (v. 24), and worse desires and actions (vv. 26–27) that affect not only individuals, but the whole of society (vv. 28–31). Paul sees the downward spiral as the outworking of God's wrath in and among people. Paul does not describe God's wrath as punishments coming from outside, but as the inner spiritual and moral corruption of humans who reject the truth about God. God "gives people over" (vv. 24, 26, 28) to their desires, and these desires destroy them. The process applies to the history of individuals, families, larger groups, nations, and the whole of humanity. It is the outworking of God's wrath that will culminate in the eschatological judgment of humans (Rom 2:5).

Paul's understanding of God's wrath is fundamentally Jewish. It reflects the teaching about sin and judgment in Genesis 1–3;[8] it also reflects the attack of Hellenistic Judaism, especially in the Wisdom of Solomon (chapters 13–15), on Gentile idolatry and sexual immorality. But in the light of the coming of Jesus, Paul goes further than Wisdom. He sees the decline into idolatry as culpable rejection of the Creator, not an unfortunate slide into folly. Paul sees subjection to sinful practices as God's judgment, not simply the result of idolatry. Paul sees his teaching in Romans 1:18–32 as applying to Jews (Rom 2), not simply to Gentiles.[9] Paul's understanding of God's wrath is applicable to all humanity: "*all* the godlessness and wickedness of human beings" (Rom 1:18).

Exposing Idolatry

The value of Paul's teaching is no less today than in his time. Fundamentally, nothing has changed with regard to fallen humans in their relationship with God and in their conduct. Only faith in Jesus begins to break the

---

7. Seifrid, "Unrighteous by Faith," 108.
8. See Hooker, "Adam in Romans 1," 73–84; Dunn, *Theology of Paul*, 91–93 (see also 79–90).
9. Seifrid, "Unrighteous by Faith," 114.

cycle of sin and wrath. People generally do not think of idolatry as applying to contemporary western society. They may speak about "pop idols," but they see idolatry as a primitive phenomenon involving gods, physical images, and sacrifices. But idolatry is still with us just as strongly as in other and ancient cultures. The issue is one of worship. What or whom do we worship? What or whom do we love and serve? If we love or serve anything or anyone above the true God, we are idolaters. This is a sobering fact in a materialistic culture where we easily end up loving and serving "Mammon" (Matt 6:24), with little reflection about what we are doing. Paul's teaching exposes idolatry.

While Paul's teaching helps us to recognize and understand what is wrong with our society, we need to be careful about what we do with our understanding. It is not so that we can stand back and criticize people or cultures. In fact, the idolatry and sins Paul describes are still present to some extent in the church. In our fallenness we continue to struggle with these things. The judgment of God is at work in the sins of all people, including Christians. We must be humble and prayerful, asking God to cleanse us from these things, and to enable us to worship him alone and to be free from the power of sin. Also, Paul's insights should give us compassion for all people, especially for those who do not know God. On the one hand, they may think they are enjoying the various (sinful) activities they are involved in. On the other hand, many are struggling with relationships, behaviors, and circumstances that they know are harmful and destructive, and from which they long to be set free. We know that only Jesus is the answer. Our responsibility is to have God's love for people in our hearts, to pray for them, and to be led by God's Spirit as we become involved in their lives, pointing them toward a saving knowledge of the Lord.

Moral Trends Today

Paul's teaching also provides us with a "benchmark" against which to discern moral trends in society that are exerting great pressure on all institutions, including the church. Two of the big moral issues of our time are abortion and homosexuality. Increasingly, governments are decriminalizing abortion and affirming the morality and normality of homosexual practice and relationships. It is argued that a mature society should recognize the right of a woman to terminate her pregnancy and of devoted homosexual couples to be married. The pressure is great and there is decreasing tolerance toward those who voice a dissenting opinion. Some professing Christians and Christian denominations have concluded that these practices are acceptable. The majority of Christians and denominations continue to regard these practices as sinful,[10] because of the Bible's teaching on marriage (Gen 1:27–28; 2:24; Matt 19:3–12)[11] and the sanctity of human life (Gen 9:6; Lev 19:18; Deut 12:31; Ps 139:13–16).[12] Paul's teaching on homosexuality in Romans 1:26–27 is very clear, showing that all homosexual practice is sinful and an outworking of God's wrath in people.[13] Paul's teaching sheds a very different light on contemporary moral shifts. Rather than seeing them as the maturing of society, we see them as evidence of moral decline and of the wrath of God at work. What we are seeing in the west is a rejection of biblical authority and morality, and a regression to a "pagan" society, in many ways closer to the social environment of the early church, with its sexual immorality, abortion, and infanticide. The early church did not give in to the cultural pressure, but was different from its society, seeking to love people and win them to the Lord.[14] The success of the early Christians in showing society God's way is an encouragement to us to do the same.

Questions concerning God's Wrath

Paul's view of God's wrath as a process of abandonment to sin, at work within human beings, raises a number of questions. Based on Paul's view

---

10. Christians are generally not opposed to abortion in every case. Most would see it as justified if the life of the mother is greatly at risk apart from an abortion. But such cases are rare today in western society.

11. See Köstenberger and Jones, *God, Marriage, and Family*.

12. See Hoffmeier, *Abortion*; Gorman, *Abortion and the Early Church*.

13. In the last fifty years various arguments have sought to limit Paul's condemnation of homosexual acts to exploitative homosexual practices, thus apparently sanctioning loving homosexual relationships. See Scroggs, *New Testament and Homosexuality*. But these arguments sideline the physical sexual complementarity of men and women as created by God—clearly revealing his will—and the foundational teaching of Genesis 1 and 2 on sexuality and marriage. They attempt to make Paul as a Jew say what is contrary to the Old Testament, early Judaism, and the New Testament. For discussions, see Dunn, *Romans 1–8*, 64–66, 74; Moo, *Romans*, 113–17; Schreiner, *Romans*, 93–97; Bird and Harris, "Paul's Jewish View of Sexuality in Romans 1:26–27," 87–104; Sprinkle, "Romans 1 and Homosexuality," 515–28; Gagnon, *Bible and Homosexual Practice*. On questions about AIDS (Acquired Immunodeficiency Syndrome) and God's judgment, see Carson, "Reflections on AIDS," 227–33.

14. See Stark, *Rise of Christianity*.

some have argued that God's wrath is a process in which he himself is not involved. Wrath is simply "an inevitable process of cause and effect in a moral universe."[15] God is ultimately behind the process in the sense that he established a moral universe. Wrath then is human beings experiencing the inevitable consequences of rejecting God's moral laws.[16] While there is some truth here, it is not an adequate view of Paul. Paul sees God as actively involved in "giving people over" to their desires (vv. 24, 26, 28). Paul does not have a deistic worldview in which God has stepped back to allow things to take their course apart from him. Rather, God is omnipresent and active in dispensing his judgment and mercy. While this does not mean that God wills or causes people to do evil, it does mean that he has decreed the consequences of their sinful actions: they will "reap what they sow" (cf. Gal 6:7–8). Such "reaping" is not apart from God; it occurs in a world sustained by God, where God is active in executing his judgment. This does not mean that God is constantly "striking" individuals or groups for every sin they commit. But it does mean that in various ways God is active in judging human sin. While it is often difficult for us to discern or understand, we ought not to separate God from his judgments. "His activity is to be discerned in those consequences."[17]

Another question is whether God's wrath is to be seen as his retribution (from Lat. *retribuĕre*: to give back, return, repay) or punishment for human sin. There is no question that Paul uses retributive terms in Romans 1 to describe God's wrath:[18]

> [27] . . . Men committed shameful acts with other men, and received in themselves the due penalty for their error . . . [32] Although they know God's righteous decree that those who do such things deserve death . . . (vv. 27b, 32a)

The idea of the punishment fitting the crime is very strong in the words, "*received* in themselves the *due penalty*" (lit. "*receiving back* the *corresponding payment* that was *necessary*") and "*deserve* death" (lit. "are

---

15. Dodd, *Romans*, 23.

16. "The act of God is no more than an abstention from interference with their free choice and its consequences" (ibid., 29). Or as has been argued more recently, "Sinful activity is the result of God's letting us go our own way—and this 'letting us go our own way' constitutes God's wrath" (Green and Baker, *Recovering the Scandal*, 55).

17. Morris, *Apostolic Preaching*, 184. For an argument against impersonal or nonemotional wrath, see McFadden, *Judgment*, 25–28.

18. See Moo, *Romans*, 116–17, 121–22.

worthy of death"). But some recent writers seek to soften Paul's words to mean simply that God oversees a process whereby people experience the inherent consequences of their actions, rather than a penalty imposed by God from the outside. Thus, the idea of retribution or punishment is toned down or even removed.[19] But such a view is hardly true to Paul. Whether or not the effect of God's wrath is seen as an inherent consequence or an externally imposed penalty, the fact is, it is decreed by God and it is a penalty, a punishment, a negative result that adversely affects the recipient. Therefore, it is retributive.[20] But this does not mean that it is malevolent. All the negative connotations of "retribution" in common English usage do not apply to God's retribution. His retribution is just, but not malicious.

A related matter is whether Paul sees any reforming purpose in God's wrath in Romans 1. Numerous commentators from Chrysostom to the present have discerned in Paul the hope that people will learn from the pain of being handed over to the consequences of their sins, and come to repentance.[21] But there is little hint of it in Romans 1, probably because Paul is emphasizing wrath and punishment here. However, shortly after, he speaks of the "kindness of God [that] would lead [sinners] to repentance" (Rom 2:4). Thus, God's kindness is at work in the midst of his wrath (cf. Rom 11:22). This is the gospel. "All of us . . . were by nature deserving of wrath. But because of his great love for us, God, who is rich in mercy, made us alive with Christ" (Eph 2:3–5). But we must understand what we have been saved from. God's wrath is real, and it is punishment.

It is significant that Paul does not focus on external punishments for sin in Romans 1. At first this seems surprising, given Paul's Jewish heritage and given that the Old Testament focuses mainly on such external punishments in the form of drought, crop failure, disease, military attack, exile, etc. But in the light of the cross Paul has gained deeper insight into the nature of human sin and of God's wrath. Paul acknowledges wrath in the form of external punishments (1 Cor 10:5–10), but he has also come to see God's wrath at work in the operation of sin within human beings. This is a greater problem than any external wrath; unless the deeper problem can be solved, there is no hope for humanity. Paul has found the solution in Jesus,

---

19. This is the main thesis of Travis's book, *Christ and the Judgement of God: The Limits of Divine Retribution in New Testament Thought* (on Romans 1:18–32, see 60–62). It is also a major thesis in Marshall, *Beyond Retribution* (on Romans 1:18–32, see 169–75). See also Moule, "Punishment and Retribution," 235–49 (on Romans 1:27, see 240).

20. See McFadden, *Judgment*, 29–32.

21. See Cranfield, *Romans*, 1:121; Marshall, *Beyond Retribution*, 173–75.

which is what he seeks to communicate to people. In so doing he focuses on the deeper problem, which may explain why in his letters Paul does not focus on external punishments with respect to unbelieving humanity. No doubt Paul still believed that God's judgments occurred in external events. But Paul's priority was on preaching the good news and bringing people to saving faith (1 Cor 9:19–22).

The temporal judgment Paul describes in Romans 1 is something we need to understand, reflect on, and pray and talk about. It is not something we should consign to the past after we become Christians. Paul wrote it to a well-established Christian church. Evidently, he thought it was necessary for them, not just as one-off instruction, but as something they would integrate into their worldview and pass on to others. Also, it seems that Paul preached the truths of Romans 1:18–32 to non-Christians as part of his gospel: the bad news together with the good news.[22] We see evidence of it in 1 Thessalonians 1:9–10 and Acts 14:15; 17:22–31; 20:21; 24:24–25; 26:20. This is instructive for us. If we are to keep the truth about humanity before us, and if we are to bring that truth to others outside the church, we cannot neglect the truths of Romans 1 in our teaching, preaching, and walk with God.

What about Human and Natural Disasters as God's Judgment?

At this point we will return briefly to the relative silence of Paul about external judgments such as wars, famines, and natural disasters. While such things are often seen as God's judgment in the Old Testament (see chapter 1), there is no clear reference in Paul's letters to such things as God's judgment. How are we to interpret such a silence? Does it mean that Paul does not share the Old Testament view of temporal judgment? Probably not. But in the light of the gospel of Christ, Paul's focus is not so much on external events, but on the more fundamental matters of human sin and the grace of God that is available to every human. Paul discerns a deeper aspect of God's judgment in the sinful condition and actions of people (Rom 1). Being set free from sin is people's greatest need; any external judgments, while serious, are secondary. What counts is entering into right relationship with God through faith in Christ. Then people are no longer under God's wrath; in the Last Day they will be saved from his wrath (Rom 5:9; 1 Thess 1:10).

22. See Seifrid, "Unrighteous by Faith," 106–7.

God's Temporal Judgment

How then are we to interpret wars, massacres, droughts, famines, bushfires, earthquakes, floods, tsunamis, tornadoes, epidemics, and the fall of political regimes in our time? How are we to interpret the terrible things that we see in communities and families around us, sometimes in our own community and family? Such things can fill our minds, causing us to ask many questions, including questions about how God's judgment may be at work. It will not do to avoid questions about God's judgment or to say that God no longer judges as he did in the Old Testament period. The Bible teaches us that God's judgment is at work. But neither should we pretend that we can clearly discern how God's judgment is at work. We do not have the insight of the Old Testament prophets. We should not make specific pronouncements about God's judgment. And we should not "miss the forest for the trees," focusing unduly on the "trees" of external events and our interpretation of them, and missing the "forest" of God's love for sinful people and how we can bring the message of that love into various situations.

So how should we understand the working of God's judgment in external events? I have found several lines of thought that are helpful to me. Firstly, Paul's understanding in Romans 8 of a fallen world is fundamental. In our brief discussion of Romans 8:20–21 in chapter 2 we focused on fallen humanity. But Paul sees this within the larger picture of "the creation" that was "subjected to frustration" (v. 20), that now "groans" (v. 22), that "will be liberated from its bondage to decay" (v. 21), and that anxiously longs for God's children to be revealed (v. 19). Paul sees the whole creation as being caught up in and affected by human sin. The ground is "cursed" (Gen 3:17). I am not competent to explain the relationship between such a worldview and the science of earthquakes, droughts, storms and the like. What I do know is that we live in a world where there is great natural danger and where humans and other creatures suffer and die because of natural events. The present creation, while being the good creation of God, falls well short of the glory of the new creation that God will bring about at the Second Coming of the Lord Jesus Christ. The present creation corresponds to a race of sinful humanity that "fall[s] short of the glory of God" (Rom 3:23). It is a creation where destructive natural events are part of God's judgment on humanity. Any of us can be affected by such events. When such events occur, it does not mean that God is directly judging the people involved. It reminds us that we live in a fallen and imperfect world that is under God's judgment. It encourages us to set our hope on God who will bring a perfect new creation (Rom 8:23–25).

Secondly, while there is clearly a connection between human sin and God's judgment, the connection is not necessarily automatic, direct, or simple; often it is not. Usually God does not act directly through external events to judge particular sinful human actions. Judgments such as that of Ananias and Sapphira (Acts 5:1–11) are the exception rather than the rule. Jesus' teaching in Luke 13 suggests this:

> 1 Now there were some present at that time who told Jesus about the Galileans whose blood Pilate had mixed with their sacrifices. 2 Jesus answered, "Do you think that these Galileans were worse sinners than all the other Galileans because they suffered this way? 3 I tell you, no! But unless you repent, you too will all perish. 4 Or those eighteen who died when the tower in Siloam fell on them—do you think they were more guilty than all the others living in Jerusalem? 5 I tell you, no! But unless you repent, you too will all perish." (Luke 13:1–5)

Jesus denies that the two events are God's direct judgment on people who are particularly sinful. Therefore those who interpreted the events as God's direct judgment would be misinterpreting the situation. We therefore should avoid such misinterpretations. We should not assume that unfortunate events mean that the people involved are "*worse* sinners." We should not be in the habit of trying to discern God's judgment in specific situations. And we should certainly not be making judgments about the people involved (Matt 7:1). We should be praying, and loving and helping people (Luke 6:27–38). The message about judgment that we need to discern in unfortunate events is that there is a judgment to come in which people will "perish" eternally unless they repent. People may "perish" now through various events, but there is a far worse future fate awaiting those who do not come into right relationship with their Creator. Thus, Jesus puts the emphasis on repentance and future salvation, not on interpreting present events. So does Paul. This is where our focus should be.

Thirdly, our understanding of God's judgment in external events needs to sit within a Christian view of God's providence, namely, the working of his mercy and judgment in history, to guide human and world history for the achievement of his redemptive purpose.[23] Within this worldview

---

23. For a helpful discussion of divine providence as an essential element of the Christian view of history, see Bebbington, *Patterns in History*, esp. 171–75.

God is sovereign and active in both mercy and judgment; he cannot be separated from either. There is no room for deism, the belief that God has left his creation to the operation of natural laws that he established, but is no longer involved in. Our belief in God's providence does not mean that we can fully explain *how* God is at work: his judgments are "unsearchable . . . and his paths beyond tracing out" (Rom 11:33). But our struggle to explain the *how* does not mean that we abandon the biblical belief *that* his judgment (or his mercy) is at work. God's judgments are at work indirectly in natural events and human actions. He sometimes also acts more directly in judgment, as in the cases of Ananias and Sapphira (Acts 5:1–11), Elymas the magician (Acts 13:6–12), and the disciplining of the Corinthian Christians (1 Cor 11:29–32). Our role is not to be skilled discerners of God's judgments, but to be humble learners of his ways as we study his Word and walk with him, believing that he is working out his saving purpose in history, and nurturing the hope that "in all things God works for the good of those who love him, who have been called according to his purpose" (Rom 8:28).

Unbelief as Temporal Judgment

We saw in the previous chapter that unbelief is part of the fallen state of humans under God's wrath (2 Cor 4:3–4). But for such a state to continue, so that a person never comes to faith in Christ, can be seen as the temporal judgment of God, with eschatological consequences. While Paul does not cover the topic extensively, he says enough to support such a view. In choosing some people (1 Cor 1:26–28), God has clearly passed over others, who remain in their unbelief. God hardens those who reject the truth and who love wickedness (2 Thess 2:10–12). In Romans 9 Paul explains the calling of some to faith and the hardening of others in unbelief, with respect to the sovereign election of God (vv. 18–24). While the interaction of divine sovereignty and human decision remains a mystery to some extent, it is clear that in the end some people are hardened in their unbelief—that is, their natural state of unbelief remains and is reinforced. It is the judgment of God.

Again, this is a sobering truth with eternal consequences. For us as Christians it brings home to us a number of things. With respect to ourselves, we need to give thanks to God for his mercy to us, whereby we came to saving faith in Jesus. And we need to remain thankful and to continue in a vital faith in the Lord (Rom 11:22; Col 1:23). We also need to encourage our Christian brothers and sisters in faithful living (1 Thess 3:1–10; Heb 10:23–25). With respect to unbelievers, we must pray for them and seek to win them to faith in Jesus, so that they find the life that is in him and are delivered from God's wrath. It is not for us to make any judgments about whom we should reach out to or about the prospects of their coming to faith. These things are God's business. Our business is to love and to share the gospel; otherwise, people will not believe and be saved (Rom 10:11–15). We have a great privilege and responsibility in working with God to bring people into his kingdom (2 Cor 5:18–20). We endure in gospel ministry, with the expectation that through it God will bring all his chosen ones to salvation (2 Tim 2:10). Further, if people oppose or mistreat us, Paul encourages us to do good to them, not evil (Rom 12:17–21; 1 Thess 5:15). We need to be kind, patient, and gentle, because in this way some will "escape the snare of the devil" and come to repentance (2 Tim 2:24–26). We need to pray for unbelievers, that they will "be saved and come to the knowledge of the truth" (1 Tim 2:1–4).

Judgment of Evil Spiritual Powers in Gospel Ministry

There is more that needs to be said about how we respond to the unbelief of people. It is easy for us to become fatalistic about the response of people to the gospel. We can adopt the attitude: "That person has heard the gospel, but not responded to it. That's their responsibility. Perhaps they are not chosen. Perhaps that's just the way it is for them." This is not a biblical attitude. It is very short on love and faith, and on understanding the spiritual battle for the lives of people in which we are engaged. We should never give up reaching out to people with God's truth and love, and praying for them to believe in Jesus. We simply do not know if or when a person will come to faith. If would have been easy for the early church to write off Saul of Tarsus as a hardened unbeliever who would probably never believe in Jesus (Acts 9:1–2). But the Lord had mercy on him (1 Tim 1:12–14). And Paul did not write off his own people—Jews who did not believe the gospel. He agonized over them (Rom 9:1–3) and kept praying for them to be saved (Rom 10:1); he took the gospel to them (Rom 10:14–15). He was not passive or fatalistic; he never gave up on them.

Spiritual warfare is a very real part of our gospel outreach.[24] As Paul says: "our struggle is not against flesh and blood" (Eph 6:12); "though we walk in the flesh, we do not wage warfare according to the flesh" (2 Cor 10:3). It is very important that we approach our evangelistic efforts with Paul's perspective. People are not freed from the unbelief which is part of the fallen human condition under Satan's influence (2 Cor 4:3–4), simply by our speaking words to them. While the gospel is the power of God for salvation (Rom 1:16) that brings people to faith (Rom 1:17; 10:17), the words we speak must come with God's power that sets people free from Satan's power. Paul knew this well. In describing the ministry of Paul and Barnabas in Iconium, Luke writes: "There they spoke so effectively that a great number of Jews and Greeks believed" (Acts 14:1). Prayer is especially important, because it is through prayer that we exercise faith in God, asking him to empower us to overcome the powers of darkness (Eph 6:10–18) and to be effective in gospel ministry (Eph 6:19–20; Col 4:2–6; 2 Thess 3:1–3), and asking him to bring people to salvation (Rom 10:1; 1 Tim 2:1–4). We cannot be dispassionate. Like Paul we must be serious about the spiritual battle, serious about living for Christ (Col 1:29), serious about winning people for the Lord (1 Cor 9:19–22), and feeling his concern for them (2 Cor 5:14, 20; 6:1–2). Then we will be in touch with God's heart and his power, and will be more effective in the spiritual battle for people's lives.

Clearly, in all this we are seeing Christ's judgment of evil powers operating here and now. Spiritual warfare is a necessary part of Christian life and service. Apart from Christ's temporal judgment of Satan no one would come to faith in Christ, and Christians would still be bound by evil powers. We must become more aware that the Lord is judging Satan now through the ministry of the gospel. We must become more engaged in the spiritual battle, asking the Lord to teach us how to discern and overcome the powers of darkness.

Judgment through Civil Authorities

Paul's teaching about God's judgment operating through civil authorities (Rom 13:1–7) is very challenging.[25] His unqualified statements about authorities being established by God (v. 1) and being servants of God

---

24. For two excellent books on spiritual warfare, see Arnold, *Powers of Darkness*; Arnold, *Three Crucial Questions about Spiritual Warfare*.

25. For a thorough discussion of the topic, see O'Donovan, *Ways of Judgment*.

(vv. 4, 6) to promote righteous behavior (vv. 3–4), are arresting. His exhortation for us to submit to authorities challenges the cynical, selfish, and negative attitudes that are often present in our society, including among Christians. While we may wish to qualify what Paul says in various ways,[26] if we are going to have a Christian worldview, then we need to integrate Paul's instruction into our view of things, and into our attitudes and actions. The context of Romans 13:1–7 encourages it. It is part of the renewed thinking of Christian disciples who are seeking to know and do God's will (Rom 12:2).[27]

What does Paul's teaching mean in practice? Paul spells out several things for us as citizens: accepting authorities as being from God and not resisting them (vv. 1–2); doing good, not evil (vv. 3–4); paying taxes (vv. 6–7) and showing respect (v. 7). These attitudes and behaviors have many implications for us today. Our failure sometimes to think through and outwork the implications shows that we have much to learn. For those who are in authority, there is the great responsibility of administering justice in society. Paul assumes a knowledge of what is good and evil; apparently, he regards it as generally present in society through the "common grace" of God. For Christians involved in civil authorities, there is the opportunity and responsibility to bring Christian influence to the understanding of right and wrong, and to the administration of justice.[28] It is a great benefit to a society if its lawmakers and law enforcers acknowledge God and ask for his help in dispensing justice in that society. For all Christians there is the responsibility to pray for our leaders:

> [1] I urge, then, first of all, that petitions, prayers, intercession and thanksgiving be made for everyone— [2] for kings and all those in authority, that we may live peaceful and quiet lives in all godliness and holiness. (1 Tim 2:1–2)

On the issue of civil authorities dealing out "wrath" (Gr. *orgē*) to offenders (Rom 13:4), we need to see it as part of the role God has given to the state. It is a major way in which God's temporal judgment operates to deal with those who do wrong. But it is not the eschatological judgment; temporal judgment does not take the place of eschatological judgment. Paul presents temporal judgment through the state as punishment: "an avenger

26. See Moo, *Romans*, 806–10.
27. Ibid., 792.
28. For a discussion of the relationship between the church and the state in promoting public justice, see Kemeny, *Church, State and Public Justice*.

who brings wrath" (Gr. *ekdikos eis orgē*) (v. 4). It is certainly retributive, but can and should also have a reformative and deterrent purpose. If the punishment of someone leads to positive change in them and also causes others to avoid wrong behavior, it is certainly to be welcomed, and should be actively promoted. The fact that God has given the role of judgment to the state means that citizens do not have the right to take their own vengeance. We are brought back to Paul's teaching in Romans 12:17–21, where he instructs us how to deal with those who harm us. But does Paul mean that we are to expect the state to "get even" for us, and then to get upset if justice is not done in our eyes? Certainly not. In line with Jesus' teaching (Matt 5:43–48) Paul teaches us to love our enemies by doing good to them (Rom 12:20–21), with the hope that they will become remorseful and perhaps even turn to God (Rom 12:20).[29] Whether it happens through civil justice or not, our desire is not for revenge but reconciliation, and hopefully even Christian conversion. If people do not change, then we leave all judgment to God, who we know will do what is right.

Paul does not address the problematic matter of the state acting unjustly.[30] With respect to God's judgment, where the state punishes someone for an action that is righteous in God's sight or for an action they did not even perform, clearly, such punishment is not an expression of God's judgment. Only when the state judges according to what is true and according to God's definition of right and wrong, is its judgment an expression of God's judgment. While Paul urges submission to authorities (Rom 13:1), surely he does not mean an undiscerning acceptance that all their actions are right, or that God's judgment is always at work through their judgments. We must discern justice and judgment according to God's Word. Where we believe that the state is acting unjustly, we should seek God and act in accordance with the wisdom he gives us in the Bible (e.g., Matt 5:10–12; Acts 4:18–20; 5:27–32, 40–42; 16:35–40; 25:10–11; 1 Pet 4:12–19).

Judgment through civil authorities is a major way in which God works out his justice in the present world, however imperfectly. Such judgment is necessary to maintain the social fabric and order of society. It gives insight

---

29. Paul says that "in so doing you will heap burning coals on his head" (v. 20). The meaning is not clear, but recent interpreters tend to see it as referring to either shame over wrongdoing, possibly leading to repentance (Cranfield, *Romans*, 2:648–50; Moo, *Romans*, 788–89); or simply repentance (Dunn, *Romans 9–16*, 750–51; Travis, *Christ and the Judgement of God*, 66–67).

30. See the discussion of political authority in O'Donovan, *Ways of Judgment*, 127–48.

into the moral nature of humans and points us to the Creator and Lawgiver, to whom each of us is ultimately accountable. His temporal judgments teach us about the way things are, and point us to the reality of the eschatological judgment. As the Preacher says:

> [13] Now all has been heard; here is the conclusion of the matter: Fear God and keep his commandments, for this is the duty of every human being. [14] For God will bring every deed into judgment, including every hidden thing, whether it is good or evil. (Eccl 12:13–14)

Disciplinary Judgment of God's People

We have seen that the Lord's disciplinary judgment of his people is a major issue for Paul, something that the church must take very seriously:

> [12] What business is it of mine to judge those outside the church? Are you [emphatic pronoun in Greek] not to judge those inside? [13] God will judge those outside. (1 Cor 5:12–13a)

Paul sees the judgment of outsiders as God's business. No doubt this explains in part why Paul does not major on the temporal judgment of unbelievers. But the judgment of believers is a different matter, something that Paul sees as necessary, that the church itself must be actively involved in, and that Paul himself will do at times. Just as God's judgment works through civil authorities (Rom 13:1–7), so his judgment works through the discipline of the church (e.g., 1 Cor 5:3–5). We have seen that for Paul the issue is holiness, both individual and corporate. God's people are not only set apart to him through the saving work of Christ and the gift of the Holy Spirit (1 Cor 1:2, 30; 6:11); they must also be holy in character and conduct (1 Cor 3:16–17; 6:19–20). Where believers do not pursue that holiness willingly, God's judgment works to get their attention and lead them on the path of holiness.

The Lord's Indirect Discipline of His People

Most of Paul's directions concerning church discipline do not mention God's judgment. But it is assumed: through the church God is evaluating behavior and doctrine so that his people learn and change. This is a big topic to which we cannot do justice here. But briefly, we will consider the situations Paul refers to, and his instructions to the church. We begin with a summary table:

Text	Situation	Instruction
1 Cor 6:1–8	Litigation between Christians in civil courts	Work it out among yourselves without litigation. Be willing to suffer wrong (and then forgive).
2 Cor 2:5–11; 7:8–12	Probably a man who had strongly opposed Paul during his second visit to the church[31]	In lost letter: punish the man (possibly a formal rebuke and exclusion from the Eucharist).[32] In 2 Corinthians: forgive and comfort the man, now that he has repented.
2 Cor 10:5–6; 12:21; 13:2, 10	Some Corinthians criticizing Paul; some sinning sexually	Stop sinning. Otherwise, Paul himself will punish them when he comes, probably with formal rebuke and some kind of (temporary) exclusion from fellowship.[33]
2 Thess 3:6–15	Some Christians living an idle and undisciplined life	At first, do not share close fellowship with them. But if they resist Paul's instruction do not allow them into church meetings; let them feel ashamed. But continue to see them and admonish them, in the hope of their coming to repentance.[34]
1 Tim 5:20	Elders who continue to sin (confirmed by two or three witnesses)	Confront them in the presence of the church. The purpose is that others will be fearful of sinning.
2 Tim 2:24–26	Some Ephesians opposing Timothy	Teach and correct (possibly, discipline) them, in the hope of their coming to repentance.
Titus 3:10–11	Those causing division in the church	Warn them once, then again if necessary. If they persist in their sin, avoid them (this is not excommunication).[35]

---

31. See Barnett, *2 Corinthians*, 124.
32. See ibid., 126.
33. See ibid., 596–97.
34. See Morris, *1 and 2 Thessalonians*, 252–61.
35. See Mounce, *Pastoral Epistles*, 454.

Paul is addressing situations where particular sins are evident in the church and are adversely affecting it. His instructions show that he never begins with public discipline, which comes only after initial attempts to correct behavior have failed. Paul is consistent with the teaching of Jesus (Matt 18:15–20), moving step by step from private to more public handling of a situation as necessary. Paul's instructions concerning public discipline are not detailed, and therefore, are not entirely clear. In some cases there is a public rebuke of the person(s). In most cases there is some degree of exclusion from fellowship. But private communication continues in the hope of the person(s) coming to repentance and being restored to fellowship.

On two occasions Paul speaks of "handing [people] over to Satan" for discipline (1 Cor 5:1–5; 1 Tim 1:19–20). These would seem to be more serious situations than the ones we have just considered. "Handing over to Satan" is not to be taken literally.[36] Rather, it is a metaphor for excommunication,[37] of excluding someone from fellowship for a time. Paul does not mean some kind of transaction with the devil,[38] but putting someone "back out into Satan's sphere . . . where Satan and his 'principalities and powers' still hold sway over people's lives to destroy them."[39] In other words, a person loses the protection from evil powers that is part of being among God's people. In both 1 Corinthians 5 and 1 Timothy 1 the purpose of such exclusion is restorative: in the former, "that [his] spirit may be saved" (1 Cor 5:5); and in the latter, "that they may be taught not to blaspheme" (1 Tim 1:20).[40] In the Corinthian situation it is difficult to know what form of punishment Paul means, when he says concerning the incestuous man: "for the destruction of the flesh" (Gr. *eis olethron tēs sarkos*) (v. 5). Some see "flesh" here as referring to the man's physical body, with him suffering sickness or even death (cf. 1 Cor 11:28–32).[41] Others

---

36. It is possible that Paul adapted his expression from Job 2:6 LXX. See South, "Critique," 550–51; Rosner, *Paul, Scripture and Ethics*, 85.

37. Fee, *1 Corinthians*, 208–9; South, "Critique," 554–55; Yinger, *Paul, Judaism, and Judgment*, 239–40.

38. It is not a curse on the man (see South "Critique," 541–43, 545–547). Some see the "handing over" as a curse formula (e.g., Lampe, "Church Discipline," 352–53; Yarbro Collins, "'Excommunication' in Paul," 255–56).

39. Fee, *1 Corinthians*, 209.

40. See Mounce, *Pastoral Epistles*, 66–70.

41. For example, Käsemann, "Sentences of Holy Law," 71; Lampe, "Church Discipline," 349–53; Roetzel, *Judgement in the Community*, 119–22; Travis, *Christ and the Judgement of God*, 121–22.

see "flesh" in the sense of fleshly desires that will be destroyed through his being excluded from the church.[42] Neither view is free from problems; quite possibly Paul means affliction that is both physical and psychological, that will lead the man to repentance.[43] However, such affliction is not the purpose, but the result of exclusion.[44] The purpose is restoration.

Regarding Paul's attitude and action in these two situations, it is clear that he regards the situations as having deteriorated to such a point that the well-being and holiness of the church is seriously under threat.[45] In Corinth the church is ignorant of the contaminating effect of serious sexual sin (1 Cor 5:1–2, 6). In Ephesus the "shipwreck" of the faith of Hymenaeus and Alexander is a danger to the faith and life of the church (1 Tim 1:19–20; cf. 2 Tim 2:17–18). The only option to protect the churches is excommunication of the offending parties, which also sends a strong message to the offenders concerning their sin and the need to repent. We note also that Paul has a strong sense of the Lord's authority in these situations. It is "in the name of our Lord Jesus" (1 Cor 5:3) and with "the power of our Lord Jesus" (1 Cor 5:4) that he acts. It is the Lord's judgment that is operating. Perhaps Paul is following the Lord's instruction in Matthew 18:15–20.[46] Paul also expects the church to be involved in the discipline: they are to "hand over to Satan" the offender (1 Cor 5:5).[47] Thus, the Lord's judgment works through Paul and the church. Finally, we note that the moral standard used by Paul to evaluate behavior is the Scriptures (1 Cor 5:11; cf. Deut 22:20–22, 30; 13:1–5; 17:2–7; 19:16–19; 21:18–21; 24:7).[48] While Christians are not "under" the law of Moses in a covenantal sense (Rom 6:14), the moral prin-

42. For example, Fee, *1 Corinthians*, 212–13; South, "Critique," 545, 552–53.

43. Gundry Volf argues that the man is not a believer. However, it is possible that his exclusion from the church could bring him to repentance (Gundry Volf, *Paul and Perseverance*, 115–16, 119–20).

44. On the Greek grammar that suggests this, see Fee, *1 Corinthians*, 209.

45. Rosner concludes his analysis of the Corinthian situation with four reasons why Paul acted as he did: "First, the man must be removed because he is guilty of covenant disloyalty, secondly, because while he remains, the church is implicated in his sin, and thirdly, because the community is the temple of the Holy Spirit . . . A fourth reason for his expulsion [is that] he must be ejected for his own sake" (*Paul, Scripture and Ethics*, 91).

46. See Lampe, "Church Discipline," 344–46; Rosner, *Paul, Scripture and Ethics*, 89–90.

47. See the grammatical note in Fee, *1 Corinthians*, 205, n. 44.

48. There are strong parallels between the sins Paul lists in 1 Cor 5:11 and the sins addressed in these various passages in Deuteronomy. See Rosner, *Paul, Scripture and Ethics*, 68–70.

ciples in the law are forever applicable to God's people, because they reveal God's will for humanity. Paul sees God's Spirit as enabling us to live in accordance with God's will (Gal 5:13—6:10). But where the behavior of God's people is in direct disobedience to God's commandments, Paul expects the church to address the situation.

The Lord's Direct Discipline of His People

Paul also sees the Lord as sometimes disciplining his people directly, apart from any action carried out by the church. The one clear case in Paul's letters is the sickness of many, and the death of some, Corinthian believers, which Paul describes as the Lord's disciplinary judgment (1 Cor 11:29–32).[49] Paul sees such judgment as coming on the church because of a failure to honor the Lord and each other at the Lord's Supper. Apparently, a good proportion of the believers are eating and drinking "in an unworthy manner" (v. 27), not examining themselves (v. 28) and not "discerning the body" (v. 29), that is, the Lord's body given for us, or the church as the "body" of Christ (1 Cor 10:17).[50] Paul's earlier description of the situation (11:17–22) is a picture of a most "unworthy" celebration of the Supper: divisions (vv. 18–19), drunkenness, and a total disregard by some for poor members (vv. 21–22). There is little real understanding of what the Supper is all about.

Paul's teaching on God's judgment in this passage raises many questions. A key question is: Why this particular kind of judgment? There are at least three reasons. Firstly, it seems that the abuse of the Lord's Supper involved quite a few church members. It was not a situation that could be easily addressed by normal means of church discipline. Secondly, the abuse cut to the heart of what it meant to be a Christian church. In its central act of corporate worship the church at Corinth was displaying ignorance and contempt toward the Lord, whom it was supposedly honoring. It was not properly acknowledging, or behaving in a way consistent with, his sacrificial death. In short, it was sinning seriously. Paul interpreted the sickness

---

49. 1 Cor 10:12, 22 and 1 Thess 4:6 are also possibilities, but Paul does not elaborate on the nature of the judgment involved. Käsemann sees 1 Cor 11:30 as the consequence in the Corinthian church of "provoking the Lord to jealousy" (1 Cor 10:22) (Käsemann, "Pauline Doctrine of the Last Supper," 125).

50. Fee argues for the latter meaning (Fee, *1 Corinthians*, 563–64). A number of commentators argue for both meanings (e.g., Moule, "Judgment Theme," 472–74; Lampe, "Church Discipline," 346).

and death of church members as God's judgment.[51] One would assume that Paul saw such direct judgment from the Lord on his people as an indication of the seriousness of their sin. Paul's letters do not indicate that such judgments are common.[52] Thirdly, such a judgment was a "wakeup call" that could hardly be ignored, as people struggled with their health and with the loss of loved ones. Paul calls the judgment "discipline" (v. 32). It was an opportunity to repent, learn, and change, to become holy in thought and action, to live as people "who are being saved" and not as those "who are perishing" (1 Cor 1:18).[53] Paul says that the purpose is "that we may not be condemned with the world" (v. 32). Repentance and growth in holiness are evidence of salvation; the absence of these is evidence of eschatological condemnation. The Lord's judgment on the Corinthians is evidence of his love for them in leading them on the path of salvation.

The Challenge for the Church Today

What do we do today with Paul's instruction concerning God's judgment in the church? To begin with, we need to see the reality of God's judgment of us. Many Christians seem unaware of it. They think that because Jesus died for us, all judgment is finished, either in the present life or in the life to come. Clearly, this is not true. God's ongoing sanctification of us in the present life is a major priority for him, and sometimes it involves judgment, either his discipline coming through the church or his direct action to get our attention, so that we become conscious of our sins, turn from them, and ask him to cleanse and renew us. The writer to the Hebrews encourages us to have a positive view of the Lord's discipline (Heb 12:5–13). It is evidence of his love for us (v. 6), whereby we share his holiness (v. 10), bear the fruit of righteousness (v. 11), and ultimately in the age to come, "see the Lord" (v. 14).

---

51. Fee says, "Most likely Paul is here stepping into the prophetic role; by the Spirit he has seen a divine cause and effect" (*1 Corinthians*, 565).

52. Travis, *Christ and the Judgement of God*, 124–25. Paul does not see Timothy's ailments (1 Tim 5:23) or Epaphroditus's sickness (Phil 2:27) as God's judgment. The book of Acts relates judgments on those who sinned, particularly against the advance of God's work—Ananias and Sapphira (5:1–6) and Elymas the magician (13:6–11)—but these judgments were extraordinary, not common.

53. On the issue of the status of the Corinthians who died, see Lampe, "Church Discipline," 348–49; Gundry Volf, *Paul and Perseverance*, 105–112. On the importance of repentance, see Yinger, *Paul, Judaism, and Judgment*, 256–58.

We also need to get serious about God's church. Paul was very serious about it, which is why he labored so hard, when humanly speaking, he could have simply gone off by himself and had a much easier life. But he was fully committed to God's purpose in and through the church. This is a challenge for us in our western individualism that tends to disconnect us from, and rob us of, the kind of fellowship to which God has called us. It is easy for us to live fairly independent lives, not deeply connected or involved with others in the church. We feel limited responsibility for or accountability to our brothers and sisters. We are uncomfortable with any form of church discipline; we do not like to receive it and do not like being involved in dispensing it. Clearly, such an attitude is a long way from God's plan for the church. With God's help we must decide to lay down our individualism and pursue a new mindset (Rom 12:2) in which we see ourselves as members of the "one body in Christ," and live accordingly (Rom 12:3–21).

The truth of God's judgment is very relevant for leaders in the church, who are called to "shepherd the church of God" (Acts 20:28; cf. John 21:15–17; Eph 4:11–13; 1 Pet 5:2–4). There are many facets to our shepherding ministry; one indispensable aspect is modelling and teaching a disciplined life, and when necessary, lovingly disciplining God's people. This is not optional if we are going to be faithful to God and his people. We need a "vision" of God's holiness and of his purifying judgment at work to "make [the church] holy, cleansing her by the washing with water through the word, and to present her to himself as a radiant church, without stain or wrinkle or any other blemish, but holy and blameless" (Eph 5:26–27). We need to seek God for his grace and wisdom, to study the Scriptures for their teaching and guidance, and to learn from each other.[54]

And what about the Lord's discipline of us? What forms can it take? How do we recognize it? The apostle describes a serious form of discipline in 1 Corinthians 11, which is probably not common. However, we can expect such judgments to still occur in the church today on occasion, as unfortunately, Christians sin in serious ways. The difficulty is in discerning it. We must take great care in our understanding and responses. People will have different interpretations about such things. Undoubtedly there are many other forms of discipline by which God seeks to correct and teach us. Some of these we would not call disciplinary judgment, but simply

---

54. For challenging and helpful books on church discipline, see Laney, *A Guide to Church Discipline*; White and Blue, *Healing the Wounded*; Jeschke, *Discipling in the Church*. See also the articles on church discipline in *Christianity Today* 49/8 (2005): 31–36.

discipline, such as when the Lord convicts us strongly for a harsh word spoken to someone. Our conscience is struck and we know we must put things right. If we believe God is sovereign, then we believe that his loving discipline can be at work through all the circumstances of life. The writer to the Hebrews encourages his audience in their hostile situation to see it as God's discipline of them for their good and their sanctification (Heb 12:1–13). The key is for us to be open to learn from the Lord in whatever situation we are in. If we are, it will be more likely that his discipline is simply discipline, and not disciplinary judgment for disobedience.

Finally, the situation in Corinth regarding the Lord's Supper indicates how important this sacrament or ordinance is for us. Clearly, the Lord thinks it is important: he instituted it and he disciplined the Corinthians when they abused it. We must allow the Lord to be the Lord at the Supper each time we celebrate it together. As we remember him we must allow him to speak and work in ways that will cause us to change as a result of being in his presence. The truth of God's judgment is an integral part of the Supper.[55] Paul's instruction to the Corinthians (1 Cor 11:23–32) is full of judgment. We remember and proclaim the Lord's death (vv. 24, 25, 26). His death speaks of judgment, the judgment of sinful humanity in the death of Christ. In various ways we are to exercise judgment as we share in the Supper. We "discern the body" (v. 29), both the Lord's physical body given for us and the church as his body of which we are a part. We recognize what he has done for us and contemplate what it means for us as members of the church. We recognize and accept again the death sentence that was executed in Christ against us as sinful humans. We realize that we have life only because of his resurrection and because we are in him. We also "discern" (v. 31) and "examine" (v. 28) ourselves, recognizing and dealing with sin in our lives, and recommitting our lives to serve the Lord by his grace. We do it "until he comes" (v. 26), with a view to the final judgment, thankful that his death will save us from condemnation, but also mindful that his discipline is at work to lead us in his way (v. 32). With the Lord's help let us seek to recover the truth of judgment in his Supper.

---

55. For a stimulating study of the theme of God's judgment in both the Lord's Supper and Christian baptism, see Moule, "Judgment Theme," 464–81.

6

God's Judgment at the Cross

WE HAVE SEEN HOW the death and resurrection of Christ stand at the center of Paul's view of God's judgment. This is because Paul sees Christ's death and resurrection as the way in which God has saved us from condemnation. When we repent and trust in Christ we begin to experience freedom from the effects of God's judgment on humanity in the present age. We also have the assurance that in the age to come we will be saved from God's eschatological wrath.

With respect to Christ's death the key question in relation to God's judgment is: *How did God's judgment work in Christ's death to free us from condemnation?* We have already begun to explore this question in chapters 2–3. After briefly summarizing our findings in those chapters we will probe more deeply into several aspects of our key question and reflect on the implications for the church today.

Summary concerning the Cross and God's Judgment

Our study in chapters 2–3 has made no attempt to be an exhaustive study of the cross in Paul.[1] Our focus has been on passages that have some relation to judgment. We have found the following:

1. The heart of the matter seems to be expressed in three or four verses: Romans 8:3; 2 Corinthians 5:21; Galatians 3:13; and possibly, Romans 3:25. We postponed consideration of the last passage until this chapter. Romans 8:3 provides the clearest statement of what happened at the cross in relation to God's judgment: God "condemned sin" in the death of Jesus. Thus, an act of divine judgment took place at the cross, judgment upon human sin. Paul is saying that our sin was judged in Christ's death. Second Corinthians 5:21 adds to the picture by

---

1. For such studies, not limited to Paul's letters, see Morris, *Apostolic Preaching*; Morris, *Cross in the New Testament*; Stott, *Cross of Christ*.

stressing Christ's sinlessness and his becoming "sin for us." The sinless one identified with sinners and represented us in his death. He died the death to which we were liable; he experienced the judgment to which we were liable. Galatians 3:13 says something similar when it says that Christ became "a curse for us." Here Paul stresses the consequences of sin. He says that Christ was cursed, which is but another way of saying that in his death Christ experienced the judgment of God for us.

2. Paul sees other aspects of the judgment that took place in Christ's death. The world, that is, the whole way of life of humans apart from and in opposition to God, was judged (1 Cor 1:20–21; 2:6; Gal 6:14). Sinful humans were judged and died with Christ (Rom 6:6, 8; Gal 2:20; Col 2:20). Evil powers were also judged in Christ's death and resurrection (Eph 1:21–22; Col 2:10, 15). Thus, Paul sees "the world, the flesh, and the devil" as having been judged in Christ. The result for believers in Christ is death to the world (Gal 2:19; 6:14; Col 2:20), death to sin (Rom 6:6, 11), and freedom from Satan's authority (Col 1:13).

3. Paul sees many benefits coming to believers through the death and resurrection of Christ, including right relationship with God (Rom 3:24; 5:9, 17–19; 1 Cor 6:11; 2 Cor 5:21; Gal 2:16; Titus 3:7), reconciliation with God (Rom 5:10; 2 Cor 5:19; Col 1:22), freedom from sin and evil powers (Rom 3:24; 6:2–11; Gal 3:13; Col 1:14; 2:13–15), the gift of God's life-giving Spirit (Rom 8:1–16; Gal 3:14; Titus 3:5), sanctification (1 Cor 6:11; Col 1:22; 1 Thess 3:13; 5:23; 2 Thess 2:13; Titus 2:11–14), and salvation from God's eschatological wrath (Rom 5:9–10; Gal 5:5; Phil 1:28; 1 Thess 1:10; 5:9; 2 Thess 1:10; 2 Tim 4:8).

Romans 3:25 and "Propitiation"

We now come to Romans 3:25, and begin by noting its immediate literary context:

> [21] But now apart from the law the righteousness of God has been made known, to which the Law and the Prophets testify. [22] This righteousness is given through faith in Jesus Christ to all who believe. There is no difference between Jew and Gentile, [23] for all have sinned and fall short of the glory of God, [24] and all are justified

freely by his grace through the redemption that came by Christ Jesus. ²⁵ God presented Christ as a sacrifice of atonement, through the shedding of his blood—to be received by faith. He did this to demonstrate his justice, because in his forbearance he had left the sins committed beforehand unpunished— ²⁶ he did it to demonstrate his justice at the present time, so as to be just and the one who justifies those who have faith in Jesus. (Rom 3:21–26)

The first half of verse 25 is significant in that it gets to the heart of Paul's understanding of what happened in the death of Christ to provide the redemption and justification of sinners, described in verse 24. Paul says that God presented Christ "as a sacrifice of atonement," which translates a single Greek word, *hilastērion*. Older versions of the English Bible tended to translate it as "propitiation," meaning "a making favorable" (from the Latin *propitiātum*), which is the literal meaning of the Greek word. Translations in the last fifty or so years have tended to translate the word differently, emphasizing the forgiveness of sins or reconciliation with God that Christ has secured. This is partly because "propitiation" is not well understood today, and partly because many scholars have had theological reservations about the idea of God being "rendered favorable."

So what does Paul mean by *hilastērion*? To find the answer we need to look into the word's ancient meaning and then follow the scholarly debate so as to identify and understand the main issues. The Greek word itself is a noun or adjective derived from the verb *hilaskomai*, which means "to appease" the gods, "to make [them] favorable," something done by humans through sacrifices or other means to secure the favor of capricious gods, and so avert their wrath.[2] Immediately, it is obvious that this cannot be Paul's meaning. The God of the Bible is not changeable and unreliable. He cannot be bribed or bought. He is constant in his holiness and love. Paul says that he is the one who provides the "propitiation"; it is not humans who present it to him. So if the idea of God being rendered favorable through the death of Christ is applicable, it does not include the pagan view of the gods or human effort in securing divine favor.

Considerable light into Paul's meaning is provided by the Septuagint (LXX), the Greek translation of the Old Testament.[3] The LXX uses *hilastērion* and its cognates to translate various Hebrew words, especially *kipper* (to cover, wipe away) and its cognates that are used to describe

---

2. See Link and Brown, "Reconciliation," 148–49.
3. This was produced in the third to second centuries BC.

how the sacrificial system was to operate "to make atonement," to provide forgiveness of Israel's sins. In his landmark study of biblical atonement C. H. Dodd argued that in the LXX *hilaskomai* and its cognates do not generally mean to propitiate God, but to expiate sin, that is, "performing an act whereby guilt or defilement is removed."[4] Thus, the issue is the forgiveness of sins, not the averting of God's wrath. God is already favorable and provides forgiveness and cleansing for his people, which is the meaning assumed by the New Testament writers.[5] Dodd's study has been very influential and many have accepted his conclusions. But Roger Nicole and Leon Morris have pointed out major flaws in Dodd's study.[6] Morris, in particular, has shown that the context in which *hilaskomai* and its cognates are used is fundamentally about the removal of God's wrath. For example:

> But he is compassionate and will forgive [or, be merciful to, Gr. *hilaskomai*] their sins and will not destroy [them]; and he will many times turn away his anger, and will not kindle all his wrath. (Ps 77:38 LXX; 78:38 Heb)[7]

> When the heaven is restrained and there is no rain because they sin against you, and they shall pray toward this place and make confession to your name, and shall turn from their sins when you have humbled them, then you will hear from heaven and will be merciful [Gr. *hileōs*] to the sins of your servant and of your people Israel (1 Kgs 8:35–36 LXX)[8]

> And Moses said to Aaron, "Take the censer and put on it fire from the altar and put incense on it and carry it away quickly into the camp and make atonement [Gr. *exilaskomai*] for them; for wrath has gone out from the presence of the Lord; it has begun to destroy the people." (Num 16:46 LXX)[9]

Thus, while the idea of expiation is present, it is part of the greater purpose of saving Israel from the wrath of God. The sacrificial system is

---

4. Dodd, "Atonement," 82–95, here 93; for a brief overview of Dodd's article, see Link and Brown, "Reconciliation," 151–53.

5. Dodd, "Atonement," 93–95.

6. Nicole, "C. H. Dodd and the Doctrine of Propitiation," 117–57; Morris, *Apostolic Preaching*, 145–78. For a brief overview of Morris's argument, see Link and Brown, "Reconciliation," 154–56.

7. See Morris, *Apostolic Preaching*, 157–58.

8. See ibid., 160.

9. Ibid., 167.

The Righteous Judgment of God

God's gracious provision whereby Israel's sins are forgiven so that Israel can continue to be and live as the covenant people of the holy God. Thus, propitiation and expiation go together; it is impossible to have one without the other.[10]

With respect to *hilastērion* itself, it is used twenty-two times in the LXX to translate *kappōreth*, the "mercy seat" (or place/means of propitiation) on the ark of the covenant (e.g., Exod 25:17–22; Lev 16:2; Num 7:89), which is where the sacrificial blood was sprinkled on the Day of Atonement (*Yom Kippur*) (Lev 16:14–15) to make atonement for the nation (Lev 16:34). Thus, there is an established use and meaning of *hilastērion* within Judaism of which Paul was no doubt aware. It was part of the sacrificial system that God had given Israel under the Mosaic Covenant.

When we come to Romans 3:25, then, it is no surprise to find that Paul's use of *hilastērion* is consistent with the Old Testament. Paul says that God provided Jesus as a *hilastērion* "in his blood." There is no pagan concept of "propitiation" here. As with Israel the Lord provides the sacrifice through which sin is dealt with and those who trust in him and his provision are graciously freed from their sins, and brought into right relationship with him (Rom 3:24). There has been much discussion about whether Paul is drawing the attention of his readers to Israel's "mercy seat" and Day of Atonement, with Jesus as the fulfillment of these things, a more popular view in recent times.[11] But some older commentators doubt that there is enough in Romans 3:21–26 to support this view.[12] For our purpose the bigger issue is Paul's understanding of what Christ's death actually involves and achieves for us. Does Paul see Christ's death as simply expiatory, as sin-focused and removing sin, along with its consequences? Or does Paul also see Christ's death as propitiatory, as God-focused, involving the wrath of God and averting it, so that the favor and mercy of God come to believers in Jesus? The question concerns the nature of God's judgment in Christ's death. Is that judgment passive, consisting only in the inevitable consequence that sin leads to death? Therefore, as Jesus identifies with sinful humanity, he dies, and that is the judgment of God. Or is God's judgment active, with God's anger against human sin manifested at the cross, with

---

10. Ibid., 211–13. "[T]he conclusion that *hilastērion* includes reference to the turning away of God's wrath is inescapable" (Moo, *Romans*, 235).

11. See Moo, *Romans*, 231–36.

12. For example, Morris, *Apostolic Preaching*, 184–98; Cranfield, *Romans*, 1:214–18.

God's Judgment at the Cross

Christ experiencing the wrath of God that humans deserve, that unbelievers will experience at the final judgment?

Clearly, Paul does not answer this question directly. And the question takes us beyond Romans 3:25. What we will attempt to do, firstly, is to see what this verse can contribute to the answer. Then we will consider the controversial topic of "penal substitution."

To begin with, we can be confident that Paul sees Christ's death as propitiatory in Romans 3:25. Given that Paul knows and accepts the theology of sacrifice in the Old Testament, he would assume that Christ's sacrifice, as the fulfillment of the Old Testament sacrifices, turned away God's wrath, that is, propitiated him. As Morris has shown, this was fundamental to Israel's sacrificial system. It is strongly supported by Paul's argument in Romans 1–5.[13] As we have seen, the argument in Romans 1:18—5:11 is framed by the wrath of God: wrath "being revealed from heaven against all the godlessness and wickedness of human beings" (1:18), godlessness that Paul goes on to demonstrate through to Romans 3:20; and eschatological wrath averted through the death and resurrection of Jesus Christ (5:9–10). Clearly, it is Christ's death as the *hilastērion* that has changed the situation completely, from being under God's wrath to being under his grace, delivered from wrath. Christ's death has averted God's wrath. It is propitiatory. Surely this is one of the main points Paul is making at the beginning of his letter. Through his death (and resurrection) Jesus has delivered us from the wrath of God. *Hilastērion* communicates it.

This conclusion is strengthened by Romans 3:25b–26, where Paul explains the purpose for Christ's death, namely, to "demonstrate [God's] righteousness." While there are various interpretations of what Paul means here by God's "righteousness,"[14] Paul is most likely explaining how God can justify sinners and still be true to himself, to his own righteous character, as Paul puts it, "so as to be just and the one who justifies those who have faith in Jesus" (v. 26).[15] In the past, under the Old Covenant, God in his forbearance "left the sins committed beforehand unpunished" (v. 25).[16] The implication is that God has now finally dealt with those past

---

13. See Morris, *Apostolic Preaching*, 198–201; Moo, *Romans*, 235; Lincoln, "From Wrath to Justification," 146–49.

14. See Moo, *Romans*, 237–42; Gathercole, "Justified by Faith, Justified by His Blood," 180–81; McFadden, *Judgment*, 130–34.

15. See the classic exposition of it in Denney, *Death of Christ*, 96–104.

16. See Moo, *Romans*, 239–40.

The Righteous Judgment of God

sins in the death of Christ. The point is that there is a serious issue of righteousness at stake. For people to be forgiven, to be justified, to escape God's wrath, it is not simply a matter of God's saying, "It's okay; I forgive you." That would be unrighteous, and contrary to God's character. The good news is that Jesus Christ has stood in for sinful people who are under God's wrath, and through his death their sin and the wrath it deserved have been removed. Justice has been done in Christ's death, and people can be forgiven, righteously.

If we do not understand this aspect of God's righteousness then we will not understand the need for God to be propitiated, for his wrath to be averted, so that his favor comes to us. God's desire to be favorable to us is not the same thing as his favor actually coming to us. On the one hand, "God is love" (1 John 4:8); he wants us to know him and to experience the many blessings of relationship with him. But on the other hand, God is holy and we are sinful. We reject, rebel against, and disobey him. He is rightfully angry against us and our sin. We are not under his favor, but under his wrath (John 3:36b). From our perspective there is an obvious tension here. God loves us and desires to favor us, but we are in his disfavor because of our sin. We need to realize that God's disfavor is real and serious. Many people have the idea that God's love somehow will cancel out whatever concerns he has about our sin. This is simply not true.[17] Such thinking shows that we have not begun to grasp the reality and greatness of God's holiness, the reality and extent of our sinfulness, and the reality and inevitability of his wrath.[18] By itself, the fact that God loves us does not save us from his wrath. God loves every person alive on earth today, but the sad reality is that most remain under the wrath of God. In this light propitiation makes sense. Something has to be done to bring us out of God's holy disfavor and wrath into the favor of his love. We cannot do it; we do not want to do it. God must do it for our sakes and in a way that is consistent with his righteousness, which is what the cross is all about. God propitiates himself. As Carson says, "God the Father is thus the propitia*tor* and the propitia*ted*, and God the Son is the propitia*tion*."[19] We experience God's favor "through faith" in his Son, Jesus Christ (Rom 3:25–26). Through the gospel we come

---

17. See the helpful practical argument in Sproul, *Reason to Believe*, 99–102.

18. "[T]he hardest truth to get across to this generation is what the Bible says about sin" (Carson, *Scandalous*, 41). For an excellent discussion of human sin and God's wrath, see Gaffin, "Scandal," 145–53.

19. Carson, *Scandalous*, 65. For further discussion along this line, see Peterson, "Atonement in the New Testament," 43–45.

to understand our rebellion and predicament under God's holy wrath. We also come to understand God's love for us and what Jesus has done for us in his death and resurrection. By God's grace we turn from our rebellion and come to him in humility, asking for his forgiveness, believing that he alone is the answer to our need, and putting our trust in him and his finished work for us. Then we enter his favor and begin to experience a wonderful new relationship with God as our Father (Rom 5:5; 8:14–17). Praise God!

Penal Substitution?

Our discussion of Romans 3:25 has concluded that salvation from God's wrath is a key issue Paul has in mind. Christ's death is the solution. In relation to the question we have asked concerning the nature of God's judgment that took place in Christ's death, our finding in Romans 3:25 tells us something about the purpose of that judgment: it is to save us from God's wrath. But our finding does not tell us how God's judgment worked at the cross to save us. We must look further. Significantly, though, it is clear that any answer to how God's judgment worked in Christ's death must address the matter of God's wrath against human sin. It must seek to explain how the cross removes not just sin, but also God's wrath.

Our study so far has shown that there is no doubt that Paul sees the cross as a place of divine judgment, where human sin was judged and condemned in Christ (Rom 8:3). While Paul does see the death of Jesus as exemplary of love, humility and obedience (Phil 2:1–8), it is more than this. Underlying the subjective influence of the message of the cross on people is an objective atonement that deals with human sin and divine wrath, and makes possible the reconciliation of people to God. The question we will now pursue is whether God's judgment that took place in Christ's death is passive or active. Does it directly involve only human sin, but not divine wrath, so that when sin is dealt with, the problem of wrath is automatically eliminated? Or does it directly involve both sin and wrath, so that in his death Jesus experiences God's wrath, his punishment, his retribution on human sin?

Since the Reformation the traditional evangelical answer to this question has been the second of these answers, namely, that Jesus experienced God's punishment for our sin. This has been called the doctrine of penal substitution, that Christ as our substitute bore the penalty due for our sin. Calvin stated it as follows:

The Righteous Judgment of God

> Christ interposed, took the punishment upon himself, and bore what by the just judgment of God was impending over sinners[20]

> In order to interpose between us and God's anger, and satisfy his righteous judgment, it was necessary that he should feel the weight of divine vengeance.[21]

Our question is whether such an understanding is an accurate reflection of Paul's theology of Christ's death.

We are thus led into a large arena of debate. Among evangelicals today there are impassioned arguments both for and against the doctrine of penal substitution. There is an increasing number of evangelicals who are rejecting the doctrine for various reasons. It is not possible here for us to go into these reasons in detail. We will begin with this viewpoint and see what it does with the idea of God's judgment at the cross. Then we will come to our final discussion.

Recent critics of penal substitution argue that the idea of Christ's enduring the wrath of God in his death is repugnant to the biblical view of God as loving and righteous. They charge penal substitution with being narrow, reflecting a non-biblical culture, abstract, legal, misunderstanding the nature of sin, irrelevant, incomprehensible, violent, abusive, vindictive, ethically unhelpful, etc.[22] They argue against trying to "pin down" the New Testament to a fundamental understanding of the atonement that makes sense of the various perspectives on it. They emphasize the variety of New Testament "metaphors" of the atonement,[23] and encourage the use of metaphors that connect with a contemporary audience.[24] For example, Chalke and Mann present the cross in terms of Jesus' "absorbing" all the pain and suffering caused by human sin in order to forgive humanity, and to demonstrate the lengths to which God would go to reconcile people to himself.[25]

---

20. Calvin, *Institutes*, 2.16.2.

21. Ibid., 2.16.10.

22. For example, Chalke and Mann, *Lost Message of Jesus*, 54–59, 182–83; Green and Baker, *Recovering the Scandal*, 23–32, 90–92, 146–50; Marshall, *Beyond Retribution*, 59–69; Jersak and Hardin, *Stricken by God?* For a response to criticisms of penal substitution, see Morris, *Cross in the New Testament*, 409–18; Packer, "What Did the Cross Achieve?", 82–100; Jeffery et al., *Pierced for Our Transgressions*, 205–328; Marshall, *Aspects of the Atonement*, 52–64; Cole, *God the Peacemaker*, 233–57.

23. Green and Baker, *Recovering the Scandal*, 58–63, 95, 98–99.

24. Ibid., 108–15, 199–221. For a critique, see Gaffin, "Scandal," 153–56.

25. Chalke and Mann, *Lost Message*, 181.

It is not always easy to find out where God's judgment fits in such views. In the light of our study of Paul this is problematic, because God's judgment is a key element in Paul's atonement theology. Nevertheless, some opponents of penal substitution do acknowledge the place of God's judgment in Paul's understanding of the cross. Green and Baker speak about Christ's substitution for humanity in finally solving "the problem of the human bias toward sin" (Rom 8:3),[26] which is "in the face of God's justice,"[27] and is an expression of God's holiness (Rom 3:25; 8:3; 2 Cor 5:21).[28] But the authors do not explain what it all means. Travis goes further,[29] arguing that on the cross Jesus experienced God's judgment but not his punishment.[30] Travis distinguishes between judgment as the inherent consequences of sin, which Jesus did experience, and punishment as God's retribution on sin, which Jesus did not experience. Travis argues that divine retribution is not a key element in Paul's theology. The cross involved human sin, not retributive wrath. As our substitute Jesus "has absorbed and taken away our sin and its consequences."[31] Marshall has a similar view. He rejects a narrow view of substitution where one person "replaces" another, and argues for a broader view of "one person *representing* all others, who are thereby made present in the person and experience of their representative."[32] Explaining 2 Corinthians 5:21 he says, "Christ absorbed human sin and its accompanying penalty, so that we might be absorbed by the saving justice of God that he embodied."[33] "It is a work of curative justice, not punitive retribution."[34] Dunn also steers away from the idea of substitution. He argues that Paul sees Christ as the representative of sinful humanity. "Jesus' death was the end of humankind under the power of sin and death, the destruction of man and woman as sinner."[35] God's wrath does not enter the equation explicitly.

---

26. Green and Baker, *Recovering the Scandal*, 63.
27. Ibid., 64.
28. Ibid., 104.
29. Travis, *Christ and the Judgement of God*, 181–204.
30. Ibid., 190, 195, 199.
31. Ibid., 186.
32. Marshall, *Beyond Retribution*, 61 (italics the author's).
33. Ibid., 57.
34. Ibid., 64.
35. Dunn, *Theology of Paul*, 223.

This viewpoint effectively does away with God's retributive wrath. It retains the idea of God's judgment, but sees it as the inherent consequences of sin that God has ordained. Thus, it is moving in the direction of C. H. Dodd's understanding of God's impersonal wrath,[36] while denying that it is impersonal. It sees the cross as dealing only with sin and its consequences, not with retributive wrath. God's judgment is built into sin itself and thus is not something distinct. When in his death Jesus experiences the inherent consequences of sin, this is God's judgment.

The problem with this view is not so much in what it affirms as in what it denies. In affirming that in his death Jesus identifies with our sin and experiences its consequences, it is true to Paul and the rest of the New Testament. In affirming that it is God's judgment on sin in Christ, it is correct. But in denying that it is God's "punishment" or his "retributive wrath," it avoids terms that are an accurate description of God's judgment, provided they are understood biblically and carefully. Travis defines retribution as judgment imposed from the outside.[37] He goes on to argue that divine retribution is limited in the New Testament. God's judgment is primarily the God-ordained inherent consequences of sin.[38] While such a definition of retribution may be suitable for human justice systems, it is hardly applicable to divine justice. However God judges sin, either by inherent consequences or by externally-imposed judgment, it is a penalty, it is retributive, it returns to people what their actions deserve (from Lat. *retribuĕre*: to give back, return, repay).[39] To deny this is to engage in semantics that may define and use terms that are acceptable to some people, but it ends up robbing people of the full truth of God's judgment. Thus, to say that our alienation from God is God's judgment but not his punishment or penalty, is simply not true. It is a penalty; it involves slavery to sin; it deprives us of God's presence and life. The ultimate alienation from God is hell. To say that hell is not a penalty or punishment is absurd; hell is the final painful experience that deprives us of all goodness and life.[40]

---

36. See the section on Romans 1:18–32 in chapter 5.

37. Travis, *Christ and the Judgement of God*, 6–10.

38. Ibid., 205–12, 256–58, 323–27.

39. See the discussion on judgment and penalties in Marshall, *Aspects of the Atonement*, 1–33. See also Gathercole, "Justified by Faith, Justified by His Blood," 175–83.

40. "I do not see how deprivation of eternal life can be understood as anything other than a penalty or punishment upon the impenitent sinner" (Marshall, *Aspects of the Atonement*, 32).

In my view the main reasons for such a redefinition of terms and the avoidance of the terminology of retribution, penalty, and punishment are cultural, not biblical. Our society holds many unbiblical ideas about God, including that he is "an angry old man with a big stick," eager to punish offenders. Our society also tends to associate terms such as retribution, wrath, penalty, and punishment with a malicious attitude that enjoys inflicting pain on others. Thus, when such terms are used in relation to God they can evoke an understanding that is far from the holy and loving God of the Bible. But the answer is not to change our theology so as to eliminate these terms. If we do, we will soon lose the biblical emphasis on God's judgment as his holy and active opposition to all that is evil. The focus will be simply on human sin and its inherent consequences, and on human responsibility. While this is a biblical focus it loses the divine dimension of the sovereignty, holiness, and judgment of God, which is the dimension that has biblical priority and that makes sense of the human dimension. Our society is already well along the road of eliminating the divine dimension; it is of no help for the church to go down this road. We must retain the Bible's theology of God's retributive wrath, but find ways of carefully explaining it, so as to faithfully represent God and to help people understand him accurately. In particular, our explanations of the cross of Christ must not be "narrow," "legal," and "cold," but must seek to paint the full picture, not only of sin and its consequences, but of God's loving, saving righteousness.

Logically, our discussion leads us to the conclusion that in his death Christ experienced God's punishment for our sin. How are we to understand it? We will begin with what Stephen Travis has to say. In his discussion Travis emphasizes two main things: firstly, that as our substitute Christ bore the consequences of our sin;[41] and secondly, that he experienced alienation from God.[42] While Travis's purpose is not to go into detail about precisely what Jesus endured on the cross, it is evident that Travis sees it as essentially an experience of separation from God. Thus, Jesus endured the alienation from God which is the consequence of sin. This alienation is what death is: separation from life, from the life of God. While Travis does not discuss in detail the nature of the death Jesus experienced, Travis sees it as more than physical. Jesus did not die only physically; he also experienced psychological "death," a feeling of complete separation from God, which is logical if Jesus experienced the consequences of human sin. Travis sees

41. Travis, *Christ and the Judgement of God*, 193, 199.
42. Ibid., 185, 186, 188.

Christ's death as necessary for the forgiveness of humanity: God does not simply "ignore sin or wave it away," but "Christ as our representative and substitute took our sins upon himself so that they no longer stand against us and we are set free to live a new life in him."[43]

While Travis argues against penal substitution, it is clear that the above description of Christ's death can be interpreted as penal substitution if God's retributive wrath is seen as operating. Thus, the consequences of human sin that Christ endures are God's righteous penalty for human sin, the expression of his active opposition against human evil. Thus, Christ bears the divine punishment which is the consequence of human rejection of God.[44] The difference from Travis' view is that the consequences are seen as God's punishment, the due penalty. Christ experiences the consequences of God's anger against sin. If this is seen as unrighteous or unnecessary, it is no more so than for Travis's view of the atonement. God cannot simply forgive humans apart from the cross. Human sin is so serious that it must be destroyed. It is destroyed by the wrath of God in the death of Christ.

We thus conclude that Paul has a penal substitutionary understanding of God's judgment in Christ's death, in which Christ experiences the punishment for our sins. This view entails not only God's wrath as being removed by Christ's death, but also Christ's death as an experience of God's wrath. It is because God's wrath on human sin has been exhausted in Christ's death that his wrath is removed from those who trust in Jesus.[45] Sin and wrath cannot be separated. Sin leads to wrath, and where sin exists, wrath will come. This is certainly true at the cross. It is illogical for Christ to deal with sin and for wrath to be absent. How can Christ bear our sins without also bearing the consequences of them? If our sins are really counted as his in the sight of God, then surely the consequences of our sins also become his. And if the wrath of God is personal, it follows that God's judgment on sin at the cross is active, not passive. God was not a passive

---

43. Ibid., 187.

44. For a discussion of the personal involvement of God with his law and in punishment, see Williams, "Cross and the Punishment of Sin," 68–99.

45. "This vicarious penal suffering, which is rightly described as the vicarious suffering of the wrath of God at sin, rests on the fellowship that Jesus Christ accepted with all of us as sinners and with our fate as such. This link is the basis on which the death of Jesus can count as expiation for us . . . Without this vicarious penal suffering, the expiatory function of the death of Jesus is unintelligible" (Pannenberg, *Systematic Theology*, 2:427).

bystander; he was active in causing his Son to experience the consequences of our rebellion—truly a sobering thought.

But what does it mean for God's judgment at the cross to be active? Does it mean that God was furiously pouring out his anger on Christ? Did he punish Christ? I would not say it this way, because I think it is easily misinterpreted. It may give the impression that God was angry with Christ, or that God enjoyed pouring out his anger, which is not true. Paul says that God "condemned sin in the flesh" of Jesus (Rom 8:3). His anger at the cross was against our sin, not against his Son. Our sin was punished in Christ; Christ experienced the punishment for *our* sins. He experienced God's wrath, wrath against our sin, not against him. Thus, I say, "God punished our sin in Christ." I do not say, "God punished Christ." Penal substitution is not the action of a sadistic God, but the love of God the Father and God the Son in paying the price to save us.

Related Matters

Gospel Traditions

We will briefly consider several related matters. The first is that the Gospel traditions regarding Jesus' contemplation of the cross and regarding his sufferings on the cross arguably support the penal substitutionary view of his death.[46] Jesus' description of his sufferings as a "baptism" or "cup" (Matt 20:22–23; 26:39; Mark 10:38–39; 14:36; Luke 12:50; 22:42), and his agony in the Garden of Gethsemane (Matt 26:37–44; Mark 14:33–36; Luke 22:41–44), indicate strongly that he saw his coming death as more than simply a painful and humiliating experience of the same character as other crucifixions. If thousands of others had faced it, many with courage and strength, it makes little sense for Jesus to struggle so much in the Garden, unless he was contemplating a death that was far worse than a normal crucifixion. Calvin asks:

> Does not that prayer, thrice repeated, "Father, if it be possible, let this cup pass from me" (Matth. xxvi. 39), a prayer dictated by incredible bitterness of soul, show that Christ had a fiercer and more arduous struggle than with ordinary death? . . . It is of

---

46. See discussion in Morris, *Cross in the New Testament*, 42–49.

consequence to understand aright how much our salvation cost the Son of God.⁴⁷

Further, Jesus' cry of abandonment from the cross, "My God, my God, why have you forsaken me?" (Matt 27:46; Mark 15:34), indicates more than a personal struggle, identification with God's suffering people (Ps 22:1), or the fulfillment of Scripture (Ps 22:1). It is the cry of someone actually experiencing what he regards as complete abandonment by God.⁴⁸ Crucifixion alone could not conceivably cause this for God's Son. For him to feel so abandoned indicates strongly that God has completely withdrawn the sense of his presence so that Jesus feels utterly alone. Logically, Jesus is experiencing the consequences of human sin, the wrath of God. Others have done their best to explain it:

> What Christ bore was not simply a sense of the connection between the sinner and the impersonal consequences of sin, but a sense of the sinner's relation to the personal *vis-à-vis* of an angry God. God never left Him, but He did refuse Him His face. The communion was not broken, but its light was withdrawn. He was forsaken but not disjoined. He was insolubly bound to the very Father who turned away and could not look on sin but to abhor and curse it even when His Son was beneath it. How could He feel the grief of being forsaken by God if He was not at bottom one with Him? Neglect by one to whom we have no link makes no trouble.⁴⁹

> [T]hese experiences of deadly fear and of desertion are of one piece with the fact that in his death . . . Jesus was taking upon Him the burden of the world's sin, consenting to be, and actually being, numbered with the transgressors⁵⁰

> [T]he cry of desolation must be interpreted as the measure of Jesus' anguish as he bears the full weight of the divine condemnation from which we are now freed.⁵¹

---

47. Calvin, *Institutes*, 2.16.12.
48. See Stott, *Cross of Christ*, 78–82.
49. Forsyth, *Work of Christ*, 243–44.
50. Denney, *Death of Christ*, 42.
51. Carson, *Scandalous*, 35.

The Trinity

Another matter is that Christ's death must be seen in the light of the truth of the Trinity.[52] The cross is not God and Christ working against each other, with different attitudes or purposes. It is not merely an angry God and a loving Christ. It is a holy, loving God who is rightfully angry at human sin, and a holy, loving Christ who is also angry about human sin. The anger of Father and Son is because of human rebellion against God and also because of the devastating effects that this rebellion has on people and the creation. At the cross the Father and the Son are working together in loving us: the Father in giving and sending his Son (Rom 5:8; 8:3, 32); the Son in suffering and dying for us (Gal 2:20), experiencing God's righteous condemnation of our sin (Rom 8:3), so that we are freed from condemnation (Rom 8:1). It is the triune God loving, suffering and demonstrating his righteousness. As we have seen, the truth of the Trinity helps us to understand why and how God propitiates himself (Rom 3:25). The truth of the Trinity also helps us to understand how God forgives our sins through the death of Christ. Forgiveness is costly to the person who forgives. They must be willing to absorb within themselves the pain of sins committed against them. In Christ's death the triune God absorbs within himself the pain of our sins in order to forgive us.

Christ as Representative and Substitute

We have also spoken about Christ as representative and substitute for humanity, without being precise concerning the meaning of each of these terms. We will now consider the difference.[53] One reason why many scholars shy away from the idea of substitution is that it is seen as exclusive: Christ dies for us so that we do not have to die. In this sense we are excluded from Christ's death. We simply participate in the benefits. Some scholars argue that this is not Paul's doctrine of atonement. Rather, Paul sees Christ as the representative of humanity who includes us in his death and resurrection, so that in him we die and are raised. It is not that he bears God's wrath for us as our substitute, but that he enters into our death

---

52. See discussions in Marshall, *Aspects of the Atonement*, 52–67; Stott, *Cross of Christ*, 156–63.

53. For discussions on substitution and representation, see Denney, *Death of Christ*, 193–98; Packer, "What Did the Cross Achieve?," 84–88; Pannenberg, *Systematic Theology*, 2:416–37; Marshall, *Aspects of the Atonement*, 64–65, 91–92.

because of sin, so that we can share his death and then enter into his life.[54] Such inclusive representation is seen to rule out exclusive substitution. But is such an understanding true to Paul? Hardly. While Paul does view Christ as our representative in whom we are included, the basis for our inclusion is the work that Christ has done for us that we cannot do for ourselves. There is an exclusive element, namely, his bearing our punishment so that we are not punished—his dying in our place so that we do not die eternally. Christ is our substitute. The inclusive and the exclusive are two ways of viewing the one wonderful work of Christ. Neither viewpoint is the whole truth. We must have both to be true to Paul.

Can we say more? In the light of our discussion of the atonement it can be argued that substitution is at the heart of Paul's understanding of Christ's work. This is because Christ's death is essentially a penalty that Christ accepts in our place. It is pain, suffering, and death. What else is it other than a penalty? But because Christ takes our place in experiencing the death that we deserved, not only do we escape death, but in God's sight we are included in Christ's death and regarded as having died in and with him. Joined with him in death we are also joined with him in resurrection life to God. Substitution is thus at the heart of the overall representative work of Christ. While the substitution is exclusive with respect to penalty endured, it is inclusive with respect to our entering into the benefits of his death and resurrection. The key Pauline texts that we have considered all support this view. When Paul speaks about the death of Christ in Romans 3:25; 8:3; 2 Corinthians 5:14–21 and Galatians 3:13, he is not simply saying or implying, "Christ took on your sin and death so that you could die and rise with him." Paul also has in mind the great personal suffering and cost, the penalty for our sin that Christ endured: what it took to avert God's wrath (Rom 3:25); what was involved for Christ when sin was condemned in his flesh (Rom 8:3); what was involved in his becoming "sin for us" (2 Cor 5:21); and the implications of his becoming "a curse for us" (Gal 3:13). It is only when the penal aspect of Christ's work is denied that substitution can be removed from Paul's view of the atonement. But then we miss the center of Christ's work. Substitution is at the heart of Paul's view of the representative work of Christ.

In effect, this conclusion claims that we can "pin down" Paul to a fundamental understanding of the atonement that makes sense of the various perspectives on it. I realize that our study has not been thorough enough

---

54. See Dunn, *Theology of Paul*, 223.

to fully substantiate such a claim. But if penal substitution is accepted as a Pauline doctrine, it is difficult to see how it cannot be at the center of Paul's atonement theology. Others have argued thus.[55] More broadly, we have found that the idea of God's judgment is fundamental to Paul's understanding of the cross (Rom 8:3). It is not possible to be true to Paul if we minimize or leave out judgment from his view of the atonement. In the light of our findings, the theme of God's judgment should help us to integrate Paul's various perspectives on the work of Christ.[56]

Final Reflections

Our focus has been on how God's judgment worked in Christ's death to save us from condemnation. We have concluded that the traditional evangelical view gives the truest and deepest insight into Paul's understanding. On this true foundation we are able to build Christian character, conduct, ministry, and mission (1 Cor 3:10–11).

I am very challenged by the topic of this chapter. This is partly because we have been exploring the heart of the gospel message. We are on holy ground, dealing with most holy things. Who is adequate to do it? But I am also challenged because in many ways we as the church do not live close to the heart of our faith. We are often content to spend most of our time and efforts on peripheral and outward matters. We do not allow the message of the cross to get deep within us so that it can work itself through us in thought, word, and action. Perhaps we are too frightened to allow the Lord access to the deepest parts of our being. But as we do give him access we find a peace and joy that the world cannot give us (John 14:27; 15:11).

The truth of God's judgment at the cross is not a truth that is easy to handle or digest. In my experience of church life it is a truth that is little known—and yet it is at the heart of the gospel. This must change. Here are some reflections on various aspects of the meaning and application of this truth that hopefully will help us to know and live it out to a greater extent:[57]

---

55. See Morris, *Cross in the New Testament*, 379–81, 404–7; Ladd, *Theology*, 464–77; Schreiner, "Penal Substitution View," 67–98; Marshall, *Aspects of the Atonement*, 51–52.

56. Building on the work of P. T. Forsyth and Karl Barth, Justyn Terry has argued that judgment is central to Paul's atonement theology, with victory, redemption, and sacrifice as subordinate metaphors (Terry, *Justifying Judgement of God*).

57. For a broader and more detailed description and discussion of what the cross achieves for God's people and their new way of life, see Stott, *Cross of Christ*, 167–351.

The Righteous Judgment of God

1. Most evangelicals know and love the good news that because Jesus suffered and died for us, we will not be condemned by God. We have the assurance of eternal life, truly a wonderful knowledge and feeling. It is the truth of penal substitution: Christ bore the penalty for my sins so that I don't have to. Praise God! Our study has shown something of the depth of this truth. It is not sufficient to have a superficial knowledge of it. We must come to know it better and allow it to affect and change us. We also need to know the other truths connected with it.

2. The truth that God condemned sin in Christ (Rom 8:3) means more than our being freed from condemnation. It means that sin has been condemned. There are huge implications. It means that sin is serious and God is holy. For God to go to the length of sending his own Son to deal with sin (Rom 8:3) sends us a strong message. It means that as the Holy One God will not ultimately allow sin in his creation. He will eradicate it completely. It also means that we are sinners, because the sin that God condemned in Christ is our sin. Apart from Christ we are sinful, condemned, and lost. For non-Christians this is the major reason to repent and believe in Jesus. For us as Christians it means we have no business "messing with sin." The good news is that because sin has been condemned, we have been freed from its power and can now begin to live righteously through the power of God's Spirit within us (Rom 8:4–14; Gal 5:16–25).

3. The truth of God's condemnation of sin in Christ also points to the great cost to the Lord Jesus in saving us. As we have seen, he experienced the wrath of God that was the consequence of our sin. We can only begin to comprehend it. The fact that he was willing to suffer in this way shows the greatness of his love for us. Paul says that his love extends to the individual: "who loved *me* and gave himself for *me*" (Gal 2:20). We need to meditate on it and give thanks to him, regularly. What devotion and commitment should it stir in me, in you?

> He became *curse* for us. He made our *doom* His own. He took on Him not only the calling of a man, but our responsibility as sinful men. It is in this that His work as Redeemer lies, for it is in this that the measure, or rather the immensity, of His love is seen.[58]

---

58. Denney, *Death of Christ*, 92.

4. The love of Christ for us *is* the love of God for us. Together, the Father and the Son love us. God sent his Son (Rom 8:3; Gal 4:4). He "did not spare [him] but delivered him up for us all" (Rom 8:32). This is how God "demonstrates his own love toward us" (Rom 5:8). The sending of Christ springs from the Father's love for us. We need to know it, give thanks to him, love him, and pursue our relationship with him as "*Abba*, Father!" (Rom 8:15).

5. The truth of the condemnation of sin in Christ causes us to reflect further on the one who stood in for us. While he was a true human, he was not a sinful human as we are. As the sinless one, God's "own Son" (Rom 8:3; 2 Cor 5:21), he was not liable to judgment. Thus, as the one appointed by God as our substitute he was able to bear our judgment without it destroying him. He was innocent. Therefore, God raised him from the dead. Jesus was the only one able to take our place in this way. He is unique. It means that only he can save us. There is no way to God other than Jesus Christ (John 14:6; Acts 4:12).

6. The truth of God's judgment at the cross causes us to reevaluate everything: God, humanity, creation and its future, the purpose of our lives, and our priorities, activities, ethics, relationships, and possessions. The cross declares that humanity apart from and in opposition to God is headed for condemnation. It has no future. The future is "a new creation" through the death and resurrection of Jesus Christ (2 Cor 5:17; Gal 6:15), "the kingdom of God" that we will inherit (1 Cor 6:9–10; 15:50; Gal 5:21; Eph 5:5). God calls us to live in the present in the light of the reality of that new creation, believing that we have died with Christ and have been raised with him (Rom 6:2–11). We no longer live for sin or for ourselves (Rom 6:12–16; 2 Cor 5:15), but for righteousness and for Christ (Rom 6:17–22; 2 Cor 5:15). This involves a major work of transformation in our lives (Rom 12:1–2), a lifelong process of renewal by the power of the Holy Spirit (2 Cor 3:18), whereby our thinking, character, and actions are conformed to Christ (Rom 8:29; Gal 4:19; Phil 2:5). It is not easy. It requires full commitment to and dependence on the Lord. It is a long and exciting "learning curve" in which we walk with him, getting to know him better and love him more, learning from him, being changed by him, doing his will, and being fruitful for his kingdom. We are very conscious of the reality of God's judgment of "the old things [that] have passed away" (2 Cor 5:17). We are surrounded by these old things. We begin

to experience the "new things [that] have come" (2 Cor 5:17), looking forward to their full realization when the Lord Jesus comes again. Paul shows us the way:

> [10] I want to know Christ—yes, to know the power of his resurrection and participation in his sufferings, becoming like him in his death, [11] and so, somehow, attaining to the resurrection from the dead. [12] Not that I have already obtained all this, or have already arrived at my goal, but I press on to take hold of that for which Christ Jesus took hold of me. [13] Brothers and sisters, I do not consider myself yet to have taken hold of it. But one thing I do: Forgetting what is behind and straining toward what is ahead, [14] I press on toward the goal to win the prize for which God has called me heavenward in Christ Jesus. (Phil 3:10–14)

Jesus puts it simply and shockingly:

> "Whoever wants to be my disciple must deny themselves and take up their cross daily and follow me." (Luke 9:23)

7. The truth of God's judgment in Christ is conveyed by the Christian ordinances of baptism (Rom 6:1–11) and the Lord's Supper (1 Cor 11:23–32).[59] These teach and remind us about God's condemnation of sin in Christ, and about the new life we have in him. We need to recover the full truth within these ordinances in our worship, preaching, teaching, and living.

8. The truth of judgment at the cross must be taught and preached if we are to be faithful to the gospel. The current tendency in many churches to preach God's love for people, with little or no mention of his judgment, is not faithful to the gospel. The message about God's love is truly the gospel only in the light of God's judgment; otherwise, the biblical meaning is lost. Communicating the truth of judgment does not mean constantly "dropping heavy truth" on God's people or on non-Christians. It means having a theological framework in which judgment has its proper place. Then as we teach and preach, the truth will come forth in a whole range of ways in practical connection with all that we say. Paul is a good model for us. While we may develop various metaphors to communicate Christ's saving work, I do not believe the central truth of Christ dying for our sins can be changed. It is not a metaphor. We are sinners for whom Christ died. In his death our sin was condemned.

---

59. See the section on judgment in the church in chapter 5.

He bore the punishment for our sins. The need today is not to find other ways of saying it, but to have the courage to say and explain it again (and again) so that people come to know the truth.[60] We must go against the tide of an increasingly biblically illiterate and practically atheistic culture. We must work hard at communicating hard truths such as God's retributive wrath. While we may use softer terms at times, we need to retain the stronger terms and teach our people what they mean. The church is supposed to be "the pillar and foundation of the truth" (1 Tim 3:15), salty "salt," and a shining "light" (Matt 5:13–16).

9. We cannot escape the implications for humanity of God's judgment at the cross. God's verdict concerning human sin has already been given at the cross. The words of John's Gospel sum up the situation:

> Whoever believes in him is not condemned, but whoever does not believe stands condemned already because they have not believed in the name of God's one and only Son. (John 3:18)

The gospel is good news for those who believe it, but bad news for those who reject it. Only those who hear it and believe enter into the salvation that Christ has secured. Here is the imperative for the church's mission to proclaim the gospel throughout the earth. May God help us to believe the gospel enough, to love God enough, and to love people enough, so that we obey the Great Commission and take the gospel to everyone.

We conclude with thanks and praise to the one who loved us and gave himself for us:

> Bearing shame and scoffing rude
> In my place condemned he stood,
> Sealed my pardon with his blood—
> Hallelujah! What a Saviour! (Philip P. Bliss)

> Amazing love! How can it be, that Thou, my God, shouldst die for me? (Charles Wesley)

> To him who loves us and has freed us from our sins by his blood, and has made us to be a kingdom and priests to serve his God and Father—to him be glory and power for ever and ever! Amen. (Rev 1:5b–6)

---

60. For some thoughts from John's Gospel on the contemporary preaching of the death of Christ, see Weston, "Proclaiming Christ Crucified Today," 136–63.

7

God's Final Judgment

By "final" judgment we mean the "last" or "eschatological" judgment at the end of the present age. We have seen that Paul speaks about or alludes to this judgment regularly. It is frequently in his mind and is a fundamental presupposition for him.

In this chapter we will not attempt to cover comprehensively Paul's doctrine of the final judgment. Rather, we will reflect on a few key aspects of Paul's teaching, especially those that are greatly needed in the church today. We will begin with a brief summary of what we found in our overview of Paul's letters.

Summary concerning the Final Judgment

1. Paul's most thorough teaching concerning the principles of the final judgment is in Romans 2:1–16. God's judgment will:
   a. Be based on truth, that is, on the facts of what has actually happened (v. 2)
   b. Be righteous (v. 5)
   c. Be in accordance with the actions of each person (v. 6), and be impartial (v. 11)
   d. Result in one of two outcomes for each person: eternal life (vv. 7, 10) or wrath (vv. 8–9)
   e. Be implemented through Jesus Christ (v. 16).
2. Paul briefly affirms the final judgment in several places (Gal 6:8–9; 1 Tim 5:24; 2 Tim 4:1).
3. When Christ returns, his people will experience bodily resurrection (Rom 8:11; 1 Cor 15:22, 42–44, 51–54; Phil 3:20–21; 1 Thess 4:16–17) and will then be judged by God through Christ (Rom 2:16; 14:10–11;

1 Cor 4:5; 2 Cor 5:10; Eph 6:7–9; Col 3:23–24; 2 Tim 4:8). Judgment will be according to actions, including motives (Rom 14:12; 1 Cor 3:12–15; 4:5; 2 Cor 5:10; Eph 6:7–9; Col 3:23). It will not result in condemnation, but salvation (1 Cor 3:15; Col 3:24; 2 Tim 4:8) and commendation/reward (1 Cor 3:14; 4:5; 2 Cor 5:10;[1] Eph 6:8). There may be little or no commendation for some (1 Cor 3:15; 2 Cor 5:10; Col 3:25[2]). The Lord's people will be saved from God's wrath (Rom 5:9–10; Phil 1:28; 1 Thess 1:10; 5:9; 2 Thess 2:13) and will live with him forever (1 Thess 4:17; 5:10). His people will judge the world and angels (1 Cor 6:2, 3).

4. Paul emphasizes two things about God's people in the present that provide assurance of salvation at the final judgment: being right with God through faith in Christ (Rom 5:9–10; 1 Cor 1:8; 6:11; Gal 5:5; Col 1:22; Titus 3:7), and living a holy life (Col 1:23; 1 Thess 3:13; 5:23; 1 Tim 2:15; 4:16; 2 Tim 1:9; 2:19; Titus 2:11–14). There is evidence in some places of tension between present conduct and final salvation (Rom 11:22; 1 Cor 9:27; 10:11–13).

5. On a number of occasions Paul affirms the condemnation of those who oppose the gospel, who work against God's purpose in the church (1 Cor 3:17; 16:22; 2 Cor 11:13–15; Gal 1:7–9; Phil 1:28; 3:18–19; 2 Thess 1:7–9; 2 Tim 4:14–15).

6. Paul describes the final destiny of unbelievers as follows:

   a. God's wrath, as a result of a sinful life and disobedience toward God (Rom 2:8–9; Eph 5:6; Col 3:5–6). The effects of God's wrath are described as "tribulation and distress" (Rom 2:9).

---

1. Second Cor 5:10 is often seen as describing the judgment of Christians only (see Barnett, *2 Corinthians*, 274), in which case the good or evil deeds that are judged are those of God's people. While the recompense for good deeds would be positive, it is not clear what the recompense for evil deeds would be. It would be some kind of loss, but not loss of salvation (cf. 1 Cor 3:15). Others see this verse as describing the final judgment of all people (Travis, *Christ and the Judgement of God*, 162–67; Yinger, *Paul, Judaism, and Judgment*, 260–70), in which case the good deeds are those of God's people, describing their faithful way of life, and the evil deeds are those of non-Christians, describing their sinful way of life. The recompense is eternal life or wrath, respectively.

2. A similar issue arises for Col 3:25 as for 2 Cor 5:10: is Paul describing the judgment of the evil deeds of a Christian (so O'Brien, *Colossians, Philemon*, 231), or of a person who proves to be an unbeliever (so Travis, *Christ and the Judgement of God*, 168–69)?

b. Not inheriting God's kingdom, as a result of a sinful life (1 Cor 6:9–10; Gal 5:19–21; Eph 5:5)

   c. Destruction (1 Cor 3:17; Phil 1:28; 3:18–19; 1 Thess 5:3; 1 Tim 6:9), perishing (Rom 2:12) or corruption (Gal 6:8)

   d. Death (Rom 1:32; 6:23)

   e. To be cursed (1 Cor 16:22; Gal 1:8–9)

   f. Judgment or condemnation (Rom 3:8; 5:16, 18; 1 Cor 11:32)

   g. Vengeance or punishment (Rom 12:19; 1 Thess 4:6)[3]

   h. Permanent exclusion from the Lord's presence, described as "tribulation," "punishment" and "eternal destruction" (2 Thess 1:6, 8–9).

7. When Christ returns, "the man of lawlessness" will be destroyed (2 Thess 2:8–10), and all evil powers will finally be abolished (Rom 16:20; 1 Cor 15:24, 26; cf. Eph 1:21; Phil 2:9–11).

The Necessity and Purpose of the Final Judgment

Can you imagine a world in which there is no final judgment? The ramifications are huge. If we take God the Judge entirely out of the picture, we are left with a world where the only judges are humans or a creation that is "judging" us for our mistreatment of it. There is no ultimate standard of right and wrong, but only changing standards that apply to us to some extent in the here and now. There is no ultimate accountability, but only a limited accountability that we may be able to avoid to some extent. There is no ultimate judgment or evaluation of life or conduct; while people may give their views concerning the moral worth of our life, we can "take it or leave it." The result is a society morally "at sea," with a plurality of "moralities," much moral tension and hurting of others, and a loss of moral virtue and wellbeing. On a cosmic scale it means that there is no guarantee that right and good (whatever they are) will ultimately prevail; humanity will probably forever be blighted by its moral failings. Certainly, wrongs and injustices that are not dealt with in the present have largely escaped justice; people have "gotten away" with the evil they have done; crime apparently

---

3. In these verses Paul does not make it clear that he is referring to the eschatological judgment alone. He may also be thinking of temporal judgment, especially in Romans 12:19. See the comments on these verses in chapters 2 and 3.

"does pay" at times. The cry in the human heart for justice is answered only partly, if at all.

Sadly, western societies are increasingly adopting such a worldview and reaping its moral fruit. But western Christians are also affected. Our moral consciousness and cohesion are declining. God as Judge is not a strong image in many Christian minds, and the final judgment is not a major consideration in the day-to-day living of most of God's people. We have been "conformed to this age" (Rom 12:2). What is the remedy? It is the one that we have encountered at various times throughout our study—simple, but radical—repentance. We must recognize the influence of a godless worldview upon us, ask God to forgive us and cleanse us from it, and with his help rediscover the biblical worldview of him as Judge, learning together as his people what it means to live in the light of his truth. Then we will "shine as lights" in our generation (Phil 2:15). Obviously, we also need to keep learning the truths of his grace. But here we are focusing on the truth of judgment.

Paul could not imagine the world without the final judgment. For him it is a corollary of God, the Creator, Judge, Redeemer, and King. God has been at work making the world right ever since humanity's Fall into rebellion. God's judgment is an essential part of his making the world right. His judgment is the punishment of sin, designed to check, curtail, and ultimately eliminate sin from his creation. His punishment teaches humans about righteousness, and prompts them to repent and walk in the way of righteousness. God judged humanity at the Fall (Rom 8:20). His judgments continue throughout history (Rom 1:18–32). His judgment on human sin was revealed at the cross of Jesus, where God "condemned sin in [Jesus'] flesh" for our salvation (Rom 8:3). But God's judgments are not complete by any means at the present time. Evil continues and at times increases. Terrible injustices are not judged or put right. Much evil is hidden and not brought to light. Most of our actions during our earthly life are not judged in any final sense. Much judgment remains to be done to bring any final justice and righteousness to the world. The final judgment does this. At the end of the present age God will complete his righteous work through judgment and salvation, ushering in the ages to come. The final judgment is an integral part of the final revelation of God's righteousness in the world. It completes a process of judgment that has continued throughout history from the Fall. That process points to a final judgment that is consistent with God's earlier judgments and with his righteous character.

While Paul does not fully spell out his theology of how the final judgment will contribute to the ultimate righting of creation, it is clearly part of God's freeing creation "from its slavery to corruption" (Rom 8:21), of ultimately reconciling "all things to himself" (Col 1:20), and of bringing "unity to all things in heaven and on earth under Christ" (Eph 1:10).[4] The corruption of the world through sin can be removed only by removing sin from the world. God will do it through final judgment of human sin and renewal of the world. Humans enter the new creation only through faith in Jesus Christ, in whom their sin has been condemned (Rom 8:3), and through whom they are made new people (2 Cor 5:17), forgiven (Rom 4:6-8; Eph 1:7) and freed from sin (Rom 6:17-18). Ultimately they will receive new bodies fit for the new creation (Rom 8:23; 1 Cor 15:50-53). People who do not put their trust in Christ cannot enter God's new creation. Their sin bars them from entry, and they do not want to enter on God's terms. They "do not obey the gospel of our Lord Jesus" (2 Thess 1:8). The only possibility for them is exclusion from God's kingdom, which occurs at the final judgment. They are "destroyed" along with their sin, outside the kingdom (2 Thess 1:9). In addition, all evil powers are "abolished" (1 Cor 15:24-26). Thus, only what has been put right by God will ultimately continue in his kingdom. The final judgment removes all rebellion, disobedience, and injustice from creation. For those who are condemned, it is a terrible and tragic reality. For creation it will ultimately be good news.

But where does the judgment of Christians by the Lord at his coming (2 Cor 5:10) fit into the picture? We need to realize that our lives as God's redeemed people here and now are part of God's new creation, of the kingdom of God already inaugurated in Christ. While our sin has been condemned in Christ (Rom 8:3) and there is no condemnation for us (Rom 8:1), we do not live in a moral vacuum.[5] God is a moral God who takes morality very seriously, especially the character and conduct of his own people. As the Judge he will judge the conduct of his people. God desires holy conduct from his people in the new creation, and at the final judgment he will judge that conduct. We are responsible and accountable to God to live obedient and fruitful lives. The purpose will not be to condemn us but

---

4. See Ladd, *Theology*, 611-14.

5. "The tribunal of Christ serves the purpose of absolute justice. It vindicates the holiness and impartiality of God. It is a salutary reminder to the Christian that, although it is true that he has been justified by faith, and is no longer under law but under grace, yet the moral values of God's universe have not therefore ceased to be his concern" (Hughes, *2 Corinthians*, 180-81).

to evaluate us, to bring to light what we are and have done by his grace and for his glory. The ultimate purpose is to bring him glory for the working of his grace in our lives in living in the way that pleases him. This was the original purpose of creation: to have "a people that are his very own, eager to do what is good" (Titus 2:14). We have the privilege of participating in it. God will give us the joy of being commended (1 Cor 4:5) for building in our lives and those of others something of true moral worth by his grace:

> [19] For what is our hope, our joy, or the crown in which we will glory in the presence of our Lord Jesus when he comes? Is it not you? [20] Indeed, you are our glory and joy. (1 Thess 2:19–20)

Of course, for God's people the final judgment leads to salvation, when we enter into all that God has prepared for us (1 Cor 2:9). Our passing through the final judgment into salvation will highlight the grace of God in saving us (Eph 2:7; 1 Pet 1:13). We will be very conscious that of ourselves we are not worthy to enter. Our focus will be on the one who has saved us from our sin. We will be deeply grateful that the punishment due for the many sins, wrongs, and injustices we committed was borne by him. Our condemnation fell upon Christ on the cross (Rom 8:3). More than that, when we see him on that future day we will be amazed at his glory and he will be glorified in us (2 Thess 1:10).

The final judgment will reveal the Lord Jesus Christ as the Judge of all humans. Paul affirms that God will judge "everyone's secrets through Jesus Christ" (Rom 2:16), that "we must all appear before the judgment seat of Christ" (2 Cor 5:10). In that day "every knee [will] bow" and "every tongue [will] confess that Jesus Christ is Lord" (Phil 2:10–11). Some will do it unwillingly, but all will acknowledge his sovereignty as Lord and Judge. We are reminded of what Jesus says: "Moreover, the Father judges no one, but has entrusted all judgment to the Son, that all may honor the Son just as they honor the Father" (John 5:22–23). Thus, the final judgment will bring glory to the Lord Jesus as God's appointed Judge. But Christ's role as Judge also has the purpose of saving people at the final judgment. His exalted role is the culmination of a righteous life lived for humanity, leading to his death "for our sins" (1 Cor 15:3) and his resurrection. Because of his life and work those who trust in him will not be condemned at the final judgment, but will be saved. In short, unless that judgment is through Christ we have no hope. A judgment apart from Christ would lead to the condemnation of all, but judgment through him will lead to the salvation of those who belong to him. This is the glorious hope of the gospel! Conversely, those who reject him are even more guilty (John 15:22–24), because they have rejected the revelation of God's judgment and salvation in his Son (John 3:19; 12:47–48).[6]

The Judgment of God's People

I do not think that Paul would be particularly pleased with what we have often done with his teaching on the eschatological judgment. We have attempted to systematize his teaching into eschatological schemata that focus on the timing of and relationship between future events. Then we have attempted to feel secure in our knowledge of what is to come, and have argued with other Christians who have a different schema. In so doing we have largely missed Paul's purpose in giving his instruction. His purpose was primarily spiritual and ethical, not just informational. He intended knowledge concerning the future to impact life in the present, so that God's people live in the light of the new creation that is coming, that they have begun to experience in the present (1 Cor 15:58; cf. 2 Pet 3:11–12).[7] In other words, Paul's teaching about judgment is intended to guide and change our way of life. The key question is: *To what extent is my life influenced by the truth that one day I will stand before the Lord and give an account to him?* We need to reflect on and pray about it often. Paul obviously did.

Judgment of Works

It is worth going back over what will be judged at the final judgment. While Paul does not go into detail, what he says enables us to go into detail for ourselves, once we get his message. Basically, Paul says that the Lord will judge everything we have done: "what they have done" (Rom 2:6); "each person's work" (1 Cor 3:13); "the things done while in the body, whether good or bad" (2 Cor 5:10). And everything means everything, even "everyone's secrets" (Rom 2:16), "what is hidden in darkness," and "the motives of people's hearts" (1 Cor 4:5). We and all we have done will be totally exposed before the Lord. Why does Paul stress it? Because he wants us to realize

---

6. See Morris, *Biblical Doctrine*, 61–62.

7. For discussions on Paul's teaching concerning the judgment of God's people, see Guthrie, *New Testament Theology*, 859–63; Ladd, *Theology*, 611–12; Dunn, *Theology of Paul*, 490–98; Travis, *Christ and the Judgement of God*, 161–80. It is notable that New Testament and Pauline theologies are sometimes quite "thin" on the topic.

that what we do is very important. It is easy to think that because we are justified by faith in Christ, our actions are secondary and not so important. Such thinking shows that our understanding of God's grace and purpose is still incomplete. Our actions reveal who we are; they are very important to God. We are saved "to do good works" (Eph 2:10), and God will hold us accountable for all that we do—a very challenging thought! As fallen humans we tend to have many things in our lives hidden or secret, either knowingly or unknowingly. Learning to open our lives to the Lord to live in his presence and to do everything "in the name of the Lord Jesus" (Col 3:17) is a lifelong discipline. Only then are we serious about living in the light of the coming Day.

Motivation for Works

The motivation to live in this way comes from our love for the Lord and our desire to please him. Love and desire must be nurtured, particularly by reflection on his love for us (2 Cor 5:14; Gal 2:20). But Paul is also motivated by "the fear of the Lord" (2 Cor 5:11), that is, by the knowledge that the Lord is our Judge, to whom we are answerable (2 Cor 5:10). This is a major aspect of Paul's motivation in mission (2 Cor 5:11–21) and in dealing with sin in his life and in the church, "perfecting holiness in the fear of God" (2 Cor 7:1). My experience of the western church in the last twenty years is that reverence for God has declined to a significant degree. We are trying to motivate ourselves and others almost exclusively from love for God, but it cannot work effectively apart from deep reverence for God. Love loses its meaning apart from respect; love and respect are "two sides of the same coin." The Lord Jesus is not first my Friend, but my Creator, Savior, Lord, and Judge. I have a serious obligation to him. As my Savior he enables me to fulfill that obligation with joy. We must regain "the fear of the Lord" in the church.[8] It will involve recovering the truth of judgment, and having the courage to preach and teach it.

---

8. Alan Stanley suggested that I add some thoughts about the fear of the Lord. These are Alan's thoughts from the Bible: Those who fear the Lord delight in God's commands (Ps 112:1) and "put their hope in his unfailing love" (Ps 147:11). Those who fear God see him as most worthy of praise (1 Chr 16:25) and trust him (Isa 50:10). The fear of the Lord is foundational and a pre-requisite to knowing him (Prov 1:7; 2:5), because the fear of the Lord is humility (Prov 22:4). The fear of the Lord is something to be delighted in (Isa 11:3, referring to the Servant). "He will be the sure foundation for your times, a rich store of salvation and wisdom and knowledge; the fear of the LORD is the key to this

Judgment according to Works and Justification by Faith

One of the potentially confusing aspects of Paul's teaching is how judgment "according to works" is consistent with justification by faith and salvation by grace. This has been a major topic of discussion among scholars.[9] It is an important topic because a failure to understand Paul's teaching on it can easily lead to a casual attitude toward ethics on the one hand, or legalism on the other. To begin with, Paul does not mean that justification by faith applies only to the beginning of the Christian life, and that the rest of our life is all about works that will determine whether or not we are saved in the end.[10] Such a view is totally at odds with Paul's view of justification by faith. His response would be: "Are you so foolish? After beginning with the Spirit, are you now trying to finish by human effort?" (Gal 3:3). Rather, Paul sees justification by faith in Christ as securing and anticipating final salvation: "But by faith we eagerly await through the Spirit the righteousness for which we hope" (Gal 5:5). The question is: why is Paul so confident, and how does he see judgment according to works in relation to final salvation?

Judgment according to works is a principle that applies to all people, both believers in Jesus and unbelievers. Everyone will come before God to give an account of his or her life (Rom 14:12). But the crucial difference is what Jesus has accomplished for those who trust in him. Unbelievers are "on their own" at the judgment. The judgment of their works will confirm their sinfulness and lead to their condemnation, because of their rebellion and disobedience to God (Rom 2:8). In contrast, believers are "in Christ." They are not judged on their own; otherwise, their end would be the same as unbelievers; even their "good" works would not cancel out their many sins. Thankfully, the work of Christ deals with their sins. Because their sin was condemned in him (Rom 8:3), they will not be condemned. In him, the risen one, they are "the righteousness of God" (2 Cor 5:21). This is why Paul is

---

treasure" (Isa 33:6). The early church lived in the fear of the Lord and grew (Acts 9:31). In sum, the fear of the Lord is not optional, because the new covenant promises that those who know God will fear him (Jer 32:39–40).

9. See Vos, *Pauline Eschatology*, 269–79; Donfried, "Justification," 140–52; Travis, *Christ and the Judgement of God*, 87–101; Yinger, *Paul, Judaism, and Judgment*, 283–91; Bird, *Saving Righteousness*, 155–87; Ortlund, "Justified by Faith, Judged according to Works," 323–39; McFadden, *Judgment*, 121–38; Stanley, *Four Views on the Role of Works*. On the law of Moses as the criterion of judgment, see Stettler, "Paul, the Law and Judgement by Works," 195–215.

10. This is basically what is argued, nuanced in various ways, in VanLandingham, *Judgment and Justification*.

confident. When believers appear before God, their works, that is, their life, will testify to the genuineness of their faith in Christ (2 Thess 1:4–5); on the basis of his work and their relationship with him through faith, they will be saved (Rom 5:9–10). For Paul the crucial issue is faith in Christ. But faith is not just words. It is heart-faith that confesses Jesus as Lord (Rom 10:9–10) and obeys him as Lord (Rom 1:5; 16:26). It is not a person's faith-claim that is judged at the final judgment, but their obedience to Christ that shows whether they have genuine faith in him; those who do will be saved. Judgment according to works does not mean salvation by works. It means, firstly, determining by a person's works, their way of life, whether they are trusting in Christ for salvation (Gal 5:6; 1 Thess 1:3; 2 Thess 1:11–12). For those who are, the final verdict of "righteous" will correspond to and fulfill the verdict that was declared concerning them when they first believed the gospel.[11]

Reward

But there is another aspect to the judgment of believers' works, namely, that of reward for faithful service to the Lord.[12] Here we must be careful, because Paul does not at all have the idea of earning wages or a reward. The reward is not what God "owes us"; it is what he freely chooses to give us through his grace. It is a gift.[13] While Paul can describe salvation itself as a "reward" (Col 3:24), he also refers to individual rewards that correspond to the life and service of each of God's people:

> ... At that time each will receive their praise from God. (1 Cor 4:5)

> because you know that the Lord will reward each one of you for whatever good you do, whether you are slave or free. (Eph 6:8)

That these rewards can vary is shown in 1 Corinthians 3:

> [12] If anyone builds on this foundation using gold, silver, costly stones, wood, hay or straw, [13] their work will be shown for what it is, because the Day will bring it to light. It will be revealed with fire, and the fire will test the quality of each person's work. [14] If what has been built survives, the builder will receive a reward. [15] If it is

---

11. See the very helpful study and discussion in Schreiner, "Justification," 71–98.

12. See Böttger et al., "Recompense, Reward, Gain, Wages," 134–45; Travis, *Christ and the Judgement of God*, 161–80.

13. "When God crowns our merits, he crowns nothing else but his own gifts" (Augustine).

burned up, the builder will suffer loss but yet will be saved—even though only as one escaping through the flames. (1 Cor 3:12–15)

Though in this passage Paul is teaching about the judgment of the work of Christian leaders, the principle is applicable to the work of all God's people.[14] Clearly, there is the possibility that some believers will receive little or no reward for their work. If we are judged according to our works, then our reward will be in proportion to the quality of those works. Experience teaches us that the quality of the works of God's people varies greatly. Some works are excellent, flowing from faith and love, and a deep desire to honor and please God, and to bless people. Some are poor, flowing from mixed motives, largely human wisdom and strength, and without a Godward focus. Some are plainly sinful. Perhaps Paul has the full range of works in mind in 2 Corinthians 5:10 and Colossians 3:23–25.[15] As to the nature of the reward or "loss" (1 Cor 3:15), it would seem that it is commendation from the Lord—"praise from God" (1 Cor 4:5; cf. Rom 2:29)—or lack of it, and the corresponding feeling of joy and satisfaction, or lack of it. The reward is primarily a relational blessing, not about spiritual "mansions" (John 14:2, KJV), "property," "wealth," or "possessions."

The judgment for reward is the Lord's evaluation of us. The issue is not salvation or condemnation; it is his assessment of our lives as his people. It is about the extent to which living for him has been the priority of our life, how much we have loved him, how much we have trusted and obeyed him in life and service. It shows that his concern is not just in saving people from condemnation, but in creating a holy people "for his name" (Acts 15:14), who pursue him, his purpose, and his glory. To be found as holy people will be our reward. For our lives now, we need to regularly ask ourselves how important the "Well done, good and faithful servant" (Matt 25:21, 23) will be to us on that day.

Faith and Works in the Christian Life

For the benefit of Protestants (I am one) I will pursue the faith-works connection a little further. While we can and must distinguish between faith and works, so as to make it clear that we are saved only through Christ's

---

14. On Paul's teaching in this passage, see Fee, *1 Corinthians*, 143–45; Kuck, *Judgment and Community Conflict*, 180–86; Yinger, *Paul, Judaism, and Judgment*, 215–22.

15. See the first two footnotes in this chapter.

work for us and not through our own works, we must also appreciate deeply the close relationship between faith and works in the Christian life. Paul makes it clear that our works are the fruit of our faith (Eph 2:8–10). Thus, true faith will inevitably produce godly character and conduct; where the latter are not found, it is unlikely that true faith is present. While in the New Testament it is James who explains the faith-works connection most clearly (Jas 2:14–26), we have also seen that it is a Pauline conviction (Rom 1:5; 6:12–23; 8:12–13; Gal 5:6, 22–24; Col 1:23; 1 Thess 1:3; 3:13; 5:23; 2 Thess 1:4–5, 11–12; 1 Tim 2:15; 4:16; 2 Tim 1:9; 2:19; Titus 2:11–14). Paul sees a life of good works as essential on the journey from justification to final salvation, not because those works save us, but because they are the fruit and evidence of saving faith. We are not talking about "sinless perfection," but growth in Christian character.[16] Its absence in a professing Christian is very problematic, placing a large question-mark (from a human perspective) over that person's faith and ultimate salvation.

The key to understanding Paul on this matter is in grasping his view of the grace of God. Paul does not see God's grace as relating only to the beginning and the end of the Christian life. Grace does not simply bring us to faith, justify us before God, and then save us on the last day. God's grace also relates to the whole of our earthly life from conversion onward. Grace sanctifies and empowers us to break free from sin, pursue godliness, and do the good works that God has called us to do (Titus 2:11–14). It is not a different grace from justifying grace or grace that saves us in the end. It is the same grace from God, but seen in its various aspects. It has one overall purpose, which is greater than simply "getting us to heaven." That purpose is that we are "conformed to the image of [God's] Son" (Rom 8:29), which involves all the aspects of God's saving work in our lives. His grace is operative in all of these.

It is when we understand God's purpose and the scope of his grace that we appreciate the necessity for character transformation and good works in our lives. This must be a major priority for us. It does not happen automatically; it happens as we deeply desire God's grace to work in our lives and allow him to do his work in us. It involves a genuine divine-human engagement. We are not passive. We must respond willingly and actively to God's gracious initiative. As Paul says:

---

16. See Travis, *Christ and the Judgement of God*, 135–51.

> ¹² ... continue to work out your salvation with fear and trembling, ¹³ for it is God who works in you to will and to act in order to fulfill his good purpose. (Phil 2:12b–13)

Paul does not say that we work our way *to* salvation. Rather, we "work *out*" our salvation. We cooperate in allowing God's salvation to have its full outworking in our lives in sanctification and good works. We do it "with fear and trembling," in "the fear of the Lord" (2 Cor 5:11), knowing that he will evaluate our lives in the end (2 Cor 5:10). We do it by the empowering grace of God, who works in us to desire and to do his will. It is very important to God; therefore, he will judge it in the end. This is why we will be judged according to our works. Where God's grace is present in a life, that person's character and works will correspond to the declaration of "righteous in Christ." We are not talking about sinless perfection, but growth in sanctifying grace. The grace that justifies and saves God's people in the end, will have also transformed them throughout their earthly life, so that they are able to present to God the Father and Judge a life that glorifies him, delights him, and that he is able to commend. Paul's description in Romans 2 of a godly person would seem applicable:

> To those who by persistence in doing good seek glory, honor and immortality, he will give eternal life. (Rom 2:7)[17]

In relation to God's people, this is not describing salvation by works, but a life that testifies to the presence of the saving grace of God.

An Empty Profession of Faith

We will briefly touch on one final matter, namely, the possibility of a professing Christian not being saved at the final judgment.[18] From our perspective it is a complicated matter, drawing us into the debate between Calvinism and Arminianism. A Calvinist view sees such a person as not being justified by faith in the first place; they have never had a genuine faith. An Arminian view may see such a person as being justified by faith in the

---

17. For a range of views on who Paul is describing at this point in his argument, see Cranfield, *Romans*, 1:151–53; Moo, *Romans*, 139–42; Yinger, *Paul, Judaism, and Judgment*, 146–82; Bird, *Saving Righteousness*, 155–87; McFadden, *Judgment*, 139–53. Even if Paul is arguing in Romans 2 that there is no one who lives in this way, his description is a helpful summary of what a Christian should and can be by the grace of God.

18. On this topic, see Travis, *Christ and the Judgement of God*, 152–60; Gundry Volf, *Paul and Perseverance*, 120–30, 196–201, 233–47; Donfried, "Justification," 140–52.

beginning of their Christian experience, but as subsequently losing faith and thus final salvation. Good works, the fruit of faith, are in the picture in both these views. If the fruit is largely absent, then it will mean either that a person was never a true believer or that they lost faith along the way. We will not pursue the debate further. However we view Paul, it is significant that he focuses strongly on the fruit of faith; it could hardly be otherwise, given that observable works are the main way that humans can discern faith. We have noted several passages where Paul asks the question about final salvation concerning himself or others. Concerning himself he says:

> No, I strike a blow to my body and make it my slave so that after I have preached to others, I myself will not be disqualified for the prize. (1 Cor 9:27)

While final salvation appears to be the issue here,[19] Paul does not entertain serious doubts about his ultimate future. What he expresses is the necessity for true faith to continue to produce the fruit of good works. Paul is determined not to grow slack in his service; otherwise, there may be a question-mark regarding the grace of God in his life. To the Gentiles in the church in Rome Paul says:

> [20] Granted. But they were broken off because of unbelief, and you stand by faith. Do not be arrogant, but tremble. [21] For if God did not spare the natural branches, he will not spare you either. [22] Consider therefore the kindness and sternness of God: sternness to those who fell, but kindness to you, provided that you continue in his kindness. Otherwise, you also will be cut off. (Rom 11:20–22)

To the Corinthians he says:

> [12] So, if you think you are standing firm, be careful that you don't fall! . . . [14] Therefore, my dear friends, flee from idolatry. . . . [22] Are we trying to arouse the Lord's jealousy? Are we stronger than he? (1 Cor 10:12, 14, 22)

These are serious warnings. They show that professing Christians can miss out on final salvation through unbelief, pride, and idolatry. Whether that means false faith from the beginning or lost faith, the fact is that a failure to bear fruit for God is a bad indication concerning future salvation. It does not mean that we are saved by our works. We are saved by God's

---

19. So Fee, *1 Corinthians*, 438–41; Yinger, *Paul, Judaism, and Judgment*, 247–53. Gundry Volf argues that the issue is not salvation, but possible disqualification from apostolic service (Gundry Volf, *Paul and Perseverance*, 233–47).

grace through faith in Christ. But if the good works are missing, grace and faith may be also, and salvation will not be ours (Titus 2:11–14). Practically speaking, good works are not perfect obedience, but growth in obedience, in works that arise from faith and the desire to glorify God (Matt 6:1–18). We must be serious about the way we live and serve. We are reminded of the Lord's words:

> [21] "Not everyone who says to me, 'Lord, Lord,' will enter the kingdom of heaven, but only those who do the will of my Father who is in heaven. [22] Many will say to me on that day, 'Lord, Lord, did we not prophesy in your name and in your name drive out demons and in your name perform many miracles?' [23] Then I will tell them plainly, 'I never knew you. Away from me, you evildoers!'" (Matt 7:21–23)

The Judgment of Unbelievers

We now come to a fundamental and sobering aspect of Paul's teaching on divine judgment that we have continued to encounter throughout our study, namely, the final judgment of those who do not believe in Christ.[20] Paul's belief about the topic is consistent with the teaching of Jesus and the rest of the New Testament.[21] Christian teaching about the final judgment is something that is known superficially in western societies that have had the gospel message for centuries. But it is neither widely understood nor taken seriously. More often it is used in humor or profanity, and many people regard belief in hell or eternal punishment to be a relic of ancient religion, no longer credible in an enlightened age. Even evangelical Christians struggle with the doctrine, some with the justice of it, all with the implications of it, and those seeking to communicate it faithfully, with how to do so in a generation that does not want to hear about it.

We begin by noting (mostly repeating) the basic principles or aspects of the final judgment:[22]

---

20. For discussions of this topic in Paul's theology, see Guthrie, *New Testament Theology*, 856–59; Ladd, *Theology*, 611–14; Schreiner, *Paul*, 467–71; Moo, "Paul on Hell," 91–109; Travis, *Christ and the Judgement of God*, 102–119.
21. See Morgan, "Three Pictures of Hell," 135–51.
22. For a helpful and challenging ten-point overview of the final judgment, see Morris, *Biblical Doctrine*, 54–72.

God's Final Judgment

1. God is the Judge, exercising his judgment through Jesus Christ (Rom 2:2, 3, 5, 16).

2. The Judge will be revealed in awesome power and glory (2 Thess 1:7).

3. Every person who has ever lived will be judged (Rom 2:6). Though Paul's letters speak about bodily resurrection only in relation to believers for judgment and salvation, evidently (cf. Acts 24:15), in line with biblical teaching, he expects every person to be resurrected and to stand before God as the Judge (Dan 12:2; John 5:28-29; Rev 20:12-13). Though in places Paul focuses on the judgment of believers (e.g., 1 Cor 3:13-15; 4:5), his references to universal judgment (Rom 2:1-16; 14:10-12; 2 Tim 4:1),[23] plus his expectation that the salvation of believers will coincide with the condemnation of unbelievers (2 Thess 1:5-10), suggest that he expects all people to be judged at the one final judgment.[24] The difference between believers and unbelievers is in the outcome.

4. It is entirely just and impartial, based on the full facts of each person's life and conduct (Rom 2:2, 5, 11, 16).

5. It is "according to the works" of each person (Rom 2:6). The outcome will correspond to God's assessment of a person's life and actions.

6. The standard by which God will judge each person is the revelation of him and his will that has been available to them.[25] There is the witness of creation to God's divinity and power (Rom 1:19-20). There is the knowledge of right and wrong, which is present in every culture (Rom 1:32; 2:14-15).[26] For some people there is the special revelation in the law of Moses (the Old Testament) (Rom 2:12; 3:2). There is also the special revelation in the gospel of Jesus Christ (the New Testament)

---

23. Some would include 2 Cor 5:10 and Col 3:22-25 here.

24. On this understanding Paul does not expect a millennial kingdom to separate the judgment of believers from that of unbelievers (Rev 20:4-6). There is no clear teaching about a millennium in Paul. On 1 Cor 15:24, see Fee, *1 Corinthians*, 753-54.

25. For a discussion of the application to Christians, Jews and others, see Stettler, "Paul, the Law and Judgement by Works," 195-215.

26. The reference to Rom 2:14-15 assumes that this passage refers to unbelieving Gentiles, who while not having the law of Moses are "a law to themselves" (v. 14), in the sense that they know some of the moral requirements of God's law. See Moo, *Romans*, 148-53; Schreiner, *Romans*, 119-24. Some commentators argue that Paul is describing Gentile Christians (e.g., Cranfield, *Romans*, 1:155-62; Gathercole, "Law unto Themselves," 27-49). McFadden argues for both (McFadden, *Judgment*, 139-53).

(Rom 1:16–17). Each person will be judged according to how they have lived in the light of the revelation they have received.

7. With respect to unbelievers, Paul gives no hope that they will be saved at the judgment. His argument is that no one has lived up to the light they have received.[27] All have disobeyed the truth they have received and all have pursued evil actions to some extent (Rom 2:8; 3:10–18).

Paul's clear message is that those who do not trust in Jesus will be condemned at the final judgment, and that it will be righteous. This is a hard truth. It raises a number of questions that Christians and others have discussed and argued about for centuries. We will touch on some of these questions.

A key issue is the nature of God's wrath and condemnation. In our summary at the beginning of this chapter we have noted the ways in which Paul describes the wrath of God. Paul's fundamental concept is that of exclusion: exclusion from God's presence (2 Thess 1:9) and his kingdom (Eph 5:5). Those who have not forsaken their sin through trust in Christ cannot live with God. However, exclusion is not nothingness, but the opposite of all that is good and pleasant: it is painful—"tribulation and distress" (Rom 2:9); it is an experience of "corruption" (Gal 6:8) and "destruction" (Phil 1:28), of the ongoing consequences of sin that corrupts and destroys all that is good; it is God's punishment (Rom 12:19; 2 Thess 1:8); it is eternal (2 Thess 1:9). While Paul is not overly graphic in his descriptions, he leaves no doubt that it is a horrific destiny that no person would desire. It is far worse than any earthly sufferings that people may experience in a fallen world. It is the deprivation of all that is good, and is an eternal existence in death, separated from the living God.

Is God's Wrath Just?

The big question that arises from Paul's understanding in our contemporary western context is how this can be just. How can it be consistent with God's love for people? How could he inflict such a destiny on his creatures,

---

27. If Paul is referring to unbelieving Gentiles in Rom 2:14–15, this would seem to be his point. The fact that people's conscience sometimes defends their actions as right does not mean they are justified before God. It means simply that sometimes they do what is right and are conscious of it. The thrust of Paul's argument is that those who have sinned apart from the law of Moses will perish (v. 12). Paul does not give any hope here of people being saved apart from faith in Christ. See Carson, *Gagging of God*, 310–12.

even if they have rebelled against him?[28] Surely he could find a way of winning them to himself, even after physical death (i.e., post-mortem evangelism).[29] Or alternately, surely in his mercy he could simply either cause or allow them to cease to exist, so that they suffer no longer. Such questions and solutions are an understandable human attempt to reconcile the teaching of Paul and the New Testament with God's love and justice. Many Christians have pondered such thoughts as they have struggled with the enormity of the doctrine of eternal punishment. I have. But for Bible-believers it is not a matter of coming up with a solution that eases our conscience or that we hope is true. That changes nothing if it is not true. And if it misrepresents the truth it does no one any good. The key issue is the truth as God has revealed it in Paul's letters and the rest of the Bible. If there are things difficult to understand, we do not put ourselves above Scripture; rather, we accept what God says, seeking to understand it as best we can, but recognizing that the ways of his holy love are ultimately beyond our limited and flawed understanding.

Unending Punishment?

So, is the traditional Christian doctrine of eternal punishment true? Is it true to Paul? Is it true to the New Testament? A number of evangelical scholars would say "no." While agreeing that unbelievers will be condemned, some argue that their condemnation is not retributive punishment. Rather, it is the inevitable consequence of rejecting God; thus, unbelievers effectively cut themselves off from the life of God.[30] Further, condemnation does not involve eternal suffering. While the consequences are eternal and irreversible, those who are condemned will either cease to exist (conditional immortality view) or God will annihilate them (annihilationism). This is the meaning of "eternal destruction" (2 Thess 1:9). Destruction is interpreted

---

28. For an emotionally-charged argument along these lines, see Pinnock, "Conditional View," 149–54.

29. "If he is all-powerful, will he not exert his infinite power to the utmost to save all the perishing? If he is all-loving, will he not save any soul with a glimmer of a belief that the rejection of Christ would deserve blame?" (Edwards, "Gospel for the World," 295; see also 302–4). This is a fundamental assumption in Bell, *Love Wins*. For a debate on Christian universalism, see Parry and Partridge, *Universal Salvation*?

30. Travis, *Christ and the Judgement of God*, 102–19; Marshall, *Beyond Retribution*, 188–97.

to mean cessation of existence.[31] The Bible does not teach the immortality of the human soul. People are in fact mortal in every respect, and unless God grants immortality, which he does only to believers in Jesus, people will ultimately cease to exist.[32] Thus, eternal condemnation does not mean eternal punishment, but forever missing out on the life with God that he has provided for humanity through his Son.

Such a view of hell has caused something of a storm among evangelical Christians in the last thirty or so years.[33] Proponents argue that they are recovering the biblical view.[34] Opponents argue that the truth is under attack from a secular society which is increasingly rejecting biblical truth.[35] We do not have the space to consider all the arguments and then come to a conclusion.[36] Rather, I will declare my view and then briefly seek to support it. I regard the traditional view of hell as eternal punishment to be correct. While I understand the reasons and arguments for conditional immortality,[37] and in some ways feel drawn emotionally toward such a view, in the end I do not regard it to be biblically or theologically sound. It may be more palatable for people today, but I do not believe it is faithful to Scripture or in the end, helpful to people, even if eases their conscience.

A major problem with the conditional immortality view is that it is driven too much by a desire to solve a theological problem, with the result that it finds in Scripture a "solution" to that problem. It is certainly possible to read Scripture in such a way, but it is at the expense of the overall voice of Scripture. Arguing that the Bible teaches conditional immortality, conditionalists then reinterpret key terms such as "eternal" (Gr. *aiōnios*) and "destruction" (Gr. *apōleia, olethros*). Some propose a logical, temporal

---

31. Stott, "Gospel for the World—Response," 315–20; Pinnock, "Conditional View," 142–47; Wenham, "Case for Conditional Immortality," 169–74.

32. Pinnock, "Conditional View," 147–49; Wenham, "Case for Conditional Immortality," 174–76; Fudge, *Fire That Consumes*, 21–40; Powys, "Hell".

33. See Wenham, "Case for Conditional Immortality," 161–68; Mohler, "Disappearance of Hell," 28–36; ACUTE, *Nature of Hell*.

34. Fudge, *Fire That Consumes*; Stott, "Gospel for the World—Response," 312–20; Wenham, "Case for Conditional Immortality," 161–91; Pinnock, "Conditional View," 135–66; Powys, "Hell," 412–20; Marshall, *Beyond Retribution*, 175–87.

35. See Mohler, "Disappearance of Hell," 36–41.

36. See discussions in Carson, *Gagging of God*, 515–36; Harmon, "Case against Conditionalism," 193–224; Chan, "Logic of Hell," 20–32; Milne, *Message of Heaven and Hell*, 150–60; Morgan, "Annihilationism," 195–218.

37. Rather than continuing to distinguish conditional mortality from annihilationism, I will now use the former term to cover both views.

God's Final Judgment

schema of judgment that often includes a short period of punishment or suffering, followed by cessation of existence (destruction) which is eternal and irreversible.[38] The problem with the schema is that in some respects it adds to what the Bible says, while in other respects it takes away from the biblical message. Let us consider Matthew 25:46:

> Then they will go away to eternal punishment, but the righteous to eternal life. (Matt 25:46)

Here the clear sense is that "eternal punishment" (Gr. *kolasin aiōnion*) is punishment that is experienced forever. Both the adjective *aiōnios* and the context point in this direction.[39] These people are going "into the eternal fire prepared for the devil and his angels" (v. 41). It is not simply fire with eternal consequences, but fire that will burn forever. While Jesus is using fire as a metaphor, it is not difficult to understand his meaning. The implication is that those in the fire will suffer forever. If the fire means destruction in the sense of consuming to the point of cessation of existence, then from this point the fire can go out; it has no further purpose. But if it continues to burn, then those in it presumably continue to exist in a state of punishment and suffering. To argue that eternal punishment means punishment for a limited duration with eternal consequences,[40] is reading into the text what is hardly plain and what Jesus' disciples could hardly be expected to have understood. The logical parallelism of "eternal punishment" (Gr. *kolasin aiōnion*) with "eternal life" (Gr. *zōēn aiōnion*) must not be missed. Eternal life is clearly everlasting life, life that is experienced forever. Similarly, eternal punishment is everlasting punishment that is experienced forever, unending punishment.

The conditional immortality view has the same problem with descriptions of hell in the book of Revelation:

> [9] A third angel followed them and said in a loud voice: "If anyone worships the beast and its image and receives its mark on their forehead or on their hand, [10] they, too, will drink of the wine of God's fury, which has been poured full strength into the cup of his wrath. They will be tormented with burning sulfur in the presence of the holy angels and of the Lamb. [11] And the smoke of their

---

38. For example, see Fudge, *Fire That Consumes*, 185–90. For a critique see Harmon, "Case against Conditionalism," 211–12, 215.

39. See discussions in Carson, *Gagging of God*, 523, 528–29; Harris, *Raised Immortal*, 180–85; McKnight, "Eternal Consequences or Eternal Consciousness?," 147–57.

40. So Fudge, *Fire That Consumes*, 119–25.

> torment will rise for ever and ever. There will be no rest day or night for those who worship the beast and its image, or for anyone who receives the mark of its name." (Rev 14:9–11)

> ¹⁰ And the devil, who deceived them, was thrown into the lake of burning sulfur, where the beast and the false prophet had been thrown. They will be tormented day and night for ever and ever. . . . ¹⁵ All whose names were not found written in the book of life were thrown into the lake of fire. (Rev 20:10, 15)

For Revelation 14 proponents argue that the torment lasts only until the people are totally consumed (i.e., cease to exist), after which the smoke rises forever as a memorial to their destruction.[41] But the text says otherwise: the smoke is the smoke of "their torment" (v. 11). Clearly, the smoke means they are still suffering, not that they suffered in the past and that now they no longer exist. The picture of everlasting suffering is clear and powerful. "For ever and ever" they have "no rest day or night" (v. 11). Revelation 20 presents the same picture: in the lake of fire the devil, the beast, and the false prophet "will be tormented day and night for ever and ever" (v. 10). Presumably, people who are thrown into the lake (v. 15) will experience the same, that is, everlasting suffering. As horrific as it is, it is the clear message of the text.

The reason why everlasting punishment is the traditional view is not because of a pre-commitment to the idea of the immortality of the soul or a desire to see the wicked suffer. The reason is that this is the direction in which the biblical texts lead us. The Bible teaches the resurrection of the dead. If God allows people to exist after physical death in *Sheol/Hades* and then raises them for judgment, then it would seem probable that they will exist forever, whether they have faith in Jesus or not. It is God's business. Further, the biblical texts do not support an interpretation of "destruction" as cessation of existence. The biblical concept of "destruction" is much broader, namely, "the situation of a person or object that has lost the essence of its nature or function," as in the "wasting" of ointment (Matt 26:8), the "ruining" of wineskins (Matt 9:17), a "lost" coin (Luke 15:9), or the "perishing" of the world in the Flood (2 Pet 3:6).[42] Thus, when Paul speaks about the "eternal destruction" of unbelievers (2 Thess 1:9), he probably does not mean irreversible cessation of existence, but everlasting ruin, their humanity devastated by the consequences of their sin, and forever missing

---

41. For example, ibid., 185–90.
42. Moo, "Paul on Hell," 105.

out on the purpose for which God created them. Finally, the traditional view is the most difficult to hold, especially today. Christians who continue to hold this view do so, not because it is pleasant or popular, but because they believe it is faithful to God and his Word.

We are left, then, with the traditional view of the final judgment for unbelievers. However, it is not simply a doctrine we hold, but a truth that should shake us to our foundations as we grapple with the revelation of God and of human sin that it conveys to us. Human-centered thinking cannot grasp it at all; hell seems the complete antithesis of love and justice.[43] But for us who believe the Bible we must allow the truth about hell to bring home to us the reality that we live in a God-centered universe, with a holy God who ultimately will not tolerate sin. We may know it theologically, but our human-centered, fast-paced, and self-serving culture easily causes the truth about God to recede from the center of our thoughts. The result is that most western Christians spend little time contemplating God's holiness and judgment. Soon the doctrine of eternal judgment seems unreal and too hard to handle. If this is true concerning us, it is time for us to return to the truth about God's holiness and judgment.

The truth about hell teaches us that it is entirely righteous for God to punish forever those who reject him. The simple logic is that those who do not acknowledge the one who created them will be condemned to an eternity apart from him. The Bible indicates that God created humans to live forever; for him the annihilation of humans is not an option. There is no way out of the reality and of the responsibility of relationship with God. Also, we need to face the fact that hell is God's retributive punishment of sinners. It is not something for us to be embarrassed about. We do God's reputation no favors by seeking to distance him from the eternal consequences of sin. Though people bring those consequences on themselves, God is the one who has decreed and who implements the consequences. They are punishment and they correspond to the sin committed. The punishment is everlasting because the sin is committed against God. To reject the everlasting God leads to everlasting consequences. Jesus teaches that there will be degrees of eternal punishment according to people's sin (Matt 11:20–24; Luke 12:47–48).[44] While God takes no pleasure in punishing sinners (Ezek 18:23, 32), he will ensure that the recompense for evil is just.

---

43. For a discussion of the justice of divine violence in relation to the final judgment, see Volf, *Exclusion and Embrace*, 295–304.

44. See Carson, *Gagging of God*, 532–33.

The Righteous Judgment of God

We must take seriously the fact that there is a Judge to whom every person will answer. This is the immovable reality of the universe that we ignore to our peril. The biblical writers knew it well:

> Nothing in all creation is hidden from God's sight. Everything is uncovered and laid bare before the eyes of him to whom we must give account. (Heb 4:13)

> It is a dreadful thing to fall into the hands of the living God. (Heb 10:31)

The Love of God

And what about God's love? Does hell reveal anything about God's love? Yes! It shows the greatness of his love in forgiving sinners who escape hell. It points us to the cross of Jesus where God through his love for us made the way of escape. It also shows his love for the world in finally condemning all evil so that his creatures can live in a world free from "death . . . mourning, crying or pain" (Rev 21:4).[45] Hell reveals that God's love does not mean that in the end he will accept everything and everyone. Such a human definition may seem to be desirable or comforting, but it is blind to the holiness of God. Every attempt to turn Christianity into a religion of universalism, in which every person will ultimately be saved, is unfaithful to the teaching of the Bible.[46] God's love is righteous, doing only what is right and truly good for his creation.[47] God's love is what he has revealed it to be, not what we reason it to be. If we desire to live within the love of God, we must respond to God's revelation of his love in Christ.[48] The truth about hell points us to that revelation. This is why the church must proclaim the

---

45. "[E]very day of patience in a world of violence means more violence and every postponement of vindication means letting insult accompany injury . . . God can create the world of justice, truth, and peace only by making an end to deception, injustice, and violence" (Volf, *Exclusion and Embrace*, 299, 300). For a discussion of hell in relation to the problem of evil, see Blocher, "Everlasting Punishment and the Problem of Evil," 283–312.

46. See Packer, "Universalism," 169–94.

47. "God's love is inseparably connected with His holiness and His justice. He must therefore manifest anger when confronted with sin and evil" (Tasker, *Biblical Doctrine*, vii).

48. For discussions of the biblical meaning of God's love, see Carson, *Difficult Doctrine*; Packer, "Universalism," 189–94.

God's Final Judgment

message about God's judgment. Otherwise, we rob our generation of the truth about God's love.

Those Who Have Not Heard the Gospel

We will finish with a difficult question: What about those people who have not had the opportunity to receive a clear and accurate presentation of the gospel, and thus the opportunity to believe in Jesus? To begin with, we need to spell out some evangelical parameters. John Stott has helpfully made clear three non-negotiables for evangelicals who are considering the question:[49]

1. All people, apart from God's merciful intervention, are perishing.
2. Human beings cannot in any way save themselves.
3. Jesus Christ is the only Savior.

Thus, people can be saved only through Jesus Christ (John 14:6; Acts 4:12). The key question therefore becomes: Is explicit faith in Christ required for a person to be saved? The answer given by the New Testament would seem to be "yes." The promise of salvation is only to those who repent and believe the gospel (John 3:16; Acts 2:38; Rom 10:9–10; 1 Pet 1:8–9). No hope of salvation is held out for others. If we leave the matter there, our answer will be that all who have not heard the gospel are eternally lost. Some evangelicals hold this view.[50] Others argue, however, that it is possible apart from hearing and believing the gospel, but through the convicting work of the Holy Spirit, for some people to come to a consciousness of their sinfulness and to throw themselves on God's mercy. For such people the saving work of Christ would avail and they would ultimately be saved.[51] It is important to spell out what such a view does not mean. It does not mean the universalist concept of "anonymous Christians," in which devout adherents

---

49. Stott, "Gospel for the World—Response," 321–24.
50. For example, Henry, "Is It Fair?," 245–55.
51. For example, Stott, "Gospel for the World—Response," 324–29; ACUTE, *Nature of Hell*, 131; Crockett and Sigountos, "Are the 'Heathen' Really Lost?," 257–64; Helm, "Are They Few That Be Saved?," 257–81. There is also the question concerning the destiny of those incapable of faith: infants and young children; and people with severe mental disabilities. On this, see ACUTE, *Nature of Hell*, 94–95; Erickson, *How Shall They Be Saved?*, 235–53.

of non-Christian religions are somehow "Christians" without knowing it.[52] Also, it does not mean the opportunity to repent and believe after death. The Bible holds out no such hope.[53]

We must be very careful regarding our beliefs and hopes regarding this matter. The New Testament gives us no clear warrant for eternal hope concerning those who have not heard the gospel. Therefore, it is unwise to assume it as a fact. For those who do assume it, it should be noted that our knowledge of sinful humans suggests that not many people would be saved in this way. Missionary experience indicates that there are not large numbers of people who are humble and contrite before God, longing to receive his mercy.[54] In the end only God knows about the matter; we leave it with him. What we know for sure is what he has revealed to us, namely, that salvation is through the proclamation of the gospel and explicit faith in Jesus Christ (Rom 1:16–17). This is the direction in which our faith, hope, and efforts must be directed. The truth about hell should strengthen the imperative for us to pray for lost people and bring the good news to them. The need is urgent, and the task is indispensable and non-negotiable.

Final Reflections

We will conclude by considering some practical implications of Paul's teaching about the final judgment.

Firstly, Paul challenges us regarding our vision of God's final judgment, a future reality very real to Paul. Therefore, he thinks about it, preaches and teaches it, lives in the light of it, and does all he can to help God's people to do the same. By and large, today's western church has lost much of Paul's vision. While we still affirm the truth of final judgment, it has largely dropped out of our practical, day-to-day, working theology. We think and speak little about it. I believe we are seeing the results of it theologically, spiritually, morally, and missionally. As God's people we must recover the truth in our daily worldview and life. Repentance is the beginning, for all of us.

52. See Conn, "Do Other Religions Save?," 195–208.

53. See ACUTE, *Nature of Hell*, 89–92. For an argument in favor of post-mortem conversion, see Parry, "Evangelical Universalism," 3–18. For a response and counter-argument, see Tidball, "Can Evangelicals Be Universalists?," 19–32. Tidball concludes (29): "The accent of New Testament teaching falls on the significance of this life and the decisions made here, with no hint of a second chance, post-mortem, or of re-education in a hell prior to release in heaven."

54. Crockett and Sigountos, "Are the 'Heathen' Really Lost?," 261.

However, one of the keys for renewal is with church leaders. The truth must get back into the church through preaching and teaching.[55] Unless we give it "air time" it will not get into people's minds and lives. It also needs to get into leaders' thinking and lives. Preaching and teaching it is not enough. It must become real to us, a deep part of the way we see the world and live our lives. Let us ask God to renew us and integrate the truth within us.

The final judgment is very significant in relation to the suffering church. As we have seen, the suffering church is a sign to the world of final salvation and judgment. Being such a sign is a great privilege and responsibility. It is also a great irony, because those who are despised are the ones who show the only way to salvation. They follow their Savior, who was "despised and rejected" (Isa 53:3). Paul's teaching on judgment is an encouragement to the suffering church, affirming their identity in Christ, strengthening their confidence in their faith and way of life, and spurring them on to persevere in living for Christ.[56] It also instructs them not to take vengeance for wrongs suffered, but to forgive, knowing that in the coming Day God will vindicate them and judge their enemies. "The certainty of God's just judgment at the end of history is the presupposition for the renunciation of violence in the middle of it."[57] It is sometimes difficult for us in the west to relate to it all. But we can and must, because we are called to stand with and serve our suffering brothers and sisters in Christ. The Lord will judge us according to our love and service to them: "Truly I tell you, whatever you did for one of the least of these brothers and sisters of mine, you did for me" (Matt 25:40).

The final judgment of unbelievers has huge implications for evangelism. This is nothing new for evangelical Christians. Hopefully, our study has reinforced the need for us to communicate to non-Christians the truth about hell as part of the gospel we proclaim.[58] We are not being faithful to God if we avoid speaking about his judgment. We are also robbing people of the full truth about God's love. Speaking about eternal judgment is not easy in our cultural context. With the help of the Holy Spirit we must rediscover ways of doing it that get through to people, without reinforcing misconceptions and stereotypes about Christians and Christianity. Our at-

---

55. A very helpful book for teaching and preaching about hell is Blanchard, *Whatever Happened to Hell?*

56. Kuck, *Judgment and Community Conflict*, 228.

57. Volf, *Exclusion and Embrace*, 302.

58. See Crockett and Sigountos, "Are the 'Heathen' Really Lost?," 261.

titude is critical. Unless we genuinely love people, and sometimes "earn the right" to share the gospel, there will be a "disconnect" between our message and our life. People must be able to see the connection. Let us pray for more love in our hearts to go and to love, for wisdom and boldness to proclaim the whole gospel, and for the grace and power of the Holy Spirit to open people's eyes and bring them to faith.

Finally, the truth about the last judgment challenges us to rediscover holiness, both personally and corporately. Our western context is one of individualism, moral relativism, materialism and associated "idolatries," and practical atheism. These things bombard us relentlessly. Paul's response to cultural pressure was to give the church a strong sense of corporate identity and distinctiveness from the world, confidence in faith and hope, and an ethic of perseverance in love, purity, and faithfulness.[59] The truth about final judgment is a key element in Paul's teaching that promotes all these things. It contributes to our knowing who we are, what we believe, what we are called to do, and what we will be. Surely, this is what the western church needs today. In our efforts to engage with the world, sadly, we have ended up becoming too much like the world (cf. John 17:16) and loving the things of the world (cf. 1 John 2:15–17). We need to relearn from Paul (and the rest of the Bible) what it means to be God's holy people in the present world. It will involve discovering how the truth of final judgment defines our identity and calling. May the Lord help us.

---

59. Adapted from Kuck, *Judgment and Community Conflict*, 228.

8

Conclusion

IN THIS FINAL CHAPTER I will not attempt to summarize all our main findings and thoughts. Rather, I wish to reflect on the "burdens" that have emerged throughout our study.

We begin with the burden of the truth of God's judgment that we have found in Paul's letters. This is a major truth for Paul, a key element of his understanding of the righteousness of God, and integrated with all other gospel truths.

1. It provides insight into the nature of God and the situation of humanity. It explains the need for and the meaning of the salvation that God has graciously provided in Christ.

2. Further, it is a truth that is always relevant for us; it is an inescapable reality. The central question is where we stand in relation to it.

3. In our pursuit of the four main aspects of Paul's understanding of God's judgment we have found powerful and relevant truths. Paul describes the human dilemma since the creation of humanity, explaining that our situation is to be understood fundamentally in relation to God's judgment. It is as we grasp this that we are able to begin to receive the freedom that Christ has provided.

4. Paul also speaks about God's judgment throughout human history, explaining how it is at work in people, both unbelievers and believers. Our eyes are opened to the various ways in which God's judgment operates. In particular, Paul instructs and challenges us concerning the Lord's discipline of his people, either directly, or indirectly through church discipline.

5. Paul also describes the center of the gospel—the cross of Jesus—in relation to God's judgment, declaring that in Christ God condemned human sin (Rom 8:3). Paul helps us to see the depth of our sin, the

necessity of its judgment, the extent of our need, the cost to God's Son, the greatness of God's love, and the implications for our lives.

6. Finally, Paul repeatedly affirms God's judgment at the end of history as the doorway through which every person will ultimately and inevitably pass into their eternal destiny. All judgment, past and present, points to the future final judgment. The new creation will emerge from it. Paul's teaching on the judgment of believers is a major component of his ethical instruction. His teaching on the judgment of unbelievers is an integral part of his gospel proclamation. Paul "jolts" us concerning the reality and seriousness of the final judgment.

We come to the main burden of this book, namely, that as the church in the west, we need to recover Paul's vision of the judgment of God. While I have not attempted to study in any detail the state of the contemporary western church in relation to Paul's teaching on divine judgment, it is fairly obvious that our vision of God's judgment is generally much smaller, fainter, and fuzzier than Paul's. Unfortunately, many Christians have little understanding of God's judgment. But even for those who know most or all the truths about judgment, these truths are often mainly theological propositions rather than an integral part of a vision of reality that governs our life on a daily basis. In short, these truths are not vitally integrated into our worldview. The reasons are not hard to find. Our society tries relentlessly to impose upon us another vision of reality, which affects us all. Unless we actively cultivate an alternate worldview, we will tend to follow our society. This has happened in the church to a significant extent, particularly with the uncomfortable and unpopular truth of God's judgment. The world rejects it. For us as Christians it is a hard truth that we wrestle with and that we struggle to communicate. The sad reality is that we have gone the easier way and begun to let go of the truth of God's judgment. We have not lost it entirely. We still hold it largely as theological assumptions, but these are brought to the surface infrequently and their connection with other truths and with our lives is becoming less clear. Our vision of God's judgment has faded, and we are experiencing its consequences in theological ignorance and misunderstanding, spiritual shallowness, moral laxity, and lack of zeal for service and evangelism. We must recover the vision.

Conclusion
Call to Action

Where do we start? Firstly, at a number of points through the book I have felt the need to challenge us to repentance. This must be our starting point in turning from our neglect of the truth of God's judgment to reintegrating it into our worldview and way of life. We must confess our sin and ask the Lord to lead us step by step as he teaches us about his judgment. We must be determined to learn and to live in the light of the truth. It will involve study of the Scriptures, prayer, reflection, and a commitment to find ways of allowing the truth to have its outworking in and through our lives. Only the Lord can enable us to recover the truth about judgment. We must seek him earnestly. As we do, we will rediscover our calling to be a holy people (2 Cor 7:1).

Secondly, the leaders of God's people have a particular responsibility and role in recovering the truth of God's judgment in the church (2 Tim 4:1–2). The truth must be preached and taught. It will be in the minds and on the lips of God's people in proportion to the "air time" that it receives in the various contexts in which people meet. Then the power of the truth will transform people's thinking and behavior. The challenge for leaders is to know and understand the truth, and to find ways of communicating it to God's people. This does not mean that we regularly preach and teach "heavy" messages about God's judgment. Rather, it means that listeners receive the fruit of the integration of the truth about judgment into the worldview of Christian leaders. Paul is a good model. Judgment was woven into his message and came to the surface regularly in ways that helped people understand the whole gospel, with judgment as a key part of it. We simply need to teach and preach from the whole Bible, not skipping the hard bits, but working through it ourselves and then explaining it to people. Explaining judgment is a challenge in our culture, but we must learn how to do it and persevere at it. Contemporary controversies among evangelicals about the atonement and hell suggest that the challenges will increase. But we cannot afford to lose any truth on these crucial matters. As we are faithful, I believe that we will see good fruit.

Thirdly, as we recover the truth about God's judgment we cannot help but be burdened for lost people, who live with the effects of God's judgment in the present, and who face God's wrath in the future. The good news is that the judgment of our sin that took place in Christ's death (Rom 8:3) is God's gracious solution for those who become aware of their predicament, and call on the Lord's name. Again, God is calling us to renew our hope in the gospel and our love for people, and to engage in spiritual warfare through prayer and bringing the gospel to people, that we might win them to the Lord (1 Cor 9:19–23). In bringing the gospel to Felix the Roman governor, Paul spoke with him about "righteousness, self-control, and the judgment to come" (Acts 24:24–25). God is challenging our hearts: Do we really believe that apart from Christ people are going to hell? Do we care about people? Do we really want them to be reconciled to God? Will we earnestly seek God to cleanse us from all complacency, hardness of heart, fear, and discouragement; and to empower us to live more fully for him, and to proclaim the truth of his judgment and salvation to all people?

Finally, we must also stand with the suffering church, particularly our brothers and sisters overseas, in prayer, fellowship, practical support, and advocacy. They know the reality of the struggle of God's people in a fallen world under God's judgment. We must support them so that they can stand firm for the Lord and be the "sign" of salvation and judgment that God has called them to be (Phil 1:27–29). They will inspire us to be more faithful in our witness, and will help to prepare us for suffering that we will encounter in the future.

Bibliography

ACUTE. *Faith, Health and Prosperity: A Report on 'Word of Faith' and 'Positive Confession' Theologies by ACUTE*, edited by Andrew Perriman. Carlisle, UK: Paternoster, 2003.
———. *The Nature of Hell: A Report by the Evangelical Alliance Commission on Unity and Truth among Evangelicals*. Carlisle, UK: Paternoster, 2000.
Alexander, T. Desmond, and Brian S. Rosner, eds. *New Dictionary of Biblical Theology*. Leicester, UK: Inter-Varsity, 2000.
Anderson, Neil T. *The Bondage Breaker*, with Study Guide. 2nd ed. Crowborough, UK: Monarch, 1996.
Arnold, Clinton E. *Power and Magic: The Concept of Power in Ephesians*. 2nd ed. Grand Rapids: Baker, 1997.
———. *Powers of Darkness: A Thoughtful, Biblical Look at an Urgent Challenge Facing the Church*. Leicester, UK: Inter-Varsity, 1992.
———. *Three Crucial Questions about Spiritual Warfare*. Grand Rapids: Baker, 1997.
Barnett, Paul W. *The Second Epistle to the Corinthians*. NICNT. Grand Rapids: Eerdmans, 1997.
Barth, Karl. *The Epistle to the Romans*. Translated by Edwyn C. Hoskyns. 6th ed. London: Oxford University Press, 1933.
Bauer, Walter, Frederick W. Danker, William F. Arndt, and Felix W. Gingrich. *A Greek-English Lexicon of the New Testament and Other Early Christian Literature*. 3rd ed. Chicago: University of Chicago Press, 2000.
Bebbington, David. *Patterns in History: A Christian Perspective on Historical Thought*. 2nd ed. Grand Rapids: Baker, 1990. Reprint, Vancouver: Regent College, 2000.
Bell, Richard H. *No One Seeks for God: An Exegetical and Theological Study of Romans 1:18—3:20*. WUNT 106. Tübingen: Mohr Siebeck, 1998.
Bell, Robert H. *Love Wins: A Book about Heaven, Hell, and the Fate of Every Person Who Ever Lived*. New York: HarperOne, 2011.
Bird, Michael F. *The Saving Righteousness of God: Studies on Paul, Justification and the New Perspective*. Milton Keynes, UK: Paternoster, 2006.
———, and Sarah Harris. "Paul's Jewish View of Sexuality in Romans 1:26–27." In *Sexegesis: An Evangelical Response to Five Uneasy Pieces on Homosexuality*, edited by Michael F. Bird and Gordon Preece, 87–104. Sydney South, Australia: New Cranmer, 2012.
Blanchard, John. *Whatever Happened to Hell?* Darlington, UK: Evangelical Press, 1993.
Blocher, Henri. "Everlasting Punishment and the Problem of Evil." In *Universalism and the Doctrine of Hell*, edited by Nigel M. de S. Cameron, 283-312. Carlisle, UK/Grand Rapids: Paternoster/Baker, 1992.
———. *Original Sin: Illuminating the Riddle*. NSBT 5. Grand Rapids: Eerdmans, 1997.

Bibliography

Bockmuehl, Markus N. A. "1 Thessalonians 2:14–16 and the Church in Jerusalem." *TynBul* 52 (2001) 1–31.

———. *Revelation and Mystery in Ancient Judaism and Pauline Christianity*. WUNT 2/36. Tübingen: Mohr Siebeck, 1990.

Böttger, P. C., et al. "Recompense, Reward, Gain, Wages." In *NIDNTT* 3:134-45.

Brown, Colin, ed. *New International Dictionary of New Testament Theology*. 4 vols. Rev. ed. Carlisle, UK: Paternoster, 1992.

Bubeck, Mark I. *Overcoming the Adversary: Warfare Praying against Demon Activity*. Chicago: Moody, 1984.

Büchsel, F. "*krinō*." In *TDNT*, 471-75.

Caird, G. B., and L. D. Hurst. *New Testament Theology*. Oxford: Oxford University Press, 1994.

Calvin, John. *Institutes of the Christian Religion*. Translated by Henry Beveridge. Grand Rapids: Eerdmans, 1989.

Carson, D. A. *The Difficult Doctrine of the Love of God*. Leicester, UK: Inter-Varsity, 2000.

———. *The Gagging of God: Christianity Confronts Pluralism*. Grand Rapids: Zondervan, 1996.

———. "Reflections on AIDS." In *How Long, O Lord? Reflections on Suffering and Evil*, 227–33. 2nd ed. Nottingham, UK: Inter-Varsity, 2006.

———. *Scandalous: the Cross and Resurrection of Jesus*. Wheaton, IL: Crossway, 2010.

Chalke, Steve, and Alan Mann. *The Lost Message of Jesus*. Grand Rapids: Zondervan, 2003.

Chan, Simon. "The Logic of Hell: A Response to Annihilationism." *ERT* 18 (1994) 20–32.

Cole, Graham A. *God the Peacemaker: How Atonement Brings Shalom*. NSBT 25. Downers Grove, IL: InterVarsity, 2009.

Conn, Harvie M. "Do Other Religions Save?" In *Through No Fault of Their Own? The Fate of Those Who Have Never Heard*, edited by William V. Crockett and James G. Sigountos, 195–208. Grand Rapids: Baker, 1991.

Cranfield, C. E. B. *A Critical and Exegetical Commentary on the Epistle to the Romans*. 2 vols. ICC. Edinburgh: T. & T. Clark, 1975, 1979.

Crockett, William V., and James G. Sigountos. "Are the 'Heathen' Really Lost?" In *Through No Fault of Their Own? The Fate of Those Who Have Never Heard*, edited by William V. Crockett and James G. Sigountos, 257–64. Grand Rapids: Baker, 1991.

Denney, James. *The Death of Christ*. Edited by R. V. G. Tasker. London: Tyndale, 1951. Reprint, Carlisle: Paternoster, 1997.

Dickson, John. *Promoting the Gospel: A Practical Guide to the Biblical Art of Sharing Your Faith*. Sydney South, Australia: Blue Bottle, 2005.

Dodd, C. H. "Atonement." In *The Bible and the Greeks*, 82–95. London: Hodder & Stoughton, 1935. Reprinted from *JTS* 32 (1931) 352–60.

———. *The Epistle of Paul to the Romans*. MNTC. London: Hodder & Stoughton, 1932.

Donfried, Karl P. "Justification and Last Judgment in Paul." *Int* 30 (1976) 140–52.

———. "Paul and Judaism: 1 Thessalonians 2:13–16 as a Test Case." *Int* 38 (1984) 242–53.

Dunn, James D. G. *The Epistle to the Galatians*. BNTC. Peabody, MA: Hendrickson, 1993.

———. *Romans 1–8*. WBC. Dallas, TX: Word, 1988.

———. *Romans 9–16*. WBC. Dallas, TX: Word, 1988.

———. *The Theology of Paul the Apostle*. Grand Rapids: Eerdmans, 1998.

Edwards, David L. "The Gospel for the World." In *Essentials: A Liberal-Evangelical Dialogue*, by David L. Edwards and John R. W. Stott, 273–305. London: Hodder & Stoughton, 1988.

Bibliography

Elwell, Walter A., ed., *Evangelical Dictionary of Biblical Theology*. Grand Rapids: Baker, 1996.

Erickson, Millard J. *How Shall They Be Saved? The Destiny of Those Who Do Not Hear of Jesus*. Grand Rapids: Baker, 1996.

Fee, Gordon D. *1 and 2 Timothy, Titus*. NIBC. Peabody, MA: Hendrickson, 1988.

———. *The First and Second Letters to the Thessalonians*. NICNT. Grand Rapids: Eerdmans, 2009.

———. *The First Epistle to the Corinthians*. NICNT. Grand Rapids: Eerdmans, 1987.

———. *God's Empowering Presence: The Holy Spirit in the Letters of Paul*. Peabody, MA: Hendrickson, 1994.

———. *Paul's Letter to the Philippians*. NICNT. Grand Rapids: Eerdmans, 1995.

Finamore, Steve. "The Gospel and the Wrath of God in Romans 1." In *Understanding, Studying and Reading: New Testament Essays in Honour of John Ashton*, edited by Christopher Rowland and Crispin H. T. Fletcher-Louis, 137–54. JSNTSup 153. Sheffield: Sheffield Academic, 1998.

Fitzmyer, Joseph A. *Romans: A New Translation with Introduction and Commentary*. AB. New York: Doubleday, 1993.

Forsyth, P. T. *The Work of Christ: Lectures to Young Ministers*. London: Hodder & Stoughton, 1910.

Fudge, Edward W. *The Fire That Consumes: The Biblical Case for Conditional Immortality*. Rev. ed. Carlisle, UK: Paternoster, 1994.

Gaffin, Richard B. "'The Scandal of the Cross': Atonement in the Pauline Corpus." In *The Glory of the Atonement: Biblical, Historical and Practical Perspectives; Essays in Honor of Roger Nicole*, edited by Charles E. Hill and Frank A. James III, 140–62. Downers Grove, IL: InterVarsity, 2004.

Gagnon, Robert A. J. *The Bible and Homosexual Practice: Texts and Hermeneutics*. Nashville: Abingdon, 2001.

Gathercole, Simon J. "Justified by Faith, Justified by His Blood: The Evidence of Romans 3:21—4:25." In *Justification and Variegated Nomism, Volume II: The Paradoxes of Paul*, edited by D. A. Carson et al., 147–84. Grand Rapids: Baker, 2004.

———. "A Law unto Themselves: The Gentiles in Romans 2.14–15 Revisited." *JSNT* 85 (2002) 27–49.

Gorman, Michael J. *Abortion and the Early Church: Christian, Jewish and Pagan Attitudes in the Greco-Roman World*. Downers Grove, IL: InterVarsity, 1982.

Green, Joel B., and Mark D. Baker. *Recovering the Scandal of the Cross: Atonement in New Testament and Contemporary Contexts*. Downers Grove, IL: InterVarsity, 2000.

Gundry Volf, Judith M. *Paul and Perseverance: Staying In and Falling Away*. Louisville, KY: Westminster/John Knox, 1990.

Guthrie, Donald. *New Testament Theology*. Leicester, UK: Inter-Varsity, 1981.

Hamilton, James M. "The Glory of God in Salvation through Judgment: The Centre of Biblical Theology?" *TynBul* 57 (2006) 57–84.

———. *God's Glory in Salvation through Judgment: A Biblical Theology*. Wheaton, IL: Crossway, 2010.

Harmon, Kendall S. "The Case against Conditionalism: A Response to Edward William Fudge." In *Universalism and the Doctrine of Hell*, edited by Nigel M. de S. Cameron, 193–224. Carlisle, UK/Grand Rapids: Paternoster/Baker, 1992.

Harris, Murray J. *Raised Immortal: Resurrection and Immortality in the New Testament*. Basingstoke, UK: Marshall, Morgan & Scott, 1983.

Bibliography

Helm, Paul. "Are They Few That Be Saved?" In *Universalism and the Doctrine of Hell*, edited by Nigel M. de S. Cameron, 257–81. Carlisle, UK/Grand Rapids: Paternoster/Baker, 1992.

Henry, Carl F. H. "Is It Fair?" In *Through No Fault of Their Own? The Fate of Those Who Have Never Heard*, edited by William V. Crockett and James G. Sigountos, 245–55. Grand Rapids: Baker, 1991.

Hoekema, Anthony A. *Saved by Grace*. Grand Rapids: Eerdmans, 1989.

Hoffmeier, James K., ed. *Abortion: A Christian Understanding and Response*. Grand Rapids: Baker, 1987.

Hooker, Morna D. "Adam in Romans 1." In *From Adam to Christ: Essays on Paul*, 73–84. Cambridge: Cambridge University Press, 1990. Reprinted from *NTS* 6 (1960) 297–306.

Hughes, Philip E. *Paul's Second Epistle to the Corinthians: The English Text with Introduction, Exposition and Notes*. NICNT. Grand Rapids: Eerdmans, 1962.

Jeffery, Steve, et al. *Pierced for Our Transgressions: Rediscovering the Glory of Penal Substitution*. Nottingham, UK: Inter-Varsity, 2007.

Jersak, Brad, and Michael Hardin, eds. *Stricken by God? Nonviolent Identification and the Victory of Christ*. Grand Rapids: Eerdmans, 2007.

Jeschke, Marlin. *Discipling in the Church: Recovering a Ministry of the Gospel*. 3rd ed. Scottdale, PA: Herald Press, 1988.

Käsemann, Ernst. "The Pauline Doctrine of the Last Supper." In *Essays on New Testament Themes*, 108–35. Translated by W. J. Montague. London: SCM, 1964.

———. "Sentences of Holy Law in the New Testament." In *New Testament Questions of Today*, 66–81. Translated by W. J. Montague. Philadelphia: Fortress, 1968.

Kemeny, P. C., ed. *Church, State and Public Justice: Five Views*. Downers Grove, IL: InterVarsity, 2007.

Kittel, Gerhard, and Gerhard Friedrich, eds. *Theological Dictionary of the New Testament: Abridged in One Volume*. Translated and abridged by Geoffrey W. Bromiley. Grand Rapids: Eerdmans, 1985.

Köstenberger, Andreas J., and David W. Jones. *God, Marriage, and Family: Rebuilding the Biblical Foundation*. Wheaton, IL: Crossway, 2004.

Kuck, David W. *Judgment and Community Conflict: Paul's Use of Apocalyptic Judgment Language in 1 Corinthians 3:5—4:5*. NovTSup 66. Leiden: Brill, 1992.

Ladd, George Eldon. *A Theology of the New Testament*. Rev. ed. Grand Rapids: Eerdmans, 1993.

Lampe, G. W. H. "Church Discipline and the Interpretation of the Epistles to the Corinthians." In *Christian History and Interpretation: Studies Presented to John Knox*, edited by W. R. Farmer et al., 337–61. Cambridge: Cambridge University Press, 1967.

Laney, J. Carl. *A Guide to Church Discipline: God's Loving Plan for Restoring Believers to Fellowship with Himself and with the Body of Christ*. Minneapolis: Bethany House, 1985.

Lincoln, Andrew T. "From Wrath to Justification: Tradition, Gospel and Audience in the Theology of Romans 1:18—4:25." In *Pauline Theology, Volume III: Romans*, edited by David M. Hay and E. Elizabeth Johnson, 130–59. Minneapolis: Fortress, 1995.

Link, H.-G., and C. Brown, "Reconciliation." In *NIDNTT* 3:148–66.

Longenecker, Richard N. *Galatians*. WBC. Dallas, TX: Word, 1990.

Marshall, Christopher D. *Beyond Retribution: A New Testament Vision for Justice, Crime, and Punishment*. Grand Rapids: Eerdmans, 2001.

Bibliography

Marshall, I. Howard. *Aspects of the Atonement: Cross and Resurrection in the Reconciling of God and Humanity*. London: Paternoster, 2007.

———. *A Critical and Exegetical Commentary on the Pastoral Epistles*. ICC. London: T&T Clark, 1999.

Marshall, Paul A. *Their Blood Cries Out: The Worldwide Tragedy of Modern Christians Who Are Dying for Their Faith*. Dallas, TX: Word, 1997.

Martyn, J. Louis. *Galatians: A New Translation with Introduction and Commentary*. AB. New York: Doubleday, 1997.

McFadden, Kevin W. *Judgment according to Works in Romans: The Meaning and Function of Divine Judgment in Paul's Most Important Letter*. Minneapolis: Fortress, 2013.

McKnight, Scot. "Eternal Consequences or Eternal Consciousness?" In *Through No Fault of Their Own? The Fate of Those Who Have Never Heard*, edited by William V. Crockett and James G. Sigountos, 147–57. Grand Rapids: Baker, 1991.

Miller, Patrick D. *Sin and Judgment in the Prophets: A Stylistic and Theological Analysis*. SBLMS 27. Chico, CA: Scholars Press, 1982.

Milne, Bruce A. *The Message of Heaven and Hell: Grace and Destiny*. Leicester, UK: InterVarsity, 2002.

Mohler, R. Albert Jr. "Modern Theology: The Disappearance of Hell." In *Hell under Fire: Modern Scholarship Reinvents Eternal Punishment*, edited by Christopher W. Morgan and Robert A. Peterson, 15–41. Grand Rapids: Zondervan, 2004.

Moo, Douglas J. *The Epistle to the Romans*. NICNT. Grand Rapids: Eerdmans, 1996.

———. "Paul on Hell." In *Hell under Fire: Modern Scholarship Reinvents Eternal Punishment*, edited by Christopher W. Morgan and Robert A. Peterson, 91–109. Grand Rapids: Zondervan, 2004.

Morgan, Christopher W. "Annihilationism: Will the Unsaved Be Punished Forever?" In *Hell under Fire: Modern Scholarship Reinvents Eternal Punishment*, edited by Christopher W. Morgan and Robert A. Peterson, 195–218. Grand Rapids: Zondervan, 2004.

———. "Biblical Theology: Three Pictures of Hell." In *Hell under Fire: Modern Scholarship Reinvents Eternal Punishment*, edited by Christopher W. Morgan and Robert A. Peterson, 135–51. Grand Rapids: Zondervan, 2004.

Morris, Leon. *The Apostolic Preaching of the Cross*. 3rd ed. Grand Rapids: Eerdmans, 1965.

———. *The Biblical Doctrine of Judgment*. London: Tyndale, 1960.

———. *The Cross in the New Testament*. Grand Rapids: Eerdmans, 1965. Reprint, Carlisle, UK: Paternoster, 1995.

———. *The Epistle to the Romans*. PNTC. Grand Rapids: Eerdmans, 1988.

———. *The First and Second Epistles to the Thessalonians*. Rev. ed. NICNT. Grand Rapids: Eerdmans, 1991.

Moule, C. F. D. "The Judgment Theme in the Sacraments." In *The Background of the New Testament and Its Eschatology*, edited by W. D. Davies and D. Daube, 464–81. Cambridge: Cambridge University Press, 1964.

———. "Punishment and Retribution: An Attempt to Delimit Their Scope in New Testament Thought." In *Essays in New Testament Interpretation*, 235–49. Cambridge: Cambridge University Press, 1982.

Mounce, William D. *Pastoral Epistles*. WBC. Nashville: Thomas Nelson, 2000.

Nicole, Roger R. "C. H. Dodd and the Doctrine of Propitiation." *WTJ* 17 (1955) 117–57.

O'Brien, Peter T. *Colossians, Philemon*. WBC. Waco, TX: Word, 1982.

———. *The Letter to the Ephesians*. PNTC. Grand Rapids: Eerdmans, 1999.

Bibliography

O'Donovan, Oliver. *The Ways of Judgment: The Bampton Lectures, 2003*. Grand Rapids: Eerdmans, 2005.

Ortlund, Dane C. "Justified by Faith, Judged according to Works: Another Look at a Pauline Paradox." *JETS* 52 (2009) 323–39.

Packer, J. I. "Universalism: Will Everyone Ultimately Be Saved?" In *Hell under Fire: Modern Scholarship Reinvents Eternal Punishment*. Edited by Christopher W. Morgan and Robert A. Peterson, 169–94. Grand Rapids: Zondervan, 2004.

———. "What Did the Cross Achieve? The Logic of Penal Substitution." In *In My Place Condemned He Stood: Celebrating the Glory of the Atonement*, by J. I. Packer and Mark E. Dever, 53–100. Wheaton, IL: Crossway, 2007. Reprinted from *TynBul* 25 (1974) 3–45.

Pannenberg, Wolfhart. *Systematic Theology*. Translated by Geoffrey W. Bromiley. 3 vols. Grand Rapids: Eerdmans, 1991, 1994, 1998.

Parry, Robin A. "Evangelical Universalism: Oxymoron?" *EQ* 84.1 (2012) 3–18.

———, and Christopher H. Partridge. *Universal Salvation? The Current Debate*. Carlisle, UK: Paternoster, 2003.

Peterson, David G. "Atonement in the New Testament." In *Where Wrath and Mercy Meet: Proclaiming the Atonement Today*, edited by David G. Peterson, 26–67. Milton Keynes, UK: Paternoster, 2001.

Pinnock, Clark H. "The Conditional View." In *Four Views on Hell*, edited by William V. Crockett, 135–66. Grand Rapids: Zondervan, 1992.

Powys, David J. *"Hell": A Hard Look at a Hard Question: The Fate of the Unrighteous in New Testament Thought*. Milton Keynes, UK: Paternoster, 1997.

Reiser, Marius. *Jesus and Judgment: The Eschatological Proclamation in Its Jewish Context*. Translated by Linda M. Maloney. Minneapolis: Fortress, 1997.

Roetzel, Calvin J. *Judgement in the Community: A Study of the Relationship between Eschatology and Ecclesiology in Paul*. Leiden: Brill, 1972.

———. "The Judgment Form in Paul's Letters." *JBL* (1969) 305–12.

Rosner, Brian S. *Paul, Scripture and Ethics: A Study of 1 Corinthians 5–7*. Grand Rapids: Baker, 1999.

Schönweiss, H., and H-C. Hahn, "Anger, Wrath." In *NIDNTT* 1:105–13.

Schreiner, Thomas R. *Galatians*. ZECNT. Grand Rapids: Zondervan, 2010.

———. "Justification apart from and by Works: At the Final Judgment Works Will Confirm Justification." In *Four Views on the Role of Works at the Final Judgment*, edited by Alan P. Stanley, 71–98. Grand Rapids: Zondervan, 2013.

———. *Paul, Apostle of God's Glory in Christ: A Pauline Theology*. Downers Grove, IL: InterVarsity, 2001.

———. "Penal Substitution View." In *The Nature of the Atonement: Four Views*, edited by James Beilby and Paul R. Eddy, 67-98. Downers Grove, IL: InterVarsity, 2006.

———. *Romans*. BECNT. Grand Rapids: Baker, 1998.

Scroggs, Robin. *The New Testament and Homosexuality: Contextual Background for Contemporary Debate*. Philadelphia: Fortress, 1983.

Seifrid, Mark A. "Unrighteous by Faith: Apostolic Proclamation in Romans 1:18—3:20." In *Justification and Variegated Nomism, Volume II: The Paradoxes of Paul*, edited by D. A. Carson et al., 105–45. Grand Rapids: Baker, 2004.

Shuster, Marguerite. *The Fall and Sin: What We Have Become as Sinners*. Grand Rapids: Eerdmans, 2004.

Bibliography

South, James T. "A Critique of the 'Curse/Death' Interpretation of 1 Corinthians 5.1–8." *NTS* 39 (1993) 539–61.

Sprinkle, Preston M. "Romans 1 and Homosexuality: A Critical Review of James Brownson's *Bible, Gender, Sexuality*." *BBR* 24.4 (2014) 515–28.

Sproul, R. C. *Reason to Believe: A Response to Common Objections to Christianity*. Grand Rapids: Zondervan, 1982.

Stählin, G., et al., "*orgē*." In *TDNT*, 716–26.

Stanley, Alan P., ed. *Four Views on the Role of Works at the Final Judgment*. Grand Rapids: Zondervan, 2013.

Stark, Rodney. *The Rise of Christianity: How the Obscure, Marginal Jesus Movement Became the Dominant Religious Force in the Western World in a Few Centuries*. New York: HarperCollins, 1996.

Steadman, Ray C. *Spiritual Warfare: Winning the Daily Battle with Satan*. Portland, OR: Multnomah, 1975.

Stettler, Christian. "Paul, the Law and Judgement by Works." *EQ* 76 (2004) 195–215.

Stott, John R. W. *The Cross of Christ*. Leicester, UK: Inter-Varsity, 1986.

———. "The Gospel for the World—Response." In *Essentials: A Liberal-Evangelical Dialogue*, by David L. Edwards and John R. W. Stott, 306–31. London: Hodder & Stoughton, 1988.

Tasker, R. V. G. *The Biblical Doctrine of the Wrath of God*. London: Tyndale, 1951. Reprinted in *Themelios* 26/2 (2001) 4–17; 26/3 (2001) 5–21.

Terry, Justyn C. *The Justifying Judgement of God: A Reassessment of the Place of Judgement in the Saving Work of Christ*. London: Paternoster, 2007.

Tidball, Derek J. "Can Evangelicals Be Universalists?" *EQ* 84.1 (2012) 19–32.

Travis, Stephen H. *Christ and the Judgement of God: The Limits of Divine Retribution in New Testament Thought*. 2nd ed. Peabody, MA: Hendrickson, 2008.

———. "Judgment." In *Dictionary of Jesus and the Gospels: A Compendium of Contemporary Biblical Scholarship*, edited by Joel B. Green et al., 408–11. Downers Grove, IL: InterVarsity, 1992.

VanLandingham, Chris. *Judgment and Justification in Early Judaism and the Apostle Paul*. Peabody, MA: Hendrickson, 2006.

Volf, Miroslav. *Exclusion and Embrace: A Theological Exploration of Identity, Otherness, and Reconciliation*. Nashville: Abingdon, 1996.

Vos, Geerhardus. *The Pauline Eschatology*. Princeton: Princeton University Press, 1930.

Wanamaker, Charles A. *The Epistles to the Thessalonians: A Commentary on the Greek Text*. NIGTC. Grand Rapids: Eerdmans, 1990.

Wenham, John W. "The Case for Conditional Immortality." In *Universalism and the Doctrine of Hell*, edited by Nigel M. de S. Cameron, 161–91. Carlisle, UK/Grand Rapids: Paternoster/Baker, 1992.

Weston, Paul. "Proclaiming Christ Crucified Today: Some Reflections on John's Gospel." In *Where Wrath and Mercy Meet: Proclaiming the Atonement Today*, edited by David G. Peterson, 136–63. Milton Keynes, UK: Paternoster, 2001.

White, John, and Ken Blue. *Healing the Wounded: The Costly Love of Church Discipline*. Leicester, UK: Inter-Varsity, 1985.

Williams, Garry J. "The Cross and the Punishment of Sin." In *Where Wrath and Mercy Meet: Proclaiming the Atonement Today*, edited by David G. Peterson, 68–99. Milton Keynes, UK: Paternoster, 2001.

Bibliography

Wright, N. T. *The Climax of the Covenant: Christ and the Law in Pauline Theology.* Edinburgh: T & T Clark, 1991.

———. *The New Testament and the People of God.* London: SPCK, 1992.

———. *What St Paul Really Said.* Oxford: Lion, 1997.

Yarbro Collins, Adela. "The Function of 'Excommunication' in Paul." *HTR* 73 (1980) 251–63.

Yinger, Kent L. *Paul, Judaism and Judgment according to Deeds.* SNTSMS 105. Cambridge: Cambridge University Press, 1999.

Modern Authors Index

Alexander, T. Desmond, xiiin4
Anderson, Neil T., 82n7
Arndt, William F., xv
Arnold, Clinton E., 44n2, 97n24

Baker, Mark D., 90n16, 116n22n23, 117, 117n26
Barnett, Paul W., 30n35, 32n38, 101n31, 131n1
Barth, Karl, 73n29, 125n56
Bauer, Walter, xv
Bebbington, David, 94n23
Bell, Richard H., 86n5
Bell, Robert H., 147n29
Bird, Michael F., x, xiv, 89n13, 138n9, 142n17
Blanchard, John, 155n55
Blocher, Henri, 15n13, 77n1, 152n45
Blue, Ken, 106n54
Bockmuehl, Markus N. A., 54n16, 86n5
Böttger, P. C., 139n12
Brown, Colin, 110n2, 111n4n6
Bubeck, Mark I., 82n7
Büchsel, F., xin1, 6n8

Caird, G. B., 54n16, 86n5
Calvin, John, 115, 116n20, 121, 122n47
Carson, D. A., 89n13, 114, 114n18n19, 122n51, 146n27, 148n36, 149n39, 151n44, 152n48
Chalke, Steve, 116, 116n22n25
Chan, Simon, 148n36
Cole, Graham A., 116n22
Conn, Harvie M., 154n52

Cranfield, C. E. B., 17n15, 19n17, 21n22, 86n5, 91n21, 99n29, 112n12, 142n17, 145n26
Crockett, William V., 153n51, 154n54, 155n58

Danker, Frederick W., xv
Denney, James, 113n15, 122n50, 123n53, 126n58
Dickson, John, 67n25
Dodd, C. H., 90n15, 111, 111n4n5n6, 118
Donfried, Karl P., 54n17, 138n9, 142n18
Dunn, James D. G., 12n9, 13n10, 16n14, 19n17n18, 20n19, 21n22, 35n40, 38n42n43, 39n46, 87n8, 89n13, 99n29, 117, 117n35, 124n54, 136n7

Edwards, David L., 147n29
Elwell, Walter A., xiiin4
Erickson, Millard J., 153n51

Fee, Gordon D., 24n24n26, 25n27, 26n28, 27n29, 28n32n33, 46n3, 54n15, 60n19, 61n21n22, 64n24, 67n26, 82n6, 103n42n44n47, 104n50, 140n14, 143n19, 145n24
Finamore, Steve, 86n5
Fitzmyer, Joseph A., 12n8, 86n6
Forsyth, P. T., 122n49, 125n56
Friedrich, Gerhard, xvi
Fudge, Edward W., 148n32n34, 149n38n40

Gaffin, Richard B., 114n18, 116n24
Gagnon, Robert A. J., 89n13

Gathercole, Simon J., 12n9, 113n14, 118n39, 145n26
Gingrich, Felix W., xv
Gorman, Michael J., 89n12
Green, Joel B., 90n16, 116n22n23, 117, 117n26
Gundry Volf, Judith M., 27n31, 103n43, 105n53, 142n18, 143n19
Guthrie, Donald, 136n7, 144n20

Hahn, H-C., 11n6
Hamilton, James M., 72n28
Hardin, Michael, 116n22
Harmon, Kendall S., 148n36, 149n38
Harris, Murray J., 149n39
Harris, Sarah, 89n13
Helm, Paul, 153n51
Henry, Carl F. H., 153n50
Hoekema, Anthony A., 62n23
Hoffmeier, James K., 89n12
Hooker, Morna D., 10n3, 87n8
Hughes, Philip E., 134n5
Hurst, L. D., 54n16, 86n5

Jeffery, Steve, 116n22
Jersak, Brad, 116n22
Jeschke, Marlin, 106n54
Jones, David W., 89n11

Käsemann, Ernst, 24n26, 102n41, 104n49
Kemeny, P. C., 98n28
Kittel, Gerhard, xvi
Köstenberger, Andreas J., 89n11
Kuck, David W., 1n1, 7n9, 8n1, 24n26, 140n14, 155n56, 156n59

Ladd, George Eldon, 125n55, 134n4, 136n7, 144n20
Lampe, G. W. H., 102n38n41, 103n46, 104n50, 105n53
Laney, J. Carl, 106n54
Lincoln, Andrew T., 12n7, 13n12, 113n13
Link, H.-G., 110n2, 111n4n6
Longenecker, Richard N., 35n40, 36n41, 39n45

Mann, Alan, 116, 116n22n25
Marshall, Christopher D., 91n19n21, 116n22, 117, 117n32, 147n30, 148n34
Marshall, I. Howard, 61n21n22, 116n22, 118n39n40, 123n52n53, 125n55
Marshall, Paul A., 81n4
Martyn, J. Louis, 35n40, 36n41
McFadden, Kevin W., 8n1, 11n4, 12n9, 13n12, 21n20, 90n17, 91n20, 113n14, 138n9, 142n17, 145n26
McKnight, Scot, 149n39
Miller, Patrick D., 3n3
Milne, Bruce A., xii, 148n36
Mohler, R. Albert Jr., 148n33n35
Moo, Douglas J., 12n9, 13n10n12, 16n14, 17n16, 19n17n18, 21n21n22, 86n5, 89n13, 90n18, 98n26, 99n29, 112n10n11, 113n13n14n16, 142n17, 144n20, 145n26, 150n42
Morgan, Christopher W., xiin2, 144n21, 148n36
Morris, Leon, xiin2, 1n1, 11n6, 20n19, 21n21, 52n11, 54n15, 56n18, 90n17, 101n34, 108n1, 111, 111n6n7, 112n12, 113, 113n13, 116n22, 121n46, 125n55, 136n6, 144n22
Moule, C. F. D., 91n19, 104n50, 107n55
Mounce, William D., 60n19n20, 61n21n22, 64n24, 67n26, 101n35, 102n40

Nicole, Roger R., 111, 111n6

O'Brien, Peter T., 43n1, 49n6, 50n7, 51n9, 131n2
O'Donovan, Oliver, 97n25, 99n30
Ortlund, Dane C., 138n9

Packer, J. I., 116n22, 123n53, 152n46n48
Pannenberg, Wolfhart, 120n45, 123n53
Parry, Robin A., 147n29, 154n53
Partridge, Christopher H., 147n29
Peterson, David G., 114n19

Peterson, Robert A., xiin2
Pinnock, Clark H., 147n28, 148n31n32n34
Powys, David J., 148n32n34

Reiser, Marius, 5n4
Roetzel, Calvin J., 1n1, 7n9, 8n1, 28n33, 102n41
Rosner, Brian S., xiiin4, 102n36, 103n45n46n48

Schönweiss, H., 11n6
Schreiner, Thomas R., 11n4, 39n44, 80n3, 89n13, 125n55, 139n11, 144n20, 145n26
Scroggs, Robin, 89n13
Seifrid, Mark A., 86n5n6, 87n7n9, 92n22
Shuster, Marguerite, 77n1
Sigountos, James G., 153n51, 154n54, 155n58
South, James T., 102n36n37n38, 103n42
Sprinkle, Preston M., 89n13
Sproul, R. C., 114n17
Stählin, G., 11n6
Stanley, Alan P., xiv, 137n8, 138n9
Stark, Rodney, 89n14
Steadman, Ray C., 82n7
Stettler, Christian, 138n9, 145n25
Stott, John R. W., 108n1, 122n48, 123n52, 125n57, 148n31n34, 153, 153n49n51

Tasker, R. V. G., xi, xin1, xiin2, 152n47
Terry, Justyn C., 125n56
Tidball, Derek J., 154n53
Travis, Stephen H., 3n3, 5n4, 6n9, 8n1, 27n30, 31n37, 51n10, 54n17, 86n5, 91n19, 99n29, 102n41, 105n52, 117, 117n29, 118, 118n37, 119, 119n41, 120, 131n1n2, 136n7, 138n9, 139n12, 141n16, 142n18, 144n20, 147n30

VanLandingham, Chris, 138n10
Volf, Miroslav, 151n43, 152n45, 155n57
Vos, Geerhardus, 11n5, 72n27, 138n9

Wanamaker, Charles A., 52n12
Wenham, John W., 148n31n32n33n34
Weston, Paul, 129n60
White, John, 106n54
Williams, Garry J., 120n44
Wright, N. T., 13n11

Yarbro Collins, Adela, 102n38
Yinger, Kent L., 1n1, 3n3, 7n9, 8n1, 24n26, 102n37, 105n53, 131n1, 138n9, 140n14, 142n17, 143n19

Subject Index

Abortion and infanticide, 88–89
Abraham, Abram, 2, 4
Adam, 10n3, 15
Atonement, the, 115, 116, 117, 120, 123–25, 159

Baptism, 17, 107n55, 128

Church
    compassion, 82, 83, 88, 94, 96, 129, 155–56, 159–60
    discipline, 100–107
    eschatological tension, 18, 29, 31, 76, 79, 82, 127–28, 131
    loving and encouraging one another, 96
    mission, 8, 65, 125, 129, 154
    prayer, 57, 59, 65, 77, 82, 88, 92, 94, 96, 97, 98, 136, 154, 156, 159, 160
    proclaiming the gospel, 30–31, 46, 48, 55, 80, 92, 93, 96, 107, 128, 129, 154, 155–56, 160
    responsible citizens, 98–99
    spiritual warfare, 44, 45, 49, 76, 82, 85, 97, 109, 160
    suffering, 18, 30, 31, 32, 34, 35, 40, 46, 48, 49, 53, 54, 55, 56, 58, 62, 63, 68, 76, 79, 80–81, 155, 160
    supporting suffering Christians, 58, 81, 155, 160
    teaching and proclaiming the truth about judgment, xi–xii, 48, 55, 92, 128–29, 137, 152–53, 155, 159, 160
    witness, 48, 55, 56, 58, 59, 62, 67, 80–81, 88, 89, 155, 160

Day of the Lord, xii, 3, 4, 10, 11, 23, 24, 25, 30, 45, 47, 48, 55, 56, 64, 65, 66, 92, 135, 136, 137, 139, 140, 141, 144, 155

Election. *See* Salvation
Eschatology, xii, 18, 22, 70–71, 79–82
    triumphalism, 81–82

Faith in God/Christ
    belief, trust, 6, 12, 14, 17, 22, 32, 36, 37, 38, 39, 45–46, 49, 57, 59, 64, 65, 71, 92, 95–96, 114, 115, 127, 129, 131, 134, 138–39, 140–41, 142–44, 146, 153–54
    faith and works, 140–42
    faithfulness, xi, xiv, 25, 48, 56, 65, 81, 96, 128, 139–40, 155–56, 160
    fear (reverential), xi, 33, 46, 51, 137, 137n8, 142
    good works, 39n44, 66–68, 135, 137, 140, 141–44
    holy living, 26, 29, 32–33, 34, 43, 50, 53, 62, 63, 64, 65, 66, 68, 82, 86, 100, 103, 105, 106, 126, 131, 134, 137, 140, 156, 159
    honoring (glorifying) him, 10, 62, 75, 78, 135, 140, 144
    learning in humility, 29, 58, 75, 95, 107, 127, 133, 137, 156, 159
    living by the Spirit, 39, 41, 76, 82, 86, 104, 126, 127
    loving him, 33, 52, 65, 95, 127, 129, 137, 140
    obedience, 6, 25, 30, 33, 127, 129, 134, 139, 140, 144

Subject Index

Faith in God/Christ *(continued)*
    pleasing him, 10, 33, 68, 74, 127, 135, 137, 140, 144
    repentance. *See* Repentance
    serving him, 43, 51, 127, 139, 140, 143, 144
    thankfulness, 74, 78, 95, 107, 126, 127, 129
    waiting for his coming, 40, 48, 52, 55, 59, 64, 65, 66, 76
Fall, the, 2, 7, 10, 15, 18, 22, 34, 35, 49, 51, 70, 71, 72, 77, 78, 81, 82, 84, 86n6, 133
Final judgment, xii, 5–6, 5n6, 10–11, 12, 14, 15, 46, 55, 58, 62, 65, 70–72, 130–56, 158
    according to works, 10–11, 31, 34, 39, 131, 136–42, 145, 146, 151, 155
    accountability to God, 13, 20, 21, 31, 47, 100, 134, 136, 137, 138, 152
    annihilation, 147–48, 148n37, 151
    condemnation, 4, 5, 6, 7, 9, 13, 14, 56–57, 71, 132, 146
    conditional immortality, 147–51, 148n37
    corruption, 39, 132, 134, 146
    curse, 28, 35, 132
    death, 132, 146
    destruction, 19, 39, 132, 134, 146, 147–51
    empty profession of faith, 142–44
    eternal, 146–51
    exclusion from God's presence and kingdom, 11, 26, 38, 43, 56–57, 71–72, 118, 132, 134, 146
    hell, 5, 22, 48, 118, 144–54, 155, 159, 160
    implications for Christians, 154–56
    justice of, 146–47
    necessity and purpose, 132–36
    of Christians, 10, 11, 24–25, 27, 31, 33, 43, 51, 56, 130–31, 134, 136–44, 158
    of non-Christians, 10, 11, 26, 38, 43, 50, 52, 56, 57, 67, 144–54
    of opponents of God's work, 21, 24, 28, 29, 34, 35–36, 46, 47, 53–54, 56, 60, 64, 67, 131
    of people who have not heard the gospel, 153–54
    of Satan and evil powers. *See* Judgment, by God
    painful, 10, 131, 132, 146, 149–51
    perishing, 12, 24, 30, 94, 132, 150, 153
    post-mortem evangelism, 147, 154
    principles, 145–46
    proclaimed by Jesus, 5–6
    proclaimed by Paul, 12, 52, 53, 69–70, 92, 154, 156, 158, 160
    punishment, 6, 56–57, 118, 132, 144, 146, 147. *See* unending punishment (below)
    reward. *See* Salvation
    salvation. *See* Salvation
    summary of Paul's view, 130–32
    unending punishment, 147–52
    universal, 10, 11, 13, 31, 38, 47, 51, 55, 56, 65, 145, 152, 158
    universalism, 47, 147n29, 152–54
    wrath, xii, 10, 11, 14, 19, 22, 35, 43, 49, 50, 52, 53, 54, 55, 57, 59, 66, 69, 71, 72, 75, 80, 86, 87, 92, 96, 108, 109, 113, 114, 130, 131, 146, 149, 159

Gentiles, 2–4, 6, 7, 10, 12, 13, 19, 36, 37, 42, 43, 53, 54, 59, 70, 87, 109, 143, 145n26, 146n27
Good news. *See* Gospel
Gospel, xi, 8, 12, 14, 16, 24, 30, 32, 34, 35, 39n44, 40, 46, 47, 48, 49, 51, 52, 53, 54, 55, 56, 57, 58, 62, 63, 64, 65, 67, 69, 71, 73, 76, 78, 79, 80, 81, 85, 86n5, 91, 92, 96–97, 114, 125, 126, 128, 129, 131, 134, 135, 139, 144, 145, 153–54, 155, 156, 157, 158, 159, 160
Grace of God, 1, 2, 4, 7, 23, 26, 30, 34, 39n44, 40, 42, 45, 46, 48, 57, 60, 62, 65, 66, 68, 72–73, 76, 82, 83, 85, 92, 98, 106, 107, 113, 115,

Subject Index

133, 134n5, 135, 137, 138, 139, 141, 142, 143, 144, 156

Hell. *See* Final judgment
Hilastērion. *See* Propitiation
Holiness. *See* Faith in God/Christ
Holiness of God, 29, 69, 73, 76, 110, 112, 114, 115, 119, 123, 126, 134n5, 147, 151, 152
Holy Spirit. *See* Faith in God/Christ, Salvation

Israel, 2–4, 6, 7, 11, 12, 13, 16, 19, 22, 27, 28, 37, 54, 70, 71, 84, 85, 111, 112, 113

Jesus Christ
  cross. *See* death (below)
  death, 6, 7, 8, 12, 14, 16, 17, 22, 23, 28, 29, 30, 31, 32, 34, 37, 38, 39, 40, 45, 49, 50, 51, 53, 59, 63, 66, 70, 71, 72, 85, 86n5, 91, 104, 105, 107, 108–29, 133, 135, 152, 157, 159
  Judge, 6, 11, 12, 31, 33, 47, 55, 56, 65, 71, 130, 134, 135, 136, 137, 145, 155
  penal substitution. *See* Penal substitution
  representative, 32, 38, 109, 117, 120, 123–24
  resurrection, 7, 8, 12, 14, 17, 22, 28, 30, 32, 37, 38, 44, 45, 47, 50, 51, 53, 63, 70, 85, 107, 108, 109, 113, 115, 123, 124, 127, 135, 138
  Savior, 22, 45, 47, 48, 55, 65, 71, 127, 135, 137, 153, 155
  Second Coming. *See* Salvation
  sinlessness, 32, 109, 127
  Son of God, 6, 8, 14, 16, 36, 38, 49, 52, 53, 69, 114, 121, 122, 123, 126, 127, 129, 135, 136, 141, 148, 158
  substitute, 32, 38n42, 109, 115–29
  Suffering Servant, 4, 7, 137n8, 155
Jews, 12, 19, 53, 54, 85, 87, 89n13, 96, 97, 145n25
John the Baptist, 5

Judgment, by God
  according to works, 1n1, 3, 5, 6, 7n9, 8n1, 10, 11, 22, 31, 34, 39, 43, 44, 51, 64, 68, 84, 100, 130, 131, 134, 136–42, 145, 146, 151, 155
  active or passive?, 112–13, 115–21
  alienation from God, 23, 43, 49, 75, 118, 119
  at the Fall, 2, 7, 10, 15, 18, 22, 34, 35, 51, 70, 71, 72, 77, 78, 81, 82, 84, 133
  based on truth, 130, 145
  condemnation, xiii, 4, 6, 13, 14, 16, 17, 18, 30, 70, 71, 72, 75, 108, 126
  corruption, 18, 75, 76, 93
  curse, 2, 4, 36, 37, 38, 40, 75, 93
  death, xiii, 2, 3, 15–18, 32, 75, 76
  decay. *See* corruption (above)
  definition of, xiii
  disasters. *See* physical judgments (below)
  eschatological judgment. *See* Final judgment
  fallen creation, 93–94
  fallen human condition, 9, 10, 15, 16, 17, 18, 30, 31, 34, 35, 36–37, 40, 42, 43, 44, 45, 46, 49, 56, 58, 62, 63, 66, 68, 74–83, 75–76 (summary), 88, 93–94, 95, 97, 137, 160
  final judgment. *See* Final judgment
  four aspects, xiii, 71–72, 74, 157
  frustration. *See* futility (below)
  fundamental to Paul's theology, 69–70, 157–58
  futility, 18, 43, 75, 93
  hell. *See* Final judgment
  historical, 70–71, 157
  impartial. *See* righteous (below)
  impersonal?, 89–90, 94–95, 118, 120
  implications for Christians, 159–60
  in Christ at the cross, 6, 14, 16, 17, 23, 28, 29, 30, 32, 34, 37–38, 39, 40, 49, 50, 63, 70, 71, 72, 107, 108–9 (summary), 108–29, 125–29 (implications), 133, 134, 135, 138, 157, 159
  in the Old Testament, 1–5

Subject Index

Judgment, by God *(continued)*
  in the teaching of Jesus, 5–7
  just. *See* righteous (below)
  moral corruption, 9–10, 84, 86–92
  mortality, 31, 35, 78, 79
  of Christians. *See* Final judgment, Temporal judgment
  of Israel, 2–4, 6–7, 12–13, 19, 27, 28, 37, 53–54, 70, 71, 84–85, 87, 111–13
  of opponents of God's work. *See* Final judgment
  of Satan and evil powers, 6, 7, 21, 23n23, 28, 29, 44, 45, 47, 49, 50, 57, 82, 85, 96–97, 109, 132, 134
  of sin, 16, 17, 29, 32, 34, 38, 49, 50, 63, 70, 107, 108, 109, 115, 118, 121, 123, 124, 126, 128, 133, 134, 138, 157, 159
  of "the world," 6, 7, 13, 23–24, 29, 30, 31, 35, 39–40, 46, 50, 56, 58, 68, 93–94, 109, 131, 133–34, 160
  penal substitution. *See* Penal substitution
  perishing, 23, 30, 57
  physical judgments, 2–4, 7, 27, 28, 54, 78, 91–95
  punishment, 3, 7, 13, 19, 20, 52, 68, 87, 90–92, 98–99, 115, 133
  restorative, 3–4, 19, 86, 91, 94, 99, 102, 103, 117, 133, 134, 152
  retribution. *See* Retribution
  reward. *See* Salvation
  righteous, xii, 10, 11, 12n7, 14, 31, 43, 44, 51, 56, 57, 58, 64, 69, 72, 73, 76, 91, 113, 114, 116, 120, 123, 130, 133, 134n5, 145, 146, 151, 152, 155
  separation from God. *See* alienation (above)
  spiritually blinded by Satan, 30, 34, 35, 37, 42, 44, 45, 49, 57, 60, 61, 65, 75, 82, 97, 102
  summary of Paul's view, 69–73
  temporal. *See* Temporal judgment
  through Christ. *See* Jesus Christ
  through earthly authorities. *See* Temporal judgment
  through the law of Moses. *See* Law of Moses
  unbelief as judgment, 19, 54, 57, 64, 84–85, 95–97
  wrath, xi, xii, xiii, 1n1, 9–14, 19, 22, 30, 37, 42, 43, 45, 50, 52, 54, 69, 70, 72, 73n29, 75, 80, 85, 86–91, 92, 109–25, 126, 129. For eschatological wrath, *see* Final judgment
Judgment, by humans
  by earthly authorities. *See* Temporal judgment
  non-retaliation, 19–20, 54, 55, 96, 99, 155
  not judging others, 20–21, 83, 88, 96

Kingdom of God/heaven, xii, 5, 18, 26, 38, 56, 65, 71, 76, 79, 96, 127, 132, 134, 145n24, 146

Law of Moses, 12–13, 16, 22, 30, 34, 36–37, 38, 40, 103–4, 138n9, 145, 146n27
Lord's Supper, 27–28, 104–5, 107, 128
Love of God
  kindness, 11, 19, 91
  love, 2, 57, 65, 93, 105, 110, 114–15, 116, 119, 121, 123, 126, 127, 128, 147, 152–53
  mercy, xiii, 19, 54, 64, 65, 73, 74, 83, 90, 91, 94–95, 112, 153–54

Nations. *See* Gentiles.
New covenant, 4, 7, 13, 30, 138n8

Original sin. *See* Fall, the

Penal substitution, 113, 115–25, 126
Promise of God, 2, 4, 13, 18, 36, 37, 81, 153
Propitiation, 14, 109–15, 123

Repentance, xiii, 3, 4, 5, 7, 11, 19, 25, 30, 33, 34, 53, 55, 64–65, 69, 80, 91,

Subject Index

94, 96, 99n29, 101, 102, 103, 105, 107, 108, 115, 126, 133, 153, 154, 159, 160
Retribution, 3, 3n3, 8n1, 20, 54, 64, 90–91, 98–99, 115–21, 129, 147–52
Righteousness of God, 9, 12n7, 13, 14, 22, 72–73, 86n5, 113–14, 116, 119, 133, 138, 152, 157

Salvation
  adoption, 18, 36, 74, 93, 115
  deliverance from Egypt, 2
  deliverance from evil powers, 44, 45, 49, 50, 51, 82, 85, 97, 109
  election, 2, 7, 19, 22, 23–24, 57, 63–64, 85, 95–96
  eternal life, 10–11, 31, 39, 67, 72, 74, 118n40, 126, 130, 131, 142, 149
  final salvation, 14, 29, 30, 46, 47, 53, 55–56, 57–58, 60, 62, 64, 65, 68, 71, 80, 92, 94, 102, 107, 131, 133, 135, 138–44, 155
  forgiveness of sins, xiii, 4, 6n8, 7, 11, 50, 65, 80, 83, 101, 110–12, 114–15, 116, 120, 123, 133, 134, 152, 155
  freedom, 14, 15–18, 32, 37, 38, 39, 40–41, 45, 48, 49, 50, 51, 66, 67, 71, 76, 78–79, 81, 82, 83, 85, 88, 92, 97, 108, 109, 112, 120, 123, 126, 129
  from God's wrath, 9, 14, 22, 25, 49, 52–53, 55, 57, 59, 62, 64, 66, 69, 70, 71, 72, 80, 91, 92, 107, 108, 109, 114, 115, 131, 135
  hope, 7, 18, 19, 30, 38, 40, 49, 55, 58, 67, 70, 74, 75, 79, 82, 91, 94, 95, 135, 138, 153–54, 156, 159–60
  inheriting God's kingdom, 26, 38, 39n44, 43, 51, 71, 79, 127, 132
  justification (final), 14, 23, 28–29, 30, 38, 40, 45, 53, 62, 65–66, 67, 138–40, 141
  justification (initial), 12–14, 15, 16, 21, 22, 26, 27, 28–29, 36–37, 38, 49, 53, 62, 67, 92, 94, 109–10,
  112, 113–14, 131, 137, 138–39, 141–42
  new creation, 18, 28, 70, 71, 76, 93–94, 126, 127, 133, 134, 136, 152, 158
  process of renewal and transformation, xiii, 23, 26, 29, 33, 42, 46, 60, 62, 66–67, 68, 74, 80, 83, 105, 107, 127, 141–42, 159
  reconciliation, 14, 32, 49, 72, 99, 109, 110, 115, 116, 134, 160
  restoration, 2, 3–4, 7, 11, 76, 94
  resurrection of the body, 16, 18, 28, 46, 71, 128, 130, 134, 145, 150
  reward, 24, 28, 43–44, 51, 68, 131, 135, 139–40
  Second Coming, xii, 18, 44, 53, 55, 56, 66, 70, 71, 79, 93, 128, 130, 132, 134
  work and indwelling of the Holy Spirit, 16, 17, 26, 36, 37, 57, 67, 68, 100, 109, 127, 153
Septuagint (LXX), 102n36, 110–12
Sin
  dishonoring God, 9, 10, 27, 104
  disobedience, 2, 4, 7, 15, 19, 33, 37, 42, 43, 56, 63, 66, 68, 71, 75, 104, 107, 114, 131, 134, 138, 146
  "flesh, the", 16–17, 38–39, 42, 50, 68, 75, 76, 82, 97, 102–3, 109
  hardness of heart, 19, 43, 54, 57, 64, 75, 84–85, 95, 160
  hostility, 3, 14, 17, 18, 23, 28, 29, 31, 34, 35, 39, 40, 46, 47, 49, 56, 64, 75, 76, 80, 85, 109, 127, 131
  idolatry, 26, 27, 29, 36, 43, 50, 52, 57, 75, 86–88, 143, 156
  rebellion, 2, 4, 6, 20, 71–72, 73, 76, 114–15, 121, 123, 133, 134, 138, 147
  rejecting God, 4, 6, 10, 23, 29, 43, 46, 48, 56–57, 60, 80, 87, 89, 90, 95, 114, 120, 129, 135–36, 147, 148, 151, 155, 158
  sexual immorality, 9–10, 25, 26, 27, 43, 50, 52, 87, 88–89, 101, 103

Subject Index

Sin *(continued)*
    sinful desires and actions, xiii, 3, 9–10, 16, 26, 27, 34, 38–39, 42, 43, 50, 52, 66, 71, 75, 77–78, 87–89, 90, 92, 94, 131–32, 140
    slavery to sin, 13, 16, 17, 36, 37, 41, 49, 51, 66–68, 71, 75, 78, 82, 118
    trespass, 4, 15, 32, 42, 122
    unbelief, 2, 19, 27, 28, 30, 57, 71, 84–85, 95–96, 129, 143
    unfaithfulness, xi, 3, 4, 128, 148, 152, 155
    wickedness, 3, 9, 11, 13, 57, 64, 66, 75, 87, 95, 113, 150
Suffering. *See* Church
Sovereignty of God, 2, 19, 25, 47, 58, 72–73, 76, 94–95, 103, 107, 119, 135
Spirit, Holy. *See* Faith in God/Christ, Salvation
Spiritual warfare. *See* Church

Temporal judgment
    generally, 22, 37, 43, 48, 52, 54, 70, 71, 72, 84–107, 84–86 (summary), 132n3
    human and natural disasters, 92–95
    in Romans 1:18–32, 9–10, 15, 52, 71, 84, 86–92, 133
    of evil powers, 44–45, 85, 96–97
    of God's people by God, 27–28, 29, 34–35, 61, 62, 71, 85–86, 95, 100–107, 105–7 (implications), 157
    of Israel, 6, 19, 27, 28, 54, 71, 84–85
    of Pharaoh, 19, 71
    through church discipline, 25, 30, 33, 34, 57, 60, 61, 67, 85–86, 100–107, 157
    through earthly authorities, 20, 21, 71, 85, 97–100
    unbelief of unbelievers, 57, 71, 85, 95–96
Trinity, the, 123

Worldview, xii, 8, 10, 22, 29, 50, 74, 77–83, 86, 90, 92, 93, 94, 98, 105–7, 127–28, 133, 136, 151, 154–56, 158–59

Scripture Index

Genesis

1–3	10n3, 87
1	89
1:27–28	89
2	89
2:16–17	2
2:24	89
3	2, 4
3:1–7	2
3:8–24	2
3:15	2
3:17	93
3:21	2
4:26	2
5:5	2
5:8	2
5:11	2
5:14	2
6:5—7:24	2
6:8	2
9:6	89
11:1–9	2
12:1–3	2
12:3	2, 4

Exodus

4:23	3
6:6	2
12:12	2
25:17–22	112
34:6	3

Leviticus

16:2	112
16:14–15	112
16:34	112
19:18	89

Numbers

7:89	112
14:26–35	2
16:46	111

Deuteronomy

4:25–31	3
10:18	3
12:31	89
13:1–5	103
17:2–7	103
19:16–19	103
21:18–21	103
22:20–22	30
24:7	103
27:26	37
28:15–68	37

Judges

2:13–14	3

Scripture Index

1 Kings

8:35–36	111

2 Kings

17:5–18	3
23:10	5n7
25:1–11	3

1 Chronicles

16:25	137n8

Ezra

1–10	3

Nehemiah

1–13	3

Job

2:6	102n36

Psalms

9:7–10	3
9:12	3
9:18–20	3
22:1	122
34:15–22	3
59:5	4
59:13	4
62:12	3, 10
77:38	111
78:38	111
78:56–64	3
79:6	4
90:11	xi
96:13	4
112:1	137n8
135:10–12	3
139:13–16	89
146:7–9	3
147:11	137n8

Proverbs

1:7	137n8
2:5	137n8
22:4	137n8
24:12	10

Ecclesiastes

12:13–14	100

Isaiah

11:3	137n8
14:12–15	61
33:6	138n8
42:1–4	4
43:25	4
45:22	4
45:23	21, 47
50:10	137n8
51:4–5	4
53	4, 7
53:3	155
59:18	3
61:1–2	4
66:15–24	4
66:22–24	5

Jeremiah

31:31–34	4, 7
32:39–40	138n8
34:17	3
46:28	3

Ezekiel

6:8–10	3
18:4	3
18:20	3
18:23	3, 11, 151
18:32	3, 11, 151
20:33–38	4
25:1—32:32	3
34:16	4
36:24–27	4
38–39	4

Daniel

12:2	145

Joel

3	4
3:4–8	3

Amos

1:3—2:3	3

Obadiah

1:15–17	4
1:15	3

Zechariah

1:6	3
14	4

Matthew

3:2	5
3:12	5
4:17	5
5:10–12	99
5:13–16	129
5:13	48
5:16	68
5:22	5
5:29	5
5:30	5
5:43–48	99
5:44–45	55
6:1–18	144
6:24	88
6:31–33	40n47
7:1–2	5n5, 21
7:1	94
7:13	5
7:21–23	5n5, 6, 29n34, 144
7:24–27	6
8:11–12	5n5, 6
9:17	150
10:14–15	5n5
10:28	5
10:32–33	6
11:20–24	151
11:21–24	5n5
12:36–37	5n5, 6
12:41–42	5n5
13:24–30	5, 5n5
13:36–43	5n5
13:40–43	5
13:47–50	5n5
16:27	6
18:9	5
18:15–20	102, 103
18:21–35	5n5
19:3–12	89
19:28	5n5
20:22–23	121
22:2–14	5n5
23:34–39	6
24:37–41	5n5
24:45–51	5n5
25:1–13	5n5
25:14–30	5n5
25:21	140
25:23	140
25:31–46	5n5, 6
25:40	155
25:41	149

Matthew (continued)

25:46	6, 149
26:8	150
26:28	7
26:37–44	121
26:39	121
27:46	122

Mark

9:43	5
9:45	5
9:47	5
10:38–39	121
10:45	7
14:33–36	121
14:36	121
15:34	122

Luke

6:27–38	94
9:23	128
12:5	5
12:47–48	151
12:50	121
13	94
13:1–5	94
15:9	150
19:41–44	6
21:20–24	6
22:37	7
22:41–44	121
22:42	121
23:27–31	6

John

3:14–16	6
3:16	153
3:17	69
3:18	129
3:19	136
3:36	114
5:22–23	135
5:24	6
5:25–27	6
5:28–29	6, 145
12:31–32	6
12:31	14, 29
12:32	6
12:47–48	136
14:2	140
14:6	127, 153
14:27	125
15:11	125
15:22–24	136
16:11	6
17:16	156
21:15–17	106

Acts

2:38	153
4:12	127, 153
4:18–20	99
5:1–11	94, 95
5:1–6	105n52
5:27–32	99
5:40–42	99
9:1–2	96
9:31	138n8
13:6–12	95
13:6–11	105n52
14:1	97
14:15	92
14:22	58
15:14	140
16:35–40	99
17:22–31	92
17:30–31	12, 69
20:21	92
20:28	106
24:15	145
24:24–25	12, 69, 92, 160
25:10–11	99
26:20	92

Scripture Index

Romans

Reference	Pages
1–5	113
1	86, 91, 92
1:1–15	9
1:5	139, 141
1:16–17	9, 86n5, 146, 154
1:16	97
1:17	9, 97
1:18—5:11	14, 113
1:18–3:20	9, 13
1:18–32	9, 15, 29, 43, 49, 52, 71, 75, 84, 86, 86n6, 87, 91n19, 92, 118n36, 133
1:18	9, 14, 75, 86n5, 87, 113
1:19–31	86n5
1:19–21	87
1:19–20	145
1:21–23	52, 87
1:21	75, 78
1:22–23	75
1:24–25	9
1:24	9, 43, 86n5, 87, 90
1:25	75, 87
1:26–27	10, 87, 89
1:26	9, 43, 86n5, 87, 90
1:27	90, 91n19
1:28–32	10
1:28–31	87
1:28	9, 43, 86n5, 87, 90
1:32	43, 90, 132, 145
2	87
2:1–16	130, 145
2:2	130, 145
2:3	145
2:4	11, 91
2:5–16	15
2:5–11	10
2:5	xii, 10, 87, 130, 145
2:6–8	39
2:6	10, 130, 136, 145
2:7	10, 130, 142
2:8–9	10, 130, 131
2:8	75, 138, 146
2:9	131, 146
2:10	130
2:11	130, 145
2:12	12, 132, 145, 146n27
2:14–15	145, 145n26, 146n27
2:14	145n26
2:16	11, 47, 69, 71, 130, 135, 136, 145
2:21–25	12
2:29	140
3:2	12, 22, 145
3:3–8	13
3:3	13
3:5–6	13
3:5	13
3:6	13
3:7	13
3:8	132
3:9	13, 16, 29, 75
3:10–18	146
3:19	13
3:20	12, 113
3:21–26	11, 14, 110, 112
3:23	93
3:24	109, 110, 112
3:25–26	113, 114
3:25	14, 16, 108, 109, 110, 112, 113, 115, 117, 123, 124
3:26	113
4:6–8	134
4:15	12, 30, 37
5–8	18
5:1–11	14
5:1	49
5:5	115
5:8	14, 123, 127
5:9–10	14, 109, 113, 131, 139
5:9	14, 49, 59, 66, 71, 92, 109
5:10	14, 49, 75, 109
5:11	17
5:12–21	15, 71, 75
5:12–19	15

Romans (continued)

Reference	Pages
5:12–18	32
5:12	2, 75
5:16	75, 132
5:17–19	109
5:18–19	66
5:18	15, 75, 132
5:20	16
5:21	74
6	16, 79
6:1–11	128
6:2–11	109, 127
6:2–6	17
6:6	17, 17n15, 109
6:8	109
6:10	17
6:11	109
6:12–23	141
6:12–16	127
6:14	103
6:16–17	16, 75
6:17–22	127
6:17–18	134
6:20–21	71
6:23	16, 74, 132
7	16
7:5	75
7:7–11	16
7:12	16
7:14	16, 75
7:15–25	16, 75
8	16, 17, 34, 79, 93
8:1–16	76, 109
8:1–2	16, 71
8:1	74, 123, 134
8:2	16, 17
8:3	16, 17, 29, 32, 38, 49, 50, 63, 70, 108, 115, 117, 121, 123, 124, 125, 126, 127, 133, 134, 135, 138, 157, 159
8:4–14	126
8:6–8	17, 75
8:9	17, 75
8:10	16, 76
8:11	16, 71, 130
8:12–13	141
8:14–17	115
8:14–16	74
8:15	127
8:17–30	79
8:17–18	18, 76, 80
8:17	35, 71, 80
8:18–25	82
8:19	18, 93
8:20–21	18, 93
8:20	75, 93, 133
8:21	75, 76, 93, 134
8:22–23	18
8:22	93
8:23–25	76, 94
8:23	18, 134
8:28	95
8:29	127, 141
8:32	123, 127
8:36–37	18, 76
9–11	19
9:1–3	96
9:11	19
9:14–23	19
9:17–18	19
9:17	71, 85
9:18–24	95
9:18	64
9:22–24	64, 85
9:22	19
9:23	19n17
10:1	96, 97
10:9–10	139, 153
10:11–15	96
10:14–15	96
10:17	97
10:21	19
11:7–10	19, 54, 71, 85
11:11	19
11:20–22	143
11:22	19, 91, 96, 131
11:25–27	19
11:26	19
11:33	95
12:1—15:13	19
12:1–2	74, 77, 127

Scripture Index

12:2	98, 106, 133
12:3–21	106
12:17–21	96, 99
12:17–19	20, 54
12:17	20
12:19	20, 85n3, 132, 146
12:20–21	99
12:20	99
13:1–7	71, 85, 97, 98, 100
13:1–4	20
13:1–2	98
13:1	97, 99
13:3–4	98
13:4	20, 98, 99
13:6–7	98
13:6	98
13:7	98
14	20, 47
14:3–4	20
14:4	20
14:7–9	20
14:10–12	20, 47, 145
14:10–11	130
14:10	20
14:11	21
14:12	25, 131, 138
14:13	20
16:17–19	21
16:17	21
16:20	21, 76, 85, 132
16:26	139

1 Corinthians

1	23, 40
1:2	29, 100
1:8	23, 131
1:18–31	23
1:18–21	23
1:18	23, 105
1:20–21	23, 109
1:21–24	23
1:26–29	23, 85
1:26–28	95
1:30	23, 100
2:6	24, 29, 109
2:8	29
2:9	135
3:5—4:5	8n1
3:10–15	24
3:10–11	125
3:10	25
3:12–15	24, 131, 140
3:13–15	145
3:13	24, 136
3:14	24, 131
3:15	24, 131, 131n1, 140
3:16–17	29, 100
3:17	24, 28, 29, 34, 36, 131, 132
4:1–5	25
4:2	25
4:5	131, 135, 136, 139, 140, 145
5	25, 102
5:1–5	27, 85, 102
5:1–2	103
5:3–5	25, 100
5:3	103
5:4	103
5:5	60, 102, 103
5:6	103
5:11	25, 103
5:12–13	100
5:12	25
5:13	25
6:1–11	26
6:1–8	86, 101
6:2	26, 131
6:3	26, 131
6:9–10	26, 75, 127, 132
6:11	26, 27, 100, 109, 131
6:19–20	29, 100
7:39	61
8:1—11:1	26
9	26
9:19–23	160
9:19–22	92, 97
9:27	27, 29, 131, 143
10:5–10	27, 71, 84, 91
10:11–13	29, 131

185

Scripture Index

1 Corinthians *(continued)*

10:12	27, 85n4, 104n49, 143
10:14–22	27
10:14	143
10:17	104
10:21	29
10:22	27, 85n4, 104n49, 143
11	106
11:17–34	27
11:17–22	104
11:18–19	104
11:18	27
11:21–22	27, 104
11:23–32	107, 128
11:23–28	27
11:24	107
11:25	107
11:26	107
11:27	29, 104
11:28–32	71, 85, 102
11:28	104, 107
11:29–32	27, 35, 95, 104
11:29	104, 107
11:30	104n49
11:31	107
11:32	28, 105, 107, 132
12:9	82
14:25	29
15	28
15:3	135
15:22	130
15:24–26	28, 134
15:24	29, 44, 85, 132, 145n24
15:26	132
15:42–44	130
15:50–53	134
15:50	127
15:51–54	130
15:54–55	28
15:58	136
16:22	28, 29, 36, 131, 132

2 Corinthians

1:3–11	30, 76
1:3–7	35
1:4	30
1:5–7	80
1:5	30
1:6	30
1:7	30
1:8	30
2:5–11	33, 86, 101
2:6	30
2:7–8	30
2:9	30
2:15	30
3	30, 37
3:7	30
3:9	30
3:16	31
3:18	127
4:3–4	30, 35, 44, 65, 75, 95, 97
4:5	31
4:6	31
4:7–12	79
4:8–12	76
4:8–9	31
4:10–12	31
4:16–18	35, 80
4:16	31, 76
4:17—5:4	31
5:9	33
5:10	25, 31, 33, 47, 131, 131n2, 134, 135, 136, 137, 140, 142, 145n23
5:11–21	32, 137
5:11	33, 137, 142
5:14–21	124
5:14	32, 33, 97, 137
5:15	32, 127
5:17	127, 128, 134
5:18–20	96
5:19	32, 109
5:20	97

5:21	32, 37, 49, 108, 109, 117, 124, 127, 138	3:14	109
		3:22	36, 37
		4:3–9	36
6:1–10	32	4:3	37
6:1–2	97	4:4	127
6:4–5	32, 76, 79	4:8–9	75
6:8–10	32, 76, 79	4:19	127
7:1	33, 137, 159	5–6	38
7:8–12	86, 101	5:5	38, 40, 66, 109, 131, 138
7:9–11	33		
7:9–10	33	5:6	139, 141
7:10	33	5:11	40, 76
7:11	33	5:13—6:10	76, 104
10:3–5	85	5:16–25	126
10:3	97	5:16–21	75
10:4–6	33	5:16	39
10:5–6	86, 101	5:17	39, 75
11:13–15	131	5:18	39
11:13	34	5:19–21	39, 75, 132
11:15	34, 36	5:19	38
11:23–30	79	5:21	38, 127
11:23–27	34, 76	5:22–24	141
12:7–10	34	5:22–23	39
12:9–10	79, 82	5:24	39, 75
12:21	101	5:25	39
13:2	34, 86, 101	5:26	39
13:10	34, 86, 101	6:7–8	90
		6:8–9	39, 130
		6:8	39, 132, 146

Galatians

		6:12	40, 76
		6:14	39, 109
1:4	76	6:15	127
1:7–9	131	6:17	40, 76
1:8–9	35, 132		
2:15	36		
2:16	36, 109	## Ephesians	
2:19–20	38		
2:19	38, 109	1:7	134
2:20	40, 109, 123, 126, 137	1:10	134
		1:19–23	44
2:21	36	1:20–22	44, 85
3:3	138	1:21–22	109
3:4	80	1:21	44, 76, 132
3:10	36, 37, 75	1:22–23	44
3:13–14	37	2:1–3	42, 49
3:13	37, 49, 108, 109, 124	2:1	75
		2:2	44, 75

Scripture Index

Ephesians (continued)

2:3–5	91
2:3	75
2:4	45
2:6	44
2:7	135
2:8–10	141
2:10	67, 68, 137
2:12	75
3:1	76
3:10	44
3:13	76
4:11–13	106
4:17–19	43, 49
4:17–18	75
4:18	75
4:19	43
5:5–7	43
5:5–6	75
5:5	127, 132, 146
5:6	50, 52, 75, 84, 131
5:26–27	106
6:7–9	43, 131
6:8	131, 139
6:10–20	85
6:10–18	44, 76, 97
6:12	44, 97
6:19–20	97
6:20	76

Philippians

1:6	45, 47
1:9	83
1:10	45, 47
1:11	45
1:13	46
1:27–30	46, 80
1:27–29	160
1:28	46, 47, 56, 109, 131, 132, 146
1:29–30	76
1:29	35, 48, 80
2	47
2:1–8	115
2:5–11	46
2:5	127
2:9–11	46, 132
2:10–11	135
2:12–13	142
2:12	46
2:13	68
2:15–16	48
2:15	133
2:16	45, 47
2:27	105n52
3:7–14	79
3:9	66
3:10–14	128
3:10	46, 48, 80
3:12–14	79n2
3:18–19	47, 131, 132
3:20–21	46, 47, 130
3:20	48

Colossians

1:5	49
1:13	49, 75, 85, 109
1:14	109
1:20	134
1:21	49, 75
1:22	49, 109, 131
1:23	49, 96, 131, 141
1:24	49, 76, 80
1:27	49
1:29	49, 97
2:1	49, 76
2:6–7	74
2:8–10	50
2:8	50
2:10	50, 109
2:13–15	50, 109
2:13–14	50
2:13	75
2:15	50, 85, 109
2:20–21	50
2:20	50, 109
3:1–4	50
3:5–6	50, 75, 131
3:6	52

3:17	137	**2 Thessalonians**	
3:22—4:1	51		
3:22–25	145n23	1:4–10	56
3:23–25	140	1:4–7	76
3:23–24	131	1:4–5	139, 141
3:23	131	1:5–10	80, 145
3:24	51, 131, 139	1:5	56, 80
3:25	51, 131	1:6	56, 132
4:2–6	97	1:7–9	131
4:3	49, 76	1:7–8	56
4:18	49, 76, 81	1:7	56, 145
		1:8–9	132
		1:8	56, 134, 146
		1:9	56, 134, 146, 147, 150
1 Thessalonians		1:10	56, 109, 135
1:3	139, 141	1:11–12	139, 141
1:6	53, 76	2:3–8	57
1:8	53	2:3	57
1:9–10	52, 53, 69, 92	2:8–10	132
1:9	52	2:9–12	57
1:10	53, 92, 109, 131	2:9	57
2:2	53, 76	2:10–12	95
2:14–16	54, 85	2:11	71, 85
2:14	80	2:13	57, 109, 131
2:16	54	3:1–3	97
2:18	53, 76	3:2	57
2:19–20	135	3:6–15	57, 86, 101
3:1–10	96		
3:2–5	53, 76		
3:3–4	53	**1 Timothy**	
3:5	53, 76		
3:7	53, 76	1	102
3:13	53, 109, 131, 141	1:1	58
4:3–6	52	1:12–16	65
4:5	53	1:12–15	65
4:6	52, 84, 85n4, 104n49, 132	1:12–14	96
4:14	53	1:15	59
4:16–17	130	1:16	59
4:17	53, 131	1:19–20	60, 85, 102, 103
5:3	52, 132	1:20	60, 64, 102
5:9	52, 109, 131	2:1–4	59, 96, 97
5:10	131	2:1–2	98
5:15	54, 96	2:5–6	59
5:23	53, 109, 131, 141	2:7	59
		2:15	60, 131, 141
		3:6	61, 86

1 Timothy *(continued)*

3:15	59, 129
4:16	60, 131, 141
5:11–15	61, 86
5:11–12	61
5:12	61
5:14	61
5:15	61
5:20	61, 86, 101
5:21	58
5:23	105n52
5:24	58, 130
6:9	60, 132
6:13–16	59
6:17	78

2 Timothy

1:6–8	62
1:8–10	63
1:8	76
1:9	63, 131, 141
1:10	63
1:12–14	62
1:16–18	64
2:1–13	62
2:10	63, 64, 65, 96
2:16–18	63
2:17–18	103
2:19	64, 131, 141
2:24–26	86, 96, 101
2:25–26	65
2:26	75
3:1–5	63
3:10–12	62
3:15	64
4:1–2	62, 159
4:1	65, 130, 145
4:5–8	62
4:8	64, 65, 66, 109, 131
4:14–15	64, 131
4:16–18	62

Titus

2:10	67
2:11–14	66, 109, 131, 141, 144
2:13	66
2:14	66, 68, 135
3:3–7	67
3:3	68, 75
3:5	67, 68, 109
3:6	67
3:7	109, 131
3:10–11	67, 86, 101
3:11	67

Philemon

1:1	68, 76
1:9	68, 76
1:10	68, 76

Hebrews

4:13	152
5:14	68
10:23–25	96
10:31	152
12:1–13	107
12:5–13	105
12:6	105
12:10	105
12:11	105
12:14	105
13:3	81

James

2:14–26	141
5:14–16	82

1 Peter

1:8–9	153
1:13	135

4:12–19	99
4:17	24
5:2–4	106

2 Peter

3:6	150
3:11–12	136

1 John

2:15–17	156
4:8	114

Revelation

1:5–6	129
3:14–22	58
12:10	61
14	150
14:9–11	150
14:11	150
20	150
20:4–6	145n24
20:10	150
20:12–13	145
20:15	150
21:4	152

www.ingramcontent.com/pod-product-compliance
Lightning Source LLC
Chambersburg PA
CBHW062038220426
43662CB00010B/1559

The Righteous Judgment of God